DATE DUE

JAMES A. MICHENER

JAMES A. MICHENER

A Critical Companion

Marilyn S. Severson

CRITICAL COMPANIONS TO POPULAR CONTEMPORARY WRITERS
Kathleen Gregory Klein, Series Editor

Greenwood Press
Westport, Connecticut • London

Library of Congress Cataloging-in-Publication Data

Severson, Marilyn S.
    James A. Michener : a critical companion / Marilyn S. Severson.
        p.   cm.—(Critical companions to popular contemporary
    writers, ISSN 1082–4979)
    Includes bibliographical references (p.   ) and index.
    ISBN 0–313–29538–7 (alk. paper)
        1. Michener, James A. (James Albert)—Criticism and
    interpretation.   I. Title.   II. Series.
    PS3525.I19Z88   1996
    813'.54—dc20   95–50461

British Library Cataloguing in Publication Data is available.

Library of Congress Catalog Card Number: 95–50461
ISBN: 0–313–29538–7
ISSN: 1082–4979

First published in 1996

Greenwood Press, 88 Post Road West, Westport, CT 06881
An imprint of Greenwood Publishing Group, Inc.

Printed in the United States of America

The paper used in this book complies with the
Permanent Paper Standard issued by the National
Information Standards Organization (Z39.48–1984).

10 9 8 7 6 5 4 3 2 1

**To my sister
for her unfailing love and support**

Contents

Contents

Series Foreword

The authors who appear in the series Critical Companions to Popular Contemporary Writers are all best-selling writers. They do not have only one successful novel, but a string of them. Fans, critics, and specialist readers eagerly anticipate their next book. For some, high cash advances and breakthrough sales figures are automatic; movie deals often follow. Some writers become household names, recognized by almost everyone.

But novels are read one by one. Each reader chooses to start and, more importantly, to finish a book because of what she or he finds there. The real test of a novel is in the satisfaction its readers experience. This series acknowledges the extraordinary involvement of readers and writers in creating a best-seller.

The authors included in this series were chosen by an Advisory Board composed of high school English teachers and high school and public librarians. They ranked a list of best-selling writers according to their popularity among different groups of readers. Writers in the top-ranked group who had not received book-length, academic literary analysis (or none in at least the past ten years) were chosen for the series. Because of this selection method, Critical Companions to Popular Contemporary Writers meets a need that is not addressed elsewhere.

The volumes in the series are written by scholars with particular expertise in analyzing popular fiction. These specialists add an academic focus to the popular success that these best-selling writers already enjoy.

The series is designed to appeal to a wide range of readers. The general reading public will find explanations for the appeal of these well-known writers. Fans will find biographical and fictional questions answered. Students will find literary analysis, discussions of fictional genres, carefully organized introductions to new ways of reading the novels, and bibliographies for additional research. Students will also be able to apply what they have learned from this book to their readings of future novels by these best-selling writers.

Each volume begins with a biographical chapter drawing on published information, autobiographies or memoirs, prior interviews, and, in some cases, interviews given especially for this series. A chapter on literary history and genres describes how the author's work fits into a larger literary context. The following chapters analyze the writer's most important, most popular, and most recent novels in detail. Each chapter focuses on a single novel. This approach, suggested by the Advisory Board as the most useful to student research, allows for an in-depth analysis of the writer's fiction. Close and careful readings with numerous examples show readers exactly how the novels work. These chapters are organized around three central elements: plot development (how the story line moves forward), character development (what the reader knows about the important figures), and theme (the significant ideas of the novel). Chapters may also include sections on generic conventions (how the novel is similar to or different from others in its same category of science fiction, fantasy, thriller, etc.), narrative point of view (who tells the story and how), symbols and literary language, and historical or social context. Each chapter ends with an "alternative reading" of the novel. The volume concludes with a primary and secondary bibliography, including reviews.

The Alternative Readings are a unique feature of this series. By demonstrating a particular way of reading each novel, they provide a clear example of how a specific perspective can reveal important aspects of the book. In each alternative reading section, one contemporary literary theory—such as feminist criticism, Marxism, new historicism, deconstruction, or Jungian psychological critique—is defined in brief, easily comprehensible language. That definition is then applied to the novel to highlight specific features that might go unnoticed or be understood differently in a more general reading of the novel. Each volume defines two or three specific theories, making them part of the reader's understanding of how diverse meanings may be constructed from a single novel.

Taken collectively, the volumes in the Critical Companions to Popular Contemporary Writers series provide a wide-ranging investigation of the complexities of current best-selling fiction. By treating these novels seriously as both literary works and publishing successes, the series demonstrates the potential of popular literature in contemporary culture.

Kathleen Gregory Klein
Southern Connecticut State University

Acknowledgments

I would like to thank my family, friends, and colleagues for their support and encouragement, Linda Lambert for her bibliographic assistance, and especially Cathy Ferrand Bullock, whose editing ability and critical insight are second to none.

1

The Life of James A. Michener: The World Is His Home

The title of James A. Michener's 1992 memoir, *The World Is My Home*, gives a pertinent focus to biographical information about this citizen of the United States, whose life and works have taken him to all corners of the earth.

James Albert Michener was born February 3, 1907; the location of his birth and the names of his biological parents are not known. He was raised by Mabel Michener, widow of a man named Edwin Michener, in Doylestown, Pennsylvania. James calls Mabel "one of those great women who serve in silence but leave behind a legacy that glows forever" (*World*, 477). As a teenager, she had served as mother to her five younger brothers and sisters when their mother died. After her husband's death in 1902, she took in a dozen or so abandoned children over the years, earning a small sum from a local charity organization.

Mabel also earned meager amounts by taking in laundry and finishing shirts brought to her from Philadelphia. James had the job of visiting the neighbors to pick up the dirty clothes for his foster mother to launder. When illness struck the family from time to time, young James lived in the county poorhouse. Material possessions were lacking, but the children under Mabel Michener's care knew love and laughter in their home: "Despite the anguish we suffered at times, we did not live tragic lives; laughter, not tears, surrounded me" (*World*, 496).

Although he may not have had a bicycle or wagon, books and music were an important part of Michener's childhood. When two women opened a small library in Doylestown, James was one of the first children to obtain a card, and by the time he was eleven, he had read all the children's books (*World*, 439). Thanks to a gift from Aunt Laura, Mabel's sister who taught in Detroit, by age twelve he had read many of the novels of Balzac, a nineteenth-century French novelist who wrote about the panorama of human experience. Music came into the home from Uncle Arthur, who gave the struggling family a Victrola, one of the early record players, and three records. The quartet from *Rigoletto* by Verdi was Michener's introduction to the world of opera and the beginning of a life-long love for opera.

Aunt Laura and Aunt Hannah, a public nurse, as well as Mabel herself, gave James role models for how a life should be lived, and Doylestown provided another model in the person of George Murray, a roofer who ran the local branch of Boys' Brigade, an organization similar to the Boy Scouts. Sports, games, summer camp, trips on the coal barges, and Sunday sermons from Murray were part of the activities. Murray's example provided the young James with the fatherly concern helpful to a growing boy. Michener deplores the waste of human talent the current culture fosters for disadvantaged youth. When he compares his situation as a child with that of today's African-American boys, he sees similarities but also underscores the family, church, and community support he received that is often lacking today. He also had dedicated teachers and a full scholarship to college. His coach told him to stay out of pool halls and avoid greasy foods; the African-American youth today gets an offer to try drugs (*World*, 498).

In addition to collecting and delivering laundry, James had his first paid job at age nine, when he gathered and sold chestnuts throughout the neighborhood. Next he worked at the local Burpee Seed Farm, cultivating phlox: "if my birthday were tomorrow and someone were to give me a bouquet of the horrid flowers, I would punch him in the nose" (*World*, 440). He also worked for a plumber as a teenager, doing very well and thinking about quitting school. Uncle Arthur stopped that idea immediately. In junior high and high school, James had a paper route and observed the complexities of small-town relationships as he rode through the streets in the early morning delivering the papers. His experiences as a cashier in Willow Grove amusement park during several summer vacations would be reflected in the activities of David Harper, his main character in *The Fires of Spring*. It was expected that cashiers selling tickets to the various rides would shortchange the public as much as possible. Those were the "honest" cashiers; the dishonest ones would also cheat the company through various scams, such as reselling the same tickets and tampering with turnstiles. Young James gained insights into the efforts of some to keep operations relatively ethical and the pressures on those trapped by their own greed. The amusement park also gave him the chance to hear good music, as concerts were presented regularly by such well-known musicians of the 1920s as John Philip Sousa and Victor Herbert.

When he was thirteen years old, James started the traveling that would always be a part of his life. He and a friend of the same age hitchhiked to New York City from Doylestown. His young friend was also an orphan who didn't do well at school but got along well with people. They hitchhiked twice more together, trying for Florida the year after the New York trip but getting sent home by policemen in a Georgia town, who felt that such youngsters should not be on their own. A year later they headed for Canada. Before graduating from college, he would visit nearly every state in the Union during these hitchhiking trips, traveling on his own after the first three trips with his friend. It was the 1920s and a more innocent era when boys could travel without fear and motorists enjoyed the adventurous young hitchhikers. Michener writes that he developed his basic attitude about accepting people pretty much as he found them, thanks to the optimistic personality and basic goodwill of his friend and the people he found who welcomed him into their cars and often into their homes (*World*, 117).

Completing high school in 1925 with a good academic record and success as an athlete in basketball, baseball, and tennis, Michener was awarded a scholarship to Swarthmore College in Pennsylvania. He did well in his studies, majoring in English and history and graduating summa cum laude. One summer vacation during his college years, Michener joined one of the last traveling Chautauqua shows. These troupes toured across the United States in the late nineteenth and early twentieth centuries, presenting such entertainment as lectures, concerts, and dramatic presentations in various towns and villages. Through this experience, Michener learned about both theatrical productions and the American countryside.

It was during his college years that Michener was confronted with the uncertainties of his background. He already knew he was different; aunts from the Michener family had made that perfectly clear while he was a child. However, it was a shattering experience to hear at age nineteen from a girl at a Michener family picnic that he was not "one of us" and that the woman he called his mother really wasn't (*World*, 486). James struggled with questions of his identity for several days. He concluded that he would never know precisely who he was and that the answer was of no importance in how he would lead his life: "From that moment of decision I never wavered or looked back. I knew who I was, a young man of nineteen with certain proved abilities and known weaknesses ready for the long haul of years that lay ahead" (*World*, 487).

At this same time Michener had been working through questions about the nature of God and religious proof. After reflecting during the same weekend when he was considering the parentage question, he decided that he wasn't competent to solve the greater questions relating to the existence of God. However, he concluded that he would try to live his life according to the principles of the biblical book of Deuteronomy and the books of the New Testament because of the excellent patterns of life these parts of the Bible set forth. He would be a practicing Christian, impartial toward denominations but supportive of churches. Michener's Quaker upbringing through the influence of Mabel Michener and Swarthmore College would affect his attitudes about how a life should be lived, but theological questions would not preoccupy him (*World*, 489).

Diploma in hand, Michener accepted his first teaching job at the Hill School, a prep school in Pottstown, Pennsylvania, where he taught English. In 1931 he was awarded the Lippincott Fellowship from Swarthmore, which would enable him to study and travel abroad for two years. At this time, the parentage question resurfaced because of his need for a passport. Mabel Michener, with the help of a lawyer, arranged a story listing herself and Edwin as James's parents, in spite of the discrepancy in dates. James did obtain the passport, and some years later when he entered the U. S. Navy, the same story of his origins was accepted.

Michener's European experience began at St. Andrew's University in Scotland. But he took full advantage of his opportunity to travel, visiting that first year the great cities of France, Italy, Spain, Belgium, and the Netherlands. During this first stay in Europe he hiked across Scotland, visited the Hebrides islands, and even spent some months on Barra, where the residents spoke mainly Gaelic and he had a chance to learn many folk songs, continuing his lifelong interest in different types of music. In Spain he toured with a group of bullfighters, developing an appreciation for this competition between man and animal. Michener was able to work on a British ship, recording updated information on navigation charts and seeing the Mediterranean Sea. He also augmented his political education through observing fascism in Italy and talking to German students. His education about communism came primarily from a student conference he attended in Brussels. After listening to all the debates and discussions, Michener discovered he had more first-hand experience with poverty and social differences than did the other participants, and he decided that communism was not a solution for America's economic depression.

After his return to the United States, Michener took a teaching position at the George School in Newtown, Pennsylvania, and taught at this Quaker institution from 1933 to 1936. He was married in 1935 to Patti Koon, whom he had met at a summer program at the University of Virginia.

Michener's next job took him to the Colorado State College of Education at Greeley, Colorado. He taught social studies in the college's laboratory school as an associate professor of education and earned a master's degree. His professors at Ohio State, where he had done graduate work, had warned him that the move was a mistake, commenting that promising young men who went West spent their time trying to work their way back East. Yet Michener had little trouble returning East; he was invited to spend the 1940–41 academic year as a visiting professor in the School of Education at Harvard University. His first publications were articles published in professional journals, and they reflected his belief that students "should be concerned with just laws, decency in public life, economic justice, the dignity of work, and the welfare of the community" (Hayes 1984, 53).

With his interest in new places and new people, Michener took advantage of the Colorado years to travel throughout the region, storing in his memory and in photographs images of the land and its residents. This material would be a starting point for his 1974 novel *Centennial*.

Michener was sure that the United States would be involved in the war already underway in Europe and Asia in 1940. Just before the bombing of Pearl Harbor by the Japanese on December 7, 1941, he had published a patriotic essay on the reasons for Americans to support the country's soon-to-come involvement in the war. He had started working for the Macmillan Publishing Company as a textbook editor after the year at Harvard and could have been exempt from military service because of his Quaker affiliation. However, before being drafted, he enlisted in the navy and was sent to the Pacific Ocean rather than to the Mediterranean, in spite of his European experience. Michener's first assignment was to visit navy air units to be sure that the units had the necessary manuals for airplane operation and maintenance. His travels to many islands in the South Pacific gave him ample opportunity to observe the land, the people, and the activities that were to figure in his early fiction. Later he became the senior naval historical officer for the area from New Guinea to Tahiti, writing extensive histories of naval operations in such places as Bora Bora and Tongatabu (Day 1964, 22).

Michener returned to his job at Macmillan after his discharge from the navy, but stories he had written for the most part in a Quonset hut on the island of Espíritu Santo by the light of a kerosene lamp were accepted by Macmillan and published as *Tales of the South Pacific* in February 1947. Because he sold two of the stories to the *Saturday Evening Post* in 1946, publication of the book was delayed until 1947. The writer feels that this delay was part of being at the right place at the right time; *Tales of the South Pacific*, a volume of connected short stories, won the 1947 Pulitzer Prize for fiction. Published a year earlier or a year later, Michener thinks, and he would not have received the award, owing to the strong candidates of those years. Comments from some critics expressed wonder that such a book was selected, since it did not fit the original criteria for the award, being neither a novel nor "distinguished." Years after the award announcement, Michener met Alice Roosevelt Longworth, daughter of President Theodore Roosevelt, and learned that she had been the person to recommend that the members of the award committee read Michener's work, which she had liked very much (*World*, 287).

Continuing as an editor of textbooks at Macmillan, Michener worked on his second novel, *The Fires of Spring*. Macmillan refused the book, and George Brett, head of the company, told the aspiring writer that he had a great future as a publisher but not as a novelist. Michener took his manuscript to Random House, which has been his major publisher since that time. His agent and other friends told Michener that if he really wanted a writing career, he needed to leave Macmillan and write full time. In 1949 he made the decision, bolstered by the success of the musical *South Pacific*, put together by Richard Rodgers and Oscar Hammerstein. Michener received the usual 1 percent royalty for having provided the original book, but once they were sure the musical would be a hit, Rodgers and Hammerstein loaned him enough money to buy a 6 percent interest in the show. He now had a steady income.

On the personal side, Michener and his first wife were divorced in 1948. Both served in the armed forces during World War II, and their separation and different experiences apparently led to the end of the marriage, as they never lived together again after the war. Michener's second marriage took place later in 1948. Vange Nord had written for magazines and worked some as an interior decorator in New York City. The couple built a home in Pipersville, Pennsylvania, not far from Doylestown. However, Michener's travels to the South Pacific and Asia on various writing assignments kept him away from home and his wife for months at a time.

With many Americans interested in other parts of the world after World War II, Michener's first series of articles on Asia in *Holiday* magazine were very well received. Travel pieces, they also included many personal observations about race, religion, trade, culture, and social and economic tensions. His agent, Helen Strauss, found him more assignments that would focus on Asia. Michener felt that Asia must develop its own strengths, basing his view on both historical perspective and his own analysis (Hayes 1984, 92). His knowledgeable viewpoint impressed the editors of *Reader's Digest*, and they requested articles, especially about the Korean War. His agent refused an exclusive arrangement, but many Michener articles have appeared in that publication over the years.

The 1950s were a prolific decade for the now full-time writer. In addition to his magazine and newspaper articles, Michener published a travel volume with short stories, a political book with sketches of Asian personalities, two short novels, three volumes on Japanese prints, a report on the Soviet suppression of the Hungarian revolt, and his first historical panoramic novel. He also collaborated on a book about colorful characters from the Pacific region. Michener had set a pattern of writing about what interested him in both fiction and nonfiction and kept himself constantly involved in projects that would continue virtually without interruption to the present time.

Not a writer in isolation, Michener experienced first-hand many of the things he would describe in his books. For example, asked by *Reader's Digest* to report on the Hungarian revolt in 1956, he interviewed hundreds of refugees as well as helped numerous refugees cross from Hungary into Austria. When he had an assignment to write about the activities of the Strategic Air Command, Michener wangled a way to fly one of the big jets. He had already experienced directly take-offs and landings on aircraft carriers when writing about the Korean War.

Michener's personal life changed in 1955 with the end of his second marriage. Vange Nord Michener asked for a divorce and custody of the Amerasian baby the couple had adopted. The divorce was final in August. Meanwhile, in December 1954, James had met Mari Yoriko Sabusawa in Chicago, where she was employed as an assistant editor of the American Library Association *Bulletin*. Michener was working on an assignment for *Life* magazine at the time—a feature concerning the marriage of a G.I. and a Japanese girl. Mari's parents were Japanese, but she had never visited Japan. Like many Japanese Americans, she spent most of World War II in an internment camp in California. Educated at Antioch College in Ohio, she worked for the government in Washington, D.C., during the last part of the war. James Michener and Mari Sabusawa were married in October 1955. Their nearly forty-year marriage ended with Mari Michener's death from cancer on September 25, 1994.

In the early 1960s Michener became involved in politics. His family had always been Republicans, but by the late 1950s Michener felt the country needed a change and the Republicans were not interested in the social issues he was. In 1960 he accepted an invitation to campaign for John F. Kennedy. He worked on the committee for Bucks County, Pennsylvania, a long-time Republican stronghold, making speeches and helping voters register. Michener also participated in a three-week campaign swing across the United States with movie and sports personalities and members of the Kennedy family. Michener has noted that Kennedy lost every state the group visited, but local candidates benefited from the media coverage of the group's appearance (*World*, 186). His experiences with the campaign were summarized in his 1961 book *Report of the County Chairman*. Additional thoughts on the U.S. system of electing a president were presented in *Presidential Lottery: The Reckless Gamble in Our Electoral System* (1969), where Michener argues for a reform of the method.

In 1962 Michener decided to run for Congress as a Democrat in a heavily Republican district of Pennsylvania. He and Mari traveled all over the district, attending every possible event, but Michener's opponent retained his seat—with a smaller than usual margin of victory, however. Michener says that his candidacy was one of the best things he has done because of the knowledge he gained about the nation and its citizens. He also feels that the election process teaches candidates humility; this conviction was reinforced for him in 1974 by the number of Richard Nixon's appointed staff who were in prison or forced to resign. They had never run for any kind of office, and they had attained great power "without ever undergoing the sobering experience of asking voters for their support or the humbling experience of having lost" (*World*, 188).

Because of his interest in things political and in good government, Michener was a delegate to the Pennsylvania Constitutional Convention, called in 1967–68 to reform the state's constitution. Most of his ideas for reform were defeated, but he still considers this participation and work as convention secretary one of the prime accomplishments of his life (*World*, 192). Following the convention, Michener served as chair of the committee implementing the changes that were accepted, so he spent nearly two years absorbed in these civic responsibilities.

Michener articulated certain of his concerns and attitudes regarding change in three works published after his work with the Constitutional Convention. *Iberia: Spanish Travels and Reflections* (1968) presents some thoughts about societies characterized by inertia, and two short works, *America vs. America: The Revolution in Middle-Class Values* (1969) and *The Quality of Life* (1970), talk about the need to adjust to change. Youthful agitation is seen as a healthful reaction to middle-class hypocrisy, but values of worth should be scrutinized and kept if they have not become ritual or mere prohibitions (Becker 1983, 183).

Michener's interest in the happenings of the world around him led him to accept a commission from Random House and *Reader's Digest* to explain what happened when four students were killed by National Guard members at Kent State University in Ohio in May 1970. Michener postponed his research for *Centennial*, donated $100,000 to the university, and began a lengthy series of interviews at Kent State, listening to all those who would talk to him, in preparation for the 1971 book *Kent State: What Happened and Why*. One critic feels that Michener's account of the tragedy is as free of bias as possible, although he does leave the reader with an overall impression of "widespread juvenile irresponsibility" (Becker 1983, 16).

Michener's involvement in governmental committees and commissions continued through the 1970s and into the 1980s. The wide variety of his activities adds to the portrait of the writer as a citizen. In the 1970s he and playwright Arthur Miller helped form a committee to protest the abuses they saw in the United Nations Educational, Scientific and Cultural Organization (UNESCO). Their issues were the UNESCO efforts to have reporters covering Third World nations licensed by those nations in order to hamper unfavorable reporting, Arab efforts to keep Israel from UNESCO operations, and anti-American propaganda. He later was part of a committee to study a possible withdrawal from UNESCO by the United States (*World*, 194–95).

Because of his knowledge of the communist bloc, gained through many trips to the Soviet Union, his experiences in Hungary during the 1956 revolt, and visits to Poland, Michener was named in 1970 to the

U.S. advisory committee on information, charged with giving counsel to the U.S. Information Service about the best ways to distribute accurate information abroad about the United States. He worked on this committee until 1976.

Michener's next assignment was serving from 1979 to 1983 on the advisory board of the National Aeronautics and Space Administration (NASA). Michener studied very hard to understand the complexities of the space program, visiting bases, trying training devices, watching launches, and working in control rooms. His new knowledge of the program and its issues would find expression in the 1982 novel *Space* (see Chapter 8).

Another assignment in the fight against communism was his selection to the U.S. International Broadcasting Board, on which he served from 1983 to 1989. The board managed American radio stations, sending programs to the USSR and Iron Curtain nations. Although Michener believed in eventual rapprochement with the Soviet Union, he also felt that broadcasting the truth of happenings in that nation and those controlled by it was important.

Michener served his country in 1983 on a committee formed to advise the military on handling the controversy that arose from its attempt to keep the Grenada invasion a secret until it had been completed. Michener's main point was that refusing to inform a society that its military units were in action is destructive to civilian morale and erodes support for the military. In a footnote in *The World Is My Home*, he writes that the military's controversial policy toward the media during the 1991 Persian Gulf conflict seemed to indicate that the committee's advice had not been taken (*World*, 214).

One additional government service for Michener was from 1983 to 1987 as a member of the U.S. Postal Service Advisory Committee. This group determines what postage stamps the government should issue. The matter of which individuals and agencies should be recognized on stamps is a highly emotional one. Michener notes that while running for Congress taught him the complexity of political life, serving on the stamp committee showed him the passion that Americans feel concerning important symbols in their lives (*World*, 223).

James Michener ended his formal work for the government in 1989, when he resigned voluntarily from his last assignment. There is some irony in that timing: that very year, citizens of the Soviet Union and eastern Europe began to enjoy those freedoms that Michener had advocated when he was on those advisory boards and committees. And his government had already recognized his work supporting the free exchange of ideas and information by awarding him the U.S. Medal of Freedom in 1977.

The service component of Michener's life and work indicates the breadth of his interests and concerns. His published writing—novels, short stories, articles, and nonfiction books—shares this breadth with his readers. His choice of subjects, his method of writing novels, and his self-assessment as a writer are all part of Michener the person.

In *The World Is My Home,* Michener talks about considering those personal characteristics that he felt would help him achieve his goals when making the decision to become a full-time writer. He had wide interests and knowledge gained from his academic work, various jobs, and travel. He was also intrigued with people and their stories, wanting to collect all he could. Another helpful skill for a writer was his ability to keep track in his mind certain details from up to five hundred books on the subject of his current research. Michener does list page numbers and perhaps one word to indicate the subject he wants to remember in the book, but he can usually find the reference he wants without his list (*World,* 301). Words have always fascinated him, and he works with a large dictionary and a synonym finder close at hand. However, as he writes, Michener does not feel the need to use all the words he knows. Instead, he tries to achieve extraordinary results with ordinary words (*World,* 306).

In his self-assessment Michener notes that neither complex characters nor intricate plots are his strong points. He accepts his characters at face value, letting them reveal themselves in their own way, but does not deal in detail with their psychological structure or problems. Instead of a plot tied up neatly at the end, he prefers to tell the story and stop it where he thinks it appropriate to do so. Michener indicates that he seems to have had some talent in creating the setting and atmosphere for his narrations, even though there are readers who can't make it through the long beginning chapters. He defines narration as knowing how to alternate effectively two types of writing, which he calls *carry* and *scene.* The carry sections convey information such as what has been happening, what the characters are working toward. Scene sections deal with characters in contact with other characters, and dialogue is important. Michener feels he has done some good work in carry, but is not as gifted with scene sections (*World,* 319).

In *About Centennial: Some Notes on the Novel* (1974) Michener summarizes his thoughts about the type of writer he is: "The purpose of a writer like me—and I am a peculiar one not well fitted to serve as a model for others—is to create a universe to which the reader must surrender himself totally for an extended period of time. If he will do so, he will acquire understandings, images and memories which will rest with him for a long time" (49).

When choosing subjects, Michener has focused often on areas he saw as gaining in international importance and has selected such places as Poland or South Africa, whose stories continued in the direction the Michener novels indicated. He frequently thinks about a possible story topic for years before consciously beginning the work that will result in a novel. And some ideas researched over the years never become a finished work. For example, Michener did a great deal of work for a projected novel about the siege of Leningrad (again called St. Petersburg) during World War II, but gave it up for health reasons.

It has been said that because of the massive factual detail in the historical, panoramic novels especially, Michener must employ an army of researchers. However, his main staff member is himself. With *Centennial*, he had the help of John Kings, who was involved in field research (see Chapter 5), and during the 1990s Mr. Kings has been serving as a manager for Michener's office, scheduling appointments and obtaining research materials, among other tasks. For *Texas* (1985), two doctoral candidates located materials (see Chapter 9), but Michener is always the one who gains the expertise necessary for the novel's subject through reading, consulting with experts, and interviewing those who are involved in the topic under consideration. He uses secretaries for putting the manuscript into the form necessary for the editor at the publishing firm, but the writing and rewriting of the story are his responsibility. Once a manuscript is in a revised draft he does request experts to check factual information and will also make changes in wording based on his editor's recommendations.

How does James Michener write? Does he suffer from writer's block on occasion? His working style is outlined in the most detail in John Kings's book *In Search of Centennial* (1978), *The World Is My Own*, and *James A. Michener's Writer's Handbook*, published in 1992. These books contain copies of manuscript pages showing the revisions that took place from the first draft through the final version. Writing a book is a long and intricate process.

When Michener has decided on a subject he wishes to pursue, he types out a statement on the reasons for his choice and makes up an outline of chapter headings for the book as he envisions it at that moment. He now has a guide that will take him through the project to its completion, often a period of up to three years. General reading on the field comes next, with no note taking but much consulting of book indexes. Concentrated reading comes when four or five ideas central to the subject have been identified. Michener says he gives himself nearly a seminar course in each area and does find that he may not use every area of research. However, the thorough preparation is useful in understanding how the various parts of the topic fit together.

Once the actual writing begins, Michener spends the morning hours, from around 7:30 A.M. to 12:30 P.M., typing with two fingers on a manual typewriter, preferably one with elite type, which enables him to get the maximum number of words on a page. He says that professional writers can't afford writer's block, and if a blank day comes along, he moves to a later part of the manuscript and work proceeds. Of course, the passage may not be usable when the writer arrives at its proper position because the flow and tone of the out-of-sequence passage do not correspond to the intervening narrative. In revising, Michener avoids altering his original pagination because he feels it would be destructive to disturb the sequence of pages and their content engraved in his mind (*World*, 382–83). He will cut and paste in order to keep the pages the same; material added will lengthen a page while deleted material shortens it. When a chapter has been edited, he turns it over to his secretary and future editing is done on the word processor. Michener sees the word processor as the necessary tool for any would-be writer, and in a 1993 *Forbes ASAP* magazine article he outlined his "dream machine." He would require at the click of a mouse or at a voice command immediate access to the research data he now finds in many books: a dictionary, a synonym finder, almanacs, encyclopedias, the Bible, atlases, access to information brokers (26–27).

The peer review is the next step—experts verify the information in the novel for errors or misinterpretations. When their suggestions have been incorporated into the text, the manuscript is sent to the editor at the publishing house. The editor and the writer exchange letters over a period of months, dealing with questions about individual passages and words. The copy editor is the next to read the manuscript thoroughly as the final authority on style. Michener cites his long-time editor, Albert Erskine, and copy editor, Bert Krantz, at Random House as two of the most outstanding examples of their professions (*World*, 384–85).

Lawyers check the text once the editors are finished. When the printer returns the galleys, an outside proofreader reads it once again, but Michener says that, in spite of all these efforts, errors and misspelled words do occur, much to his embarrassment. He feels that the care with which his books have been written and published explains in large part their wide acceptance and longevity (*World*, 386).

This wide acceptance has earned James Michener a great deal of money. His attitude toward money and wealth, and what he has done with much of his earnings, adds another facet to the portrait of the writer as a man. He says his attitude is "bizarre and contradictory" (*World*, 450), and owing to the poverty of his childhood, he eliminated money as a dominant factor in his thinking. However, as a writer he has earned large sums of money, although he says he pays no attention to royalty percentages or yearly balances. And he lives personally as though hard times will come again, preferring slivers of soap to buying a can of shaving cream (Nicklin 1993, A27).

Michener feels that when publishers use the profits earned by the company through sales of best-sellers to publish beginning writers, a balance has been achieved. However, recent changes in the publishing industry endanger this practice, he feels. When it was rumored that Random House would be purchased by a buyer Michener considered unqualified to run the business, he began a movement with other Random House writers to leave if the sale went through. More qualified buyers became the new owners (*World*, 467, 469).

James Michener has done his part to encourage writers and higher education by giving away much of what he has earned by writing. The University of Iowa's Writer's Workshop received $500,000 in 1980 and another $500,000 in 1990. These gifts have been used to set up fellowship programs for new writers. The Texas Center for Writers at the University of Texas at Austin has benefited from Michener's financial encouragement for a total of $19 million: $1 million in 1986 to set up the center, $3 million in 1990 to create fellowships, and $15 million in 1992. The University of Miami was given $1 million in 1990 after Michener used the campus library for research on the Caribbean; the money established a writing program for graduate students, especially for those from the Caribbean. Eckerd College, in St. Petersburg, Florida, received $1 million in 1992, which is being used to endow scholarships; Michener began teaching writing classes at Eckerd in 1989. He has donated a total of $7 million to his alma mater, Swarthmore College, part of which has been used to fund a program to help professors in fields other than English teach their students discipline-specific ways of writing. Another alma mater, the University of Northern Colorado (formerly the Colorado

State College of Education), received $600,000 in 1992 to endow a campus library that had been constructed and named after Michener in the 1970s. Another example of the writer's financial support to colleges with which he has been associated is the $750,000 given since 1988 to Sheldon Jackson College in Sitka, Alaska. Michener lived in a log cabin near the college while writing *Alaska* (1988). The collection of twentieth-century American art that James and Mari Michener collected over the years has been donated to the University of Texas at Austin. The collection contains 376 paintings, with a stated value of $19 million (Nicklin 1993, A27–28). The Michener collection of Japanese prints has been given to the University of Hawaii. Other gifts from royalties have gone to programs to help poets get published, to support young writers in Canada and Poland, to set up graduate internships at a university press for students interested in making books, to fund scholarships for children of war correspondents and space experts, and to support a society that cares for older writers in financial difficulties (*World*, 474). If Michener has spoken and written about the inequities of royalties, this preceding record of his philanthropies shows he has done something about them.

James Michener's latest novel, *Miracle in Seville*, was published in the autumn of 1995, when the writer was eighty-eight years old. How does a man of advanced years who had a severe heart attack in his fifties and quintuple bypass surgery and a hip replacement in his seventies, and who is undergoing kidney dialysis in his eighties continue to publish books that are read by innumerable readers? He likens himself to the old apple tree that bore a tremendous crop after the farmer drove rusty nails into its trunk: The health problems evidently stimulated Michener to increased effort. From 1986 to 1995 he wrote and published a total of fifteen books. As he states in his memoir, "I write at eighty-five for the same reasons that impelled me to write at forty-five: I was born with a passionate desire to communicate, to organize experience, to tell tales that dramatize the adventures which readers might have had" (*World*, 6). He has done just that and will be remembered as he wishes for that long row of solid books that say "By James A. Michener." The following chapters will give an overview of the fiction from that long row and discuss nine novels more thoroughly.

2

Michener's Fiction:
An Overview

James A. Michener tells stories. He has told them in some twenty-five fictional works, many of which are hundreds of pages long. Does he fit into a well-defined literary genre or does his work resist categorization? This chapter will discuss the genre question, the development of Michener's fiction, and his recurring themes, ideas, and concerns. These twenty-five works will be considered along with the reasons for the choice of the eight novels that are presented in separate chapters. Michener's latest fictional work, *Miracle in Seville* (1995), will be introduced in a final chapter.

MICHENER AND LITERARY GENRE

Michener writes narratives; he tells what happens to selected people at certain times in certain places. His work does not fit neatly into a category like science fiction, mystery or suspense stories, or psychological novels. Many of his major novels can be called historical in that they reconstruct past ages. However, Michener cannot be identified with historical fiction, which presents exploits that are grounded in fact but rely on extravagant adventures. His historical, panoramic novels are a serious effort to explain or interpret the past by showing how events involve human beings and are influenced by them. He grounds them in great amounts of fact, a tactic that eliminates those readers uninterested in his subject.

Setting and theme are important in all of Michener's fiction. As he says in his *Literary Reflections,* "An effective novel starts with characters, grows with them, and matures intellectually and spiritually with them. But they must be seen in their setting, engaged by the great themes of their time" (99). Even in the shorter novels, he creates a sense of place that situates the reader directly in the world where the narrative takes place. And in all his fiction, there is the impact of a view of life, of certain values that are promoted.

Michener has enjoyed success with the public, if not always with critics. Readers choosing a Michener novel know they will get a well-told story about people living in an interesting place at an interesting time. They will learn about areas of their own country or of the world, they will find out a number of details about how life was and is lived, and they will discover an attitude toward life. A. Grove Day finds Michener similar to "those crusaders like Jack London and Upton Sinclair who found in fiction a broader extension of their revelatory reportage" (Day 1964, 150). Another critic notes that Michener is a writer of serious purpose: "he wants to instruct, to take his readers through history in an entertaining fashion, to introduce them to lands and peoples they do not know" (*Contemporary Authors* 1995, 45: 288). In the shorter as well as the panoramic novels, the story teaches as well as entertains. Michener himself explains his success partially as one of timing: "I published my books at the precise time when Americans were beginning to look outward at the entire world rather than inward at themselves. They were spiritually and intellectually ready and even eager to read the exploring kinds of books I wanted to write. And with the intrusion of a largely banal television many were prepared to seek refuge in long books" (*World,* 464).

Michener started his storytelling career with shorter works such as *Tales of the South Pacific* (1947), *The Fires of Spring* (1949), *Return to Paradise* (1951), *The Bridges at Toko-Ri* (1953), and *Sayonara* (1954). Except for the autobiographical *The Fires of Spring,* the places were the South Pacific, Korea, and Japan—areas brought to American interest because of recent wars. It was with *Hawaii* in 1959 that the writer found the historical, panoramic formula that would present long spans of time and the interweaving of historical facts with the fictional participation of several families of characters. *Caravans* (1963) would take the reader to Afghanistan with a return to a more focused group of characters and story line. *The Source* (1965) would develop further the historical panorama of people in a well-defined place, this time in Israel, over hundreds of years. *The Drifters* (1971) would leave the panorama of centuries of time to concentrate on the story of youth searching for meaning in a series of well-defined places in contemporary time. With *Centennial* (1974), *Chesapeake* (1978), and *The Covenant* (1980), Michener continued his historical panoramas, using two areas of the United States and also South Africa. In *Space* (1982) he chose to present the panorama of the development of space exploration through the involvement of four fictional families. His fiction during the rest of the 1980s and the early 1990s would include five more historical, panoramic novels: *Poland* (1983), *Texas* (1985), *Alaska* (1988), *Caribbean* (1989), and *Mexico* (1992). Six shorter novels during this same period tell more concentrated stories but share the ongoing Michener concerns for personal fortitude and social problems: *The Legacy* (1987), *Journey* (1989), *The Eagle and the Raven* (1990), *The Novel* (1991), *Recessional* (1994), and *Miracle in Seville* (1995). *Creatures of the Kingdom* (1993) is a collection of animal stories; most are from previously published novels, one is new. This summarized listing shows that while Michener may be best known for his historical fiction, he conveys a similar sense of place and values to the reader when he tells stories more restrained in scope.

RECURRING THEMES, IDEAS, CONCERNS

One of the values Michener holds as extremely important is human tolerance, which becomes an evident theme in the majority of his fictional works. Whether the issue is one of race, religion, or culture, Michener's books promote respect for all human beings. Nurse Nellie Forbush in *Tales of the South Pacific* realizes that her attitude toward those with different skin color blinds her to their worth as people. *Hawaii* illustrates the superiority complex of the white Americans toward the islands' other groups. *Centennial* and *Chesapeake* reveal the dismal American record toward the Indians, the blacks, and the Mexicans. *Caribbean* shows how racial discrimination has hampered the development and well-being of the islands' varied population. These novels and the others in Michener's long row of solid books do not provide answers to the problems of prejudice. They present prejudice in action and show different ways of reacting to it and against it.

The environmental theme is less persistent in Michener's works, but concern for the land is often evident. People cannot flourish without using the land and its products, but it is difficult to find the balance in the struggle to make the land fruitful without ruining it. In *The Source* the reader sees the transformation of a promised land into a desert. At times it is lack of understanding that harms the land: the dry land farmers in *Centennial* set up the fields for erosion with their straight-line plowing; the cotton farmers in *Texas* do not at first realize that their deep wells are depleting the underground source of water. But it is greed that motivates the Russian seal and otter hunters and the American salmon canning industry in *Alaska*. Again, there are no easy answers, and at the close of such novels as *Chesapeake* and *Alaska* the reader sees an indication that an interest in profit may outweigh a consideration for an ecological equilibrium.

The similar values of courage and hard work are also important thematic considerations in Michener's fiction. Human courage is defined by the actions of many Michener characters as the fortitude necessary to press onward against difficulties, whether those difficulties are caused by climate, terrain, wars, or other people. Harry Brubaker in *The Bridges of Toko-Ri* will continue to fly missions over Korea because his sense of doing the job well will overcome a sense of bitterness about leaving his family to fight in another war. Levi and Elly Zendt in *Centennial* push on across the plains although the hardships of the journey seem overwhelming. Michener characters on the whole are willing to exert themselves to achieve goals. The Chinese and Japanese of *Hawaii* exemplify drive; the Hawaiians show more willingness to enjoy a relaxed life-style. Another example of lack of will or inertia is the Virginia planter in *Chesapeake* who buys more than he can pay for with what his slaves produce. His apathy leads to moral as well as economic bankruptcy, according to the Michener view of life.

Another Michener concern is the condition of women: "I have found all societies, all religions fearfully unfair to women and, whenever possible, have done my best to redress the imbalances" (*World*, 317). The women characters in the early novels are not especially memorable, but from *Hawaii* on, the novels have important women characters. Their activities reflect the standards and patterns of their culture, but such characters as Lady Gray Eyes in *Mexico*, who manages to halt the human sacrifices required by her Indian culture's religion, and Biruta Buk in *Poland*, who smuggles food to members of the resistance, illustrate the fortitude that characterizes the best of human endeavor.

Michener's thematic concerns and values are evident in all of his fiction, although individual books emphasize different aspects of his view of life.

MICHENER'S WRITING STYLE

Michener's style is characterized by his ability to tell a story while giving the reader a large amount of factual information. At his best, Michener's descriptions of setting and happenings are so graphic that the reader becomes part of the world and the event the writer is depicting. It would be hard to find a more engrossing account of rounding South America in a sailing ship than in *Hawaii* or a more understanding portrayal of a bullfight than in *Mexico*. At times, the images can be trite: Lloyd Gruver in *Sayonara* decides that home must be where he and some woman could become "part of the immortal passage of human beings over the face of the earth" (186). But the average reader, caught up in the story, moves from one page to the next and notes only in passing a phrase here or a sentence there that does not ring as true as most of the narrative.

In analyzing his writing, Michener says he prefers the simpler sentence because his goal is clarity: "I tend to think linearly, with a strong start, a clean, sharp active verb and a reasonable conclusion" (*World*, 308). He goes on to indicate that his tendency is to use too many declarative sentences connected by *and*. He corrects this by beginning a sentence with a dependent clause and finishing it with a strong independent one. Michener remarks that while he has not conquered the English sentence, he believes he has wrestled it "to an honorable draw" (*World*, 309). Most of his readers would agree.

Regarding character development, Michener's own analysis summarizes his achievements: "I tend to accept characters more or less at face value, preferring to have them reveal themselves in their own way.... I have tried to create men and women who capture the imagination and hold it" (*World*, 313). He has succeeded often in this endeavor even if in-depth characterization is not his strongest point.

Perhaps Michener's greatest achievement beside his ability to tell a meaningful story is his talent in creating a sense of place. He feels that humans and their societies must be seen as part of a natural setting in order to be fully understood or appreciated. Readers can visualize the plains of Poland or the mountains of Korea, the waterways leading to the Chesapeake or the beaches of Madagascar, the remote peaks and valleys of Afghanistan or the vastness of space. The story, the people, the place come together to create that total universe that the reader will inhabit for the duration of the narrative.

MICHENER'S FICTIONAL WORKS

Michener is best known for his fictional works that illuminate the history of a particular area. The following chapters of this study focus on six of the historical, panoramic novels in order to give a clear picture of the ways Michener brings together story, setting, and people to create an interesting and engrossing historical world. In *Hawaii, Centennial, Chesapeake, Texas,* and *Alaska* he deals with five different parts of the United States, presenting a revealing portrait of the American national tradition and telling stories of particular interest to American readers who want to learn about their history. *The Covenant* takes place in South Africa, an area very much in the international spotlight when it was published in 1980 and again at the present time. Its story is representative of Michener's ability to bring to life another part of the world, instructing his readers as well as entertaining them. This novel is also interesting for its portrait of the relationships between different racial groups, an issue of concern in many parts of the world, including the United States.

The Fires of Spring (1949) is part of the study as an example of Michener's early work and as an illustration of how he handles a story centered on one character. *Space* comes along thirty-three years later and focuses on one specific historical phenomenon, the exploration of outer space. This topic, with its celebration of human intelligence and ingenuity, is one of continuing interest to readers wanting to grapple with ideas while caught up in a narrative about people exploring frontiers. *Miracle in Seville* (1995) appeared in bookstores as this study was going into publication. A discussion of the book is included to illustrate Michener's continuing ability to tell a story and involve his readers in the values of a particular culture.

The remaining sixteen novels can be considered only briefly. The novels whose scope is more limited in space and time and whose stories deal with a variety of subjects will be discussed first, in the order they were published, with the presentation of the other four historical, panoramic narratives following.

Tales of the South Pacific (1947), Michener's first published novel, won the Pulitzer Prize for fiction in 1947 and inspired a long-running Broadway musical and then a film. The book is a collection of vignettes about Americans involved in World War II in the South Pacific in 1942–43, when the forthcoming major battle will happen at a fictional place called

Kuralei. There are recurring characters in the stories; they along with several other memorable characters are drawn deftly and completely. Some grow in the war; others can't stand up to the waiting and crumple when action is to begin. The narrator is a navy commander who is sent to various islands carrying messages and observing how people react to war. All the tales lead to the moment of the big battle, and along the way the reader gets an introduction to the island cultures as well as the natural world of the South Pacific: the islands, the sea, the beaches, the mountainous terrain, the majestic pine trees that must be destroyed to create an air strip. The final chapter is set in a hilltop cemetery where all men are heroes. The battle is over; where will the world get the good men to replace those who have been killed? Courage is celebrated in this first novel along with the theme of tolerance and the brotherhood of human beings in spite of skin color. And the sense of place is created with care as Michener describes the islands in vivid detail. The South Pacific, those who lived there, and those who came there for the purposes of war, come alive in these tales.

Return to Paradise (1951) is a combination of essay and story. Each essay talks about a different part of the South Pacific, covering several islands as well as glimpses of New Zealand and Australia. The short story following each essay takes place on the island just discussed or has a connection with it. Michener says he wrote the book because he saw increasing American links with this part of the world and the need for understanding: "Thus the reader could see from the essay what I thought about a given island; while from the fictional story he could determine what the island thought about itself"(2).* The descriptive essays are the best part of the book in their creation of a sense of place, but some of the stories catch the reader in the adventures of memorable people of different cultures. The theme of interracial relations and the need to treat people of all colors as human is interwoven into many of the stories, as is the impact Americans have on the different cultures during World War II.

Michener moves his setting to Korea in his short novel about the Korean War, *The Bridges at Toko-Ri* (1953). The first section of the story presents the sea with a description of freezing weather and turbulent waves as seen from the deck of a U.S. Navy aircraft carrier and by pilots trying to land their planes on the heaving deck. The reader can feel a

---

*Quotes from Michener's fictional works are from the paperback editions listed at the end of this study, except for citations from *Miracle in Seville*.

part of life on this ship and of the process of bringing the planes in to land in terrible conditions. The dramatic rescue of a downed pilot from the icy water is routine to these men of courage who are doing the job that needs to be done even though, as the Admiral says, "All wars are stupid. . . . But we'd better learn to handle the stupidity" (41). His rescued pilot will go on doing his job and will bomb those bridges at Toko-Ri.

The story moves to the land when the pilot, Harry Brubaker, gets three days' leave with his wife and children in Japan. Nancy Brubaker learns more about her husband's job and its importance; the admiral believes she must have some understanding of what this war is about even though most Americans at home couldn't care less. The Brubaker family shares a Japanese bath with a Japanese family, a peaceful moment of human brotherhood.

In the last section the bridge bombing operation is set up and carried out. Michener moves the story along with his authentic descriptions of what it feels like to fly "through the vast upper reaches of the world. Sea and sky fell away and he was aloft in the soaring realm of the human spirit" (75). The mission accomplishes the military objective at the cost of human lives; Harry Brubaker and the two men sent to rescue him after the plane is shot down are killed by enemy fire. The admiral asks again, "Why is America lucky enough to have such men?" (126).

The story is engrossing and moving, the characters lively and individualized in flashes as their story is told. The description of what it was like to live on an aircraft carrier and fly a jet plane during war is the most authentic part of the narrative, and the theme of courage is well illustrated: we have to fight wars that are, by nature, stupid; the burden will always fall on a few stalwart souls, we don't know why, but the courageous will always perform when needed.

Japan is the scene of Michener's next short novel, *Sayonara* (1954). The story of American air force major Lloyd Gruver, who falls in love with a Japanese dancer, deals with prejudice as well as devoted love between a man and a woman. American military men are not to marry Japanese women, and against his wishes and better judgment, Gruver must try to help Joe Kelly, an enlisted man in his unit, overcome this regulation. In the process he meets and falls in love with Hana-ogi, a dancer with the Takarazuka theater, and changes his attitude about the Japanese completely. Neither love affair is destined for a happy ending. Kelly kills himself and his wife rather than leave her in Japan, Hana-ogi leaves for Tokyo, and Gruver returns to the "real" world of his military career, saying good-bye to the Japan of the crowded islands and the people who share the good and bad traits of people everywhere: "I was forced to acknowledge that I lived in an age when the only honorable profession was soldiering, when the only acceptable attitude toward strange lands and people of another color must be not love but fear" (208).

The novel's setting brings the reader pictures of Japanese cities and byways, from the paper-walled houses of Osaka to the shrines of Kyoto to the meticulously tended tiny plots of land. Since Gruver is the story's first-person narrator, the reader sees through his eyes these scenes and the deftly drawn people who inhabit them. Gruver is also the one who illustrates the effort of one culture to understand another. He contrasts the devotion of many Japanese wives with the ambitious coldness of American military wives he knows. He participates in the cultural clashes as he confronts the lieutenant colonel who hates the Japanese and Americans who marry them, and he fights with some Japanese who hate Americans for sleeping with their women. Examples of prejudice are very evident in this narrative, but Gruver and Hana-ogi show that it can be overcome, if only for a moment. With his authentic story and sense of place, Michener gives the reader a broader understanding of Japan and its people.

Afghanistan in 1946 is the setting for *Caravans* (1963), Michener's novel portraying a culture in transition and its effect on those who encounter it. In the story of Ellen Jasper he is also presenting the theme of young people who have rejected their culture's values but have found no replacement. Ellen has disappeared after marrying a man from Afghanistan whom she met as a college student in the United States. An American foreign service officer must find out what has happened to her. In his search Mark Miller experiences the Afghan culture and land in its variety through jeep trips across the country and a journey with a group of nomads. Ellen, he discovers, is so disconnected that she has left her husband to join the nomads. While traveling with the caravan, she connects with a German doctor who is a war criminal because of medical experiments performed during World War II. She tries to develop a relationship with Mark, saying she wishes she had met him in America. Finally Ellen is to be sent on with another caravan into the Soviet Union, to be repatriated to the United States from there, but the reader wonders what opportunistic path she will choose for herself. To her, the world is insane: "I've rejected all the lives I've known, so I'm dead too. I can live only at the bottom . . . at the bottom dregs of an insane world. Where hope is being reborn" (297). Ellen is an interesting character, but her search for the essence of living takes her from one man to another; the hope that she thinks is being reborn is never defined.

Caravans is a memorable novel for its engrossing story, seen against a fascinating land and culture in transition. Michener gives a thorough and pertinent explanation of Afghanistan's geographical and political situation and brings the country alive to the reader with information about its history and people. Mark's travels with the caravan are especially vivid, and the portrait of the caravans of nomads originating in several countries and gathering in a mountain valley for trade and social interaction is striking in its depiction of a vanishing world. The old freedoms are slipping away, says the leader of the group with which Mark has been traveling. He has been saving money to purchase the land reclaimed when a new irrigation dam is built; groups who adapt to change will survive.

Michener develops the story of young people like Ellen more thoroughly in *The Drifters*, the novel he published in 1971. Again, the story unfolds in places that are well defined, almost in travelog fashion. The narrative focuses on six young people adrift in Europe and Africa in 1968–69. The cultural and social context is very important in the novel; the stories are told against the background of the Vietnam War, racial tensions, the drug culture, emerging African nations, and "free love" or casual sex. American involvement in the Vietnam War is now in the historic past, but the other social issues remain relevant in the 1990s. To structure the story, Michener uses a first-person narrator, George Fairbanks, a sixty-one-year-old businessman with an international corporation who knows several of the six and meets the others when connecting with the group at different points in their wandering. He treats them like people and is therefore accepted—but does not hesitate to say when he disagrees with the behavior and the ideas expressed.

Each of the six is introduced in a separate chapter that explains why they "dropped out" and how they found their way to Torremolinos on the Spanish coast, where they meet each other. Their discussions with each other and with Fairbanks as they move from place to place bring out much information about the concerns of young people on the verge of adulthood. Their reactions and experiences in such locations as Portugal, Moçambique, and Marrakech educate them and the reader about different cultures, religions, and histories. The recurring themes of the relationship of humans to each other and their environment are an important part of this narrative of the youth revolution of the late 1960s,

as they are in all Michener's novels. And the search for self, or the coming-of-age theme, is also part of the story of *The Drifters*. The narrator's
conclusion is that those young people who follow the conventional path
to adult responsibilities through education and jobs would ensure the
continuation of society. However, the survivors among the drifters might
very well be the spiritual guides of the world because they "would see
the world whole . . . would comprehend life as a terrifying reality, a combination of accomplishment and failure" (701). Of his group of drifters,
one dies, but the others will continue their journey, results unknown.

Michener concentrated on his historical, panoramic novels for the rest
of the 1970s and well into the 1980s, but he had some more stories to
tell in the shorter format. In 1987 he published *The Legacy*, his reaction
to the hearings about U.S. military aid to the *contras* involved in the
struggle for control of Nicaragua. Major Norman Starr is to testify at
Senate hearings about the alleged cover-up by the president's National
Security Council. The reader never learns what he has actually done; the
book is more a summary of the efforts of his forebears to create and
support the U.S. Constitution than a narrative of one man's decision.
Major Starr realizes that the Constitution is his legacy to defend: "I now
saw the Constitution which my ancestors had helped create, interpret
and enlarge as a treasured legacy whose provisions bind the various
regions and interests of our nation together" (176). He will not use the
phrase "I was following orders" as a defense. The book celebrates the
bicentennial of the Constitution and has worthy objectives and a main
character with courage, but it is not an engrossing story. The final pages
are a complete reprinting of the Constitution.

The story told in *Journey* (1989) was originally part of *Alaska* and was
cut when Michener's editors convinced him to keep the latter narrative
under one thousand pages in the hard-bound version. The chapter titles
tell the tale of the expedition of five Englishmen to the Klondike gold
rush in the last years of the nineteenth century: "Hope," "Courage,"
"Desolation," "Requiem." Lord Luton, an English nobleman, finances
and leads this adventure, accompanied by his cousin, his nephew, and
a friend, plus a gamekeeper from Lord Luton's Irish estate. Because this
English lord refuses to set foot on American territory, he decides to approach the Klondike overland, from Edmonton in Alberta, Canada, via
the Mackenzie River system. The terrain, the weather, and Lord Luton's
refusal to listen to advice result in the deaths of three of the party:
"Never, not even in his lonely, unspoken reflections, did he acknowledge
personal culpability for the growing disaster; he viewed it as either a

capricious act of God or the manifestation of the malevolent forces of nature" (197). The expedition members are realistically drawn young men facing adversity with character and fortitude, but the beautiful and terrifying land and the variable weather play equally important roles in this entertaining story of hazardous adventure.

Michener begins *The Eagle and the Raven* (1990) with a prologue telling how this book, like *Journey*, was born from a deleted chapter of a historical, panoramic novel, in this case *Texas*. Santa Ana, the Mexican general and ofttimes president of Mexico, is the eagle who defeated the Texans at the Alamo. Michener presents him as a flamboyant leader with no real understanding of government. Sam Houston is the raven, depicted as quite a good leader, true to his principles and with a concept of honor. The book is a fictionalized biography based on Michener's usual thorough research. He supplements the narrative with line drawings of the characters in action, maps showing the worlds of the eagle and the raven, and a reproduced painting of the battle of San Jacinto, where the raven's forces defeated the eagle's. Actual letters from the two historical personages, a comparative chronology of the two lives, and a suggested reading list complete the book. The narrative is an interesting interpretation of two historical figures but not a compelling story.

Michener leaves his usual pattern in *The Novel* (1991). Instead of a historical panorama, he presents the world of books. Each section features the first-person narrative of a different inhabitant of this world: the writer, the editor, the critic, the reader. Lukas Yoder is a successful writer who thinks he has written his final book, until he becomes obsessed with writing about a murder that takes place in the Pennsylvania community where Yoder lives. Yvonne Marmelle, Yoder's editor, tells of the process by which she became an editor and of her efforts to protect her integrity and her author when the publishing firm is the target of a corporate takeover. Teacher, aspiring novelist, and critic Karl Streibert has problems with Yoder's success and his own ambitions. Jane Garland, a millionaire widow, becomes involved in the discussions about the novel of the future and is directly affected by the murder. In addition to creating the suspense of a murder mystery, Michener uses the story to bring out ideas about literature and the novel as genre and to provide information about the writing, editing, and publishing process. And the narrative's structure gives opportunity for more in-depth presentation of each of the principal characters. Each one also undergoes a life crisis that gives dramatic interest to the section he or she dominates. *The Novel* is an absorbing narrative and shows that James Michener at age eighty-four had not lost his touch as a storyteller.

In his foreword to *Creatures of the Kingdom* (1993) Michener talks about his feelings for animals, his sorrow that many species are disappearing, and some of his personal experiences with animals. The stories in this volume come from several novels: *Hawaii, Centennial, Chesapeake, The Covenant, Texas, Alaska*. The one previously unpublished selection is set in Texas and features Lieutenant Colonel Bedford Cobb, a member of the family so prominent in *Texas*, and his skirmishes with a gray squirrel. The confrontation is related in a light tone, with all the devices used to thwart the squirrel described in detail. When Cobb's wife wants him to shoot the squirrel, however, Cobb refuses. The creature is the honorable enemy, and like the Chinese Cobb opposed in Korea, it is not to be denigrated by epithets or killed dishonorably.

The book jacket for Michener's *Recessional* (1994), summarizes the story's focus: "to illuminate the challenges of aging, and the opportunities and dilemmas older adults and their families encounter today." The novel follows several residents of the Palms, a Florida retirement center, over the course of a year through the unfolding of their various activities and concerns. It is also the story of the center's new director, Andy Zorn, and his effort to find meaning in his life after feeling forced from his chosen vocation—medicine—because of unjustified malpractice suits. His emotional awakening comes from his relationship with Betsy Cawthorn, who has lost both legs in an auto accident.

The medical profession, with its wonderful accomplishments, its ultimate lack of definitive answers for certain situations, and its complicated billing procedures, is detailed through the lives of the residents and the staff. Alzheimer's disease, breast cancer, the right to die and the ramifications of living wills, even AIDS, are part of the characters' lives. Women's roles and the environment are also touched on. The first ordained woman pastor in an unnamed Protestant denomination discusses with other residents of the Palms how women have been treated in the world's religions. And the natural world plays its role with the portrait of the rattlesnake whose world shrinks and drives him to strike. In addition, the savanna, a stretch of untamed land near the Palms, must give way to development. Sensible, concerned people will win some battles and lose others as they face the problems of living and dying in a complex and confused world. Michener's gift for storytelling has not diminished in this recent narrative. He has created memorable characters and illustrated values and attitudes that deserve his readers' thoughtful consideration.

The four historical, panoramic novels not discussed in individual chapters form a contrast to the novels just considered. Even though many of the same themes recur, these works concentrate on the history of particular places through the stories of fictional characters. *The Source* (1965) is Michener's next effort after *Hawaii* (1959) to tell this type of story. After ten years of studying the world of Islam, Michener had an opportunity to visit Haifa, Israel, including a site important during the Crusades. Michener describes the effect of this excursion: "as I stood alone in the dungeon of that ancient fortress, with the shadowy forms of warriors long dead moving in the dust, I suddenly conceived my entire novel *The Source*" (quoted in Day 1977, 120). For the novel an imaginary archeological site called Makor, meaning "the source," is created in Israel. It will be excavated by a team financed by a wealthy American Jew, headed by an American Catholic of Irish descent, with Israeli and Arab archeological experts. This team forms the framework story for the historical panorama of fifteen separate episodes. Nearly one-third of their story is told at the novel's beginning, other small fragments are interspersed throughout the book, another third is related in the next to last chapter, and the conclusion comes in the final chapter. The historic time begins with the inhabitants of the area ten thousand years before the present era and continues through the Hebrews of Old Testament time, the Roman occupation, the Crusades, the later immigrants to the Jewish Holy Land, and the establishment of the modern state of Israel in 1948. Michener notes that the novel has a complex structure and one he would not recommend to another novelist or use again, but in this story, it worked (*About Centennial*, 46). The reader's orientation to the story's events is helped by the two maps for nearly every episode: one of the region and one of Makor for the specific time period. Other linkage is provided through the objects found in the excavation at Makor, which recreate the history. Each of the fifteen objects refers in a symbolic way to the episode's narrative.

Religion and how humans react to it, live it, and die for it are the main themes of this novel. Two questions are underlying: Can Jews, Christians, and Moslems learn to coexist in respectful tolerance? Why do Jews make things so difficult for themselves? "The historical continuity that causes these questions to arise, or that shows actions in the public arena that exacerbate them, is the thread that binds the fifteen historical narratives together. What we are shown as far as Jews are concerned is testimony of heroic endurance almost beyond belief, balanced against a rigidity of law so austere as on occasion to be antihuman" (Becker 1983, 81–82). Ilan Eliav, the Israeli member of the archeological team who is slated for a post in the Israeli cabinet, reflects at the book's end that the law needs to be brought up to date, but he notes also, "no religion defended so tenaciously the ordinary dignity of living" (1086–1087). The Jewish people are shown enduring centuries of catastrophe because of the coherence and steadfastness of their faith, yet in their state of Israel how will the problems of existence with the Arabs be solved? As usual, Michener brings his story to a close without proposing definitive answers to complex questions. Instead, he enlivens history with interesting and memorable people, sheds light on beliefs that sustain human existence, and creates a vivid sense of place with his description of Makor and its land, rocks, trees, animals, and plants.

Poland was published in 1983, but Michener began working on the novel in 1977, believing that the country would soon become a focal point of international interest, as it did with the emergence of the Solidarity movement and the declaration of martial law in 1981. His last research trip to the country ended a week before martial law was declared. The narrative deals with seven hundred years of Polish history, covering several invasions and partitionings of the country, the Nazi occupation during World War II, and a modern struggle of farmers trying to form a labor union. The lives of three fictional families in a village Michener calls Bukowo present these historical events: the Counts Lubonski are the nobility, the Bukowskis represent the gentry or petty nobility, and the Buk family is part of the peasant heart of Poland. Before beginning the narrative, Michener gives a summary of what is fiction and what is fact in the narrative. He also explains how the Polish people were organized into social categories during most of the time period covered in the story. Maps help orient the reader.

The first and last chapters take place in 1981 and frame the historical panorama. The narrative captures the story of Poland's struggle and development, but the numerous characters make it difficult to track the personal histories of more than a few characters. The early chapters concentrate more on battles than on people and are not among Michener's best, but the reader does begin to understand this battleground for armies from both the east and the west. The social stratification is also very clear; after a battle the nobility gains the most, the gentry may profit slightly, but the peasant receives nothing for his effort. Once the story reaches the seventeenth century, some interesting characters begin to emerge from the swirling mass of soldiers. The picture of how the various classes live, the battle preparations and fighting, the political maneuvering become real as members of the three families of Bukowo participate in the events. The chapter about the Nazi occupation, the Polish resistance, and life in a concentration camp is one of the most gripping in its intensity, as it recreates the horror and shows the courage of individuals faced with terror. When the story stops, the farmers have no union, a Communist official has added more names to the list of Poles to be arrested when the crackdown comes, but Szymon Bukowski marries Biruta Buk, and "for the time being the Russian tanks remained well hidden, deep within the Forest of Szczek" (616). The little village of Bukowo still exists, exemplifying the endurance of Poland.

The next historical, panoramic novel, *Caribbean* (1989), moves to an island world: "The chief character in this narrative is the Caribbean Sea, one of the world's most alluring bodies of water, a rare gem among the oceans, defined by the islands that form a chain of lovely jewels to the north and east" (1). The first sentence of *Caribbean* establishes the sense of place for this historical, panoramic novel. The maps at the beginning of the book help the reader's geographic orientation, and the episodes taking place on specific islands set the historical scene of this region. The various stories show how the invading European peoples—Spanish, English, French—come with their sense of superiority and treat the original inhabitants with scorn and cruelty. One Spanish priest, in the Caribbean shortly after Columbus's voyages, is in a minority when he reflects, "The history of this island, and all of the islands Spain has captured in this lovely sea, will involve the slow and even reluctant admission that the big black man down there has a soul" (87). *Caribbean* is a story of conflict, greed, racial tension, domination, and submission played out against an idyllic background of sea, sun, sand, mountain, lush vegetation, and fertile soil. Like *Chesapeake* and *The Covenant*, it illustrates the loss of human potential when prejudice and discrimination treat certain groups as less than human and deny them access to educational and economic opportunities. In the late twentieth century the islands' problems continue. Is their economic welfare to depend on cruise ships of wealthy tourists? How are young people to find the opportunities for study and jobs? The story closes with two of the characters, a young Haitian woman and a young man whose ancestors came to Trinidad from India in the 1850s, finding happiness. They will help this region find answers to its problems.

The novel's ending is upbeat, but its story is complex. Because of the number of islands playing a role in the narrative, there are more stories than can be easily absorbed—and more characters. Michener cannot follow selected families through the ages in the same way he has done in other novels; family names do recur and he brings descendants of many of the characters together as lecturers on a cruise ship in the final chapter, a rather neat tying together of the strands of the saga. However, the depiction of the battles, the slave revolts, the cultural struggles, the way various groups lived is done with his usual concern for authenticity and vitality. The novel is readable history; readers are educated and entertained.

Mexico (1992), Michener's most recent historical, panoramic novel, traces that country's history through an intermingling of present and past. A chronology of the three cultural strands and maps orient the reader at the book's beginning. Norman Clay, a journalist who was raised in the fictional city of Toledo, is returning home to report on a series of bullfights between two matadors of different styles and heritages. He is also searching for meaning in his own life, and his trip to Toledo gives him the opportunity to ponder his Indian, Spanish, and American cultural heritage. The heritages of the two matadors, Victoriano Leal of the Spanish tradition and Juan Gómez from an Indian family, are also presented. The final part of the search is Norman's effort to understand Mexico itself: "But of Mexico as a unique land, with its own promise and its own problems, no one had written. And least of all the Mexicans themselves. For anyone in this land who took up his pen did so either as a Spanish apologist, or as an Indian, or as an anti-American, or as a pro-Russian. But as a Mexican? Never" (91).

The narrative's structure differs from previous novels: the present as a result of the past is an essential part of the novel. Michener devotes only six of the twenty chapters to the history of the past and uses Norman Clay as the first-person narrator to show the need to be connected in some fashion to one's heritage. The six historical chapters punctuate the ongoing narrative; two present the Indian history and culture, two bring the Spanish into the story, and two introduce the Clays. The usual Michener themes of how different races treat each other, the harm bigotry in religion can cause, and the relationship of humans to their land are very important in this book and are illustrated with vivid examples. In addition the authenticity of his presentation of the art of bullfighting gives the reader new insight into this confrontation between man and animal. *Mexico* shows that Michener has not lost any of his ability to tell a good story while providing his readers with interesting information about how different cultures live and think and interact.

In a career writing fiction that spans more than forty years, James Michener's output has been remarkably even. He has refined the art of telling an engrossing story while presenting massive amounts of factual information. He has created remarkable worlds for his readers to inhabit and has given them a sense of humanity's strength and weakness in twenty-five books.

3

The Fires of Spring
(1949)

The Fires of Spring, Michener's second novel, published in 1949, is a book about Americans in America. It is also a coming-of-age novel, in the sense that it follows the experiences of David Harper from his childhood in the poorhouse of Doylestown, Pennsylvania, to early adulthood. The book reflects some of Michener's early experiences and thoughts about life. Although critics were not overly enthusiastic about the book, its author noted in the 1960s that he had received more mail about this work than about anything else he had written. These readers appreciated the story's frankness and its reflection of their own attitudes (Day 1964, 57).

In this chapter the development of the plot, the characters, and the themes will be discussed. Also, a feminist critical perspective will be defined and the novel looked at from the viewpoint of a feminist critic.

PLOT ORGANIZATION AND DEVELOPMENT

To focus the story of David Harper's growing up, each section of *The Fires of Spring* is organized around the episodes and the people that are part of David's life at a particular point on his path to becoming an adult. The reader sees the events mainly through David's eyes as he searches for his identity in the 1920s and 1930s, progressing from the poorhouse to the streets of New York City. At times what happens in David's life is more sensational than real, yet Michener is able to involve his reader in the journey and make it interesting.

At the start of the story David is ten years old, an orphan living in the poorhouse where his Aunt Reba is in charge of the women's section. Aunt Reba is so full of anger at the direction of her life that she has no love to give, but the old men cherish the boy. He learns lessons during the year that he will not understand until later, as he watches the heartbreak of the people forced by circumstances into the poorhouse and absorbs the stories told by such residents as Old Daniel. David also sees death and dying, but he has many moments of joy, such as the party by the canal, a place which was already real to him because of Old Daniel's stories. Another highlight is the trip to Paradise Amusement Park with the Paxsons, a local family whom he meets when a Quaker fellowship comes to lead Sunday worship at the poorhouse. The taste of loganberry juice, which he can buy for the family thanks to the generosity of the old men who give him their carefully hoarded pennies, is a special treat. His desire to write is born when he is disillusioned by the ending of the *Iliad*, which his fifth-grade teacher reads to the class. David is going to tell stories that end as he thinks they should end.

The story moves next to David's high school years. He gets his first job at the Paradise Amusement Park, where he learns about differing degrees of dishonesty and different types of people during his summer vacations. At the carnival David also discovers art and literature thanks to the European musician Klementi Kol, who takes him to visit a private art collection in Philadelphia and gives him novels by the French writer Balzac. He also starts learning about love by falling in love with the little prostitute Nora. And in high school he learns about the magic of mathematics and the fun of being a star basketball player. It's a schizophrenic life, all-American student during the school year and short-change cashier during the summer. David grieves over the death of Nora in a fire at the amusement park, but the amusement park phase of his life ends when he receives a scholarship to college from an anonymous donor. Perhaps his dreams will become a reality.

Dedham College, patterned after Michener's alma mater Swarthmore, is another awakening. Discussions with professors and fellow students are eye-opening—as is watching his acquaintance from Paradise, Mary Meigs, sing in a Philadelphia vaudeville show. David wishes for "a world of neat categories organized into known patterns" (187) when he takes Professor Tschilezynski's math classes. But he knows after listening to Joe Vaux, the campus social radical, talk about the poor and the exploited that he doesn't see people as representative of abstract ideals and ideas: "Joe talks about abstract things, but I don't care about them. It's real people I like" (213). David continues his confused groping toward figuring out who he is and what he wants to do throughout his college years. Interspersed with classes and professors who open his mind to new ideas and others who are dull and boring is his affair with Mona, formerly Mary Meigs. She goes off to make her mark in Hollywood, and David makes his way through his exams, receiving highest honors in English and history. He has a graduate fellowship to study literature at Chicago with an eventual goal of being a college professor, but is that where his dreams should lead him?

A phone call from Mona inviting him to join a traveling theatrical group changes David's direction in the section titled "Chautauqua." He realizes he has not seen America and traveling throughout a summer with a theater-variety troupe will let him avoid decisions about the future, including marriage to Marcia Paxson. As he says to Marcia, "I'm not as old as you are. Spiritually, I mean. . . . I'm not sure of myself, Marcia. You might not want to marry me when you see the kind of man I become. If we could wait . . ." (269). Marcia can't wait and tells David not to return to her when everything doesn't turn out the way he wants. The first blow is to discover that Mona is sleeping with the troupe's director and leading man, and he is hired only because college boys come cheap. Since the traveling theater troupes are about to vanish from the American scene thanks to radio, the movies, and the automobile, David's travels with the Cyril Hargreaves troupe are stories that won't be repeated. However, the experiences with people, those in the troupe and others encountered along the way, are another important part of his education. And he gains an awareness of his land, the America of the road, the churches, the schools, the hillsides, the pastures. Michener gives a special sense of place to this section, and the reader sees the land and its people along with David.

The final segment of David's coming of age takes place in New York City, in "The Valley" of Greenwich Village set among the skyscrapers of Manhattan, where he is determined to become a writer. The time is the Depression of the 1930s, and David's first job is as an assistant editor for Clay Publications (a magazine publisher). Stories of crime and sexual passion are the focus of the firm's publications, and David learns how to edit so that the stories suggest everything but say nothing directly. Again he comes into contact with many different types of people, all adding to his education. His efforts give Michener a chance to talk about novels and the writing process. Because of the Depression, David loses his job with the magazine publisher and is unemployed for three years. After composing his whole novel in his mind but writing little on paper, he finally renounces his dream. Marcia Paxson, now doing social work in New York, comes back into his life, and her scorn at what she sees as his cowardice in giving up completes the coming-of-age process. When Morris Binder, the editor at the publishing company, is killed, David turns down the job to work as assistant cook at Mom Beckett's boardinghouse where he has been living and resumes his writing. The narrative has taken the reader through many stages of one young man's development to the point where he finds himself.

The reader who accepts the book as a series of interesting episodes, and doesn't become preoccupied by the sensational events such as the carnival fire and Morris Binder's murder, whose timing is overly coincidental, finds it an engaging story, a panorama featuring the episodes affecting one character seen against several memorable backgrounds. Michener used many personal experiences in this story, and A. Grove Day feels that *The Fires of Spring* "purged its author of the autobiographical itch" (1964, 65). None of his subsequent novels would focus on so personal a story.

CHARACTER DEVELOPMENT

Michener gives his main character, David Harper, an unconventional background: he spends his childhood in a poorhouse, works as a shortchange artist as a teenager, becomes a protégé of bootlegger Max Volo, and travels with a theatrical troupe. And David's reactions to events are at times opportunities for Michener to provide more commentary than is needed to illustrate the character. Yet David's reflections about what happens to him and around him are such that a reader can care about him and identify with his thoughts, if not his experiences.

David accepts life in the poorhouse as it is, without comprehending completely all the heartbreak of the residents. He feels enough love from the old men to counteract the hate and abuse he receives from his aunt. He is shown as the idealistic child who wants Hector the Trojan to always win. Michener's image of a David protected from the poorhouse tragedies because he resides on an island formed by his own imaginative dreams is not completely effective, as the writer develops the image with too much detail. However, "the boy's quiet love for other people" (73) is a characteristic that remains part of his identity throughout the story.

David grows throughout the novel but does not really change in any significant way. He never loses his idealism or his loyalty to his friends, in spite of the problems they cause him. David continues to give money to people like Nora or Mona Meigs, who uses him for her own ends, and refuses Mr. Stone's opinion of humanity: "Certain people, David, are going to wind up in the garbage heap no matter what you or I or they or God Himself does" (161). During his tour on the Chautauqua circuit, he begins to see things more as they are—part of the growing process. He learns that people's motives are often mixed, even his own. He is also able to rise to the occasion when courage is needed, trying unsuccessfully to get Nora out of the amusement park fire but helping to save lives when a tornado and then a fire strike during a Chautauqua theatrical performance. For Michener, David appears to be an embodiment of ideas and attitudes, an interesting illustration of the coming-of-age process seen against a panorama of American life.

Marcia Paxson enters David's life during his childhood in the poorhouse. She represents the contrast to Nora and Mona Meigs, with high standards for herself and David. Marcia reappears in the story when David reaches a new turning point. When they meet again in New York, she won't marry him until he has the courage to refuse Binder's job of pandering to the lowest possible taste and resume working toward his dream of becoming a writer. Michener portrays Marcia as the high-principled woman who prods, encourages, and tries, as Mom Beckett says, to make something of her man. She is sympathetic yet never quite comes to life.

The secondary characters who come in and out of David's life represent certain types, but already in this early novel Michener shows a knack for making them memorable. A certain trait or comment, and the character is vividly believable. In the poorhouse it's Old Daniel who gives David worthwhile advice, even as he illustrates the futility of unrealized dreams: "Think to the limit of your mind. . . . Whatever you do, David, do it to the absolute best of your ability" (42).

At Paradise Nora initiates David into the world of sexual relationships, and although she is not the misunderstood girl he wants to think she is, her hard frailty and wish to protect David for his own good make her sympathetic. For David, Nora illustrates Klementi Kol's definition of love: "But if any love makes you stronger and more determined to share, then it's much finer than most people ever attain" (134). Other sharply

drawn characters introduced in this section along with Kol are Mona
Meigs and Max Volo. Kol opens David's mind to good literature, art,
and music, taking him to concerts and museums and sending him books.
He comes across as basically a sad man, with no illusions about his place
as an orchestra conductor nor his relationship with Mona. Mona, on the
other hand, is all ambition, ready to gratify her desires with anyone who
pleases her but never losing sight of the fame and fortune she must
pursue at all costs. David will never understand her hard and bitter
concentration. However, he cannot resist her pleas for help when she
needs money for that one last push toward stardom. Mona is pictured
with sharp edges and a physical magnetism that make her a vivid figure
but not necessarily a likeable one. Max Volo is the stereotype of the crook
who is out to make a fast buck, yet he too acts from mixed motives.
When he hears lies about David's relationship with Mona, he has his
henchmen beat up the young man. However, Max has always admired
David's courage since the fire at Paradise, and he is the anonymous
donor who paid for David's college scholarship.

At Dedham three professors and a student enliven the portrait of a
college education. Student Joe Vaux is memorable for his belief in the
cause of mankind, even if he sees human beings as part of the mass
rather than as individuals. Professors Tschilezynski, Chisholm, and
Thorpe are to be remembered for their intense love of learning. Tschilezynski is described as a vast, untidy man, enthralled by the beauty of
mathematical equations and the excitement to be found in books. Chisholm is almost a caricature with an exaggerated Texas accent, playing a
guitar and singing American folk songs. He, however, is the teacher who
asks David, "What books have blasted yore mind loose, Mr. Harper?"
(225). Thorpe, in standing up for his beliefs about art and literature,
teaches David about honor. These three people are brought to life briefly
in the story by their ideas.

In the chapter titled "Chautauqua" the reader does not forget the
members of the Cyril Hargreaves troupe who add to David's knowledge
about people. There is Hargreaves himself, who cuts financial corners by
handling several roles via the stage telephone and is jealous, at age sixty-
six, of any young man who might take his place in Mona's bed. Wild
Man Jensen, the truck driver interested in the stock market, discovers a
willing girl in every town but also wants to help the dwarf Vito Bellotti
find a girl dwarf to marry. Emma Clews, middle-aged, fat, unattractive,
and a poor actress, arouses David's pity. This cast plays assigned roles,

yet its members have enough life to remain vivid to David and the reader after the tent is struck for the last time.

The characters who become part of David's life in New York are also interesting types with roles to play in his story. Alison Webster, whom David met during Chautauqua days, is now on the way up in the writing world. She is ambitious like Mona but more independent, refusing to allow David to be part of her life; she is going to be a writer, and nothing will interrupt her. Morris Binder and Miss Adams at Clay Publications almost seem to be designed as stereotypes—the gifted editor subject to convulsions and the prim secretary who cherishes and cares for Binder. Their melodramatic end advances David's growth by forcing him to ponder their bleak lives and lack of "singing accomplishments" (472) and his own lack of courage in dropping his dreams. They are also vehicles for expressing ideas about writing. Mom Beckett, who runs the boardinghouse where David lives, is the stock character with a checkered past and a heart of gold. She supports Claude, a gifted poet who is ineffectual in earning money to live on, and treats David with exuberant but motherly warmth. All the characters are necessary to push David onward to adulthood and they provide a variety of human types to intrigue the reader.

THEMATIC CONSIDERATIONS

Since the main theme of *The Fires of Spring* is the coming of age of a young man, it is not surprising that this theme is reinforced by many observations on life and love and education. In addition, the young man wants to be a writer, which gives Michener the opportunity to talk about literature as well as the process of writing. Novels of this sort lend themselves to their author's reflections, and Michener expresses his with a sermonlike intensity. Moralistic he may be, but certain phrases and thoughts catch the reader's attention.

Michener uses the novel's sensational events to highlight some ideas about the meaning of life. When David acts courageously during the tornado, he is pleased that he did not run from the disaster. He expresses thoughts about the significance of his place in the universe, seeing for the first time that he is not the center of the world. The realization, Michener indicates, frees him because he now understands that whether he lives or dies is not important in the overall scheme of things.

Through the successes and failures of the various characters, Michener wants to show too that dreams are important in order to live life fully. David concludes that Binder and Miss Adams had lived on the edge of life with their "series of filthy magazines stretching from the sewage pits of society to the minds of morons" (472). The image is contrived but reveals David's thoughts about his own direction. He sees from their example that he must go back to his novel and never surrender.

In this story Michener also makes pronouncements about the nature of love. While he is growing up, sexual passion is David's view of love. He does learn on the Chautauqua circuit how tangled relationships can be and how impossible love is to define. After the trick played on Hargreaves so David can spend the night with Mona, David reflects that each person knows love as a different miracle (314). The images in his interior monologue are obvious—"No aspect of life is more complex, and none so simple" (314)—yet the ideas are part of the maturing process and real from that standpoint.

David's experiences in high school and college give Michener a chance to talk about what formal education should be. An essential element is the desire to learn, and the subject studied is of secondary importance. Miss Chaloner at Doylestown High assumes that her students will want to know about hundreds of things and is the first to show David the order and beauty of the universe of mathematics. Dedham has professors who also stimulate the love of learning, but Michener also criticizes American higher education of the 1920s for its emphasis on English culture and neglect of American history and literature as well as art and music. However, a few determined faculty members at Dedham institute an experimental curriculum for some of the top students. David will spend his last two years reading in English and history, writing papers, and discussing with professors. At the end of this intensive study he will be examined by outstanding scholars from other colleges and universities. This meeting of minds is a challenge to both students and professors, forcing both to think and develop their critical faculties.

In addition to discovering the world of books, David is fortunate enough to meet those along his way who introduce him to art and music. Michener's own tastes appear through the works David appreciates. For example, he finds the novels of the nineteenth-century French novelist Balzac "a complete interpretation of life" (119), and Michener mentions this writer as one of his favorites in his memoirs, *The World Is My Home.* The Johnson collection of paintings in Philadelphia that David sees with Klementi Kol resembles the private Barnes collection that Michener visited by posing as a culture-struck steel-mill worker. David hears the majestic music of such composers as Wagner for the first time during his summers at Paradise, and classical music continues to be part of his maturing in New York, when he listens with Morris Binder to "music that would sing in his memory forever" (402). David's reactions to the selections he hears reflect Michener's own introduction to the world of music.

The definition of a novel that Claude the poet gives makes sense to David: " 'A novel,' he said, 'is a golden kettle into which you pour all of experience' " (385). Claude also notes that novelists who don't understand words or feelings write long books rather than trying to say it all in a few words, as a poet does. David continues to think about what it means to write and has his moment of revelation after watching the play of light and shadow on a brick wall for several hours: "Writing is like that. Seeing what no one has ever seen before and writing it down so simply that everyone will say, 'Of course! I knew that all along' " (406). Miss Adams reads his first efforts and is encouraging, although she criticizes his extensive use of adjectives and adverbs. David retorts that he wants everything to be perfectly clear to his readers. He has had a vision and wants to sing it. Miss Adams insists that true art is the vision with discipline. Michener in this story is inclined more toward David's point of view. He puts everything into the "golden kettle" and works hard to make everything perfectly clear.

However, in this early novel Michener shows the sense of place and history that enhances all his fiction. The reader is part of life in the poorhouse, sharing the residents' sense of failure and seeing how American society treated its unfortunates in the first decades of the twentieth century. Homeless shelters in the 1990s are the poorhouse counterpart; Michener might well wonder if the lessons of the past have been learned. The Chautauqua circuit is a part of the past not likely to be repeated, and it is seen in the story against the prosperity of small-town America in the 1920s. The reader participates also in the Depression of the early 1930s with the long-term unemployment. David, laid off by Clay Publications, lives on Mom Beckett's handouts and searches for a job. His experiences illustrate the discouragement of the time for so many. The historical context of each section of *The Fires of Spring* adds to the story's interest and provides a special framework for David's growing process. Michener will never see a character's story apart from the society and the place that surrounds him.

David Harper's story lacks the focus to become the definitive coming-

of-age novel. Michener has taken the opportunity too often to make pronouncements and overwork an image or a comparison. However, the
story is compelling, the narrative pace keeps the reader involved in what
happens, and the writing is often vigorous and sincere. James Michener
has said what he wanted to say in *The Fires of Spring*.

A FEMINIST READING OF *THE FIRES OF SPRING*

Literary criticism from a feminist viewpoint appeared first in the late
1960s. From the beginning, the focus has been on the images of women
presented in literature: How are women portrayed in the work? Are they
stereotypes based on a male view of women, or are they authentic human beings? When women are viewed stereotypically, they fall into two
distinct categories: spiritual or material—in other words, good or evil.
"Under the category of the good-woman stereotypes, that is, those who
serve the interests of the hero, are the patient wife, the mother/martyr,
and the lady. In the bad or evil category are deviants who reject or do
not properly serve men or his interests: the old maid/career woman, the
witch/lesbian, the shrew or domineering mother/wife" (J. Donovan,
1983, 48). The stereotypical woman, good or evil, is defined by her relationship with men. Does she serve or thwart the interests of men?

Authentic women characters, on the other hand, act as independent
beings. They have a reflective, critical consciousness; they are "self"
rather than "other." However, women in Western society are usually
perceived as the "other," not the "self." The "self" is the socially dominant group or the norm—that is, men. The "other" is subordinate or
deviant, inessential—that is, women. Critic Josephine Donovan writes,
"Women in literature written by men are for the most part seen as Other,
as objects, of interest only insofar as they serve or detract from the goals
of the male protagonist" (1983, 41).

In addition, a feminist perspective about a literary work goes beyond
the "self/other" opposition to consider the social and legal status of the
women in the culture and time period portrayed in this work. "Feminist
criticism is ultimately cultural criticism," notes Cheri Register (1989, 10).
But it becomes moral criticism, too, assuming that literature can change
attitudes and even behaviors in readers. As Donovan states, "Feminist
criticism is moral because it sees that one of the central problems of
Western literature is that in much of it women are not human beings,

seats of consciousness. They are objects, who are used to facilitate, explain away, or redeem the projects of men. . . . For a feminist, moral literature is one which affirms the life of women, as well as all other creatures" (1983, 52).

"The demand for authenticity supersedes all other requirements" (Register 1989, 21). Therefore, a feminist perspective will require a reading that evaluates the independent reality of a work's characters, the female characters specifically. This type of reading will also look for role models among the female characters, for women whose identities are not dependent on men, who are involved in work or activities that give them an opportunity for self-realization. Finally, it will require consideration of the social, economic, and political environment that frames the story.

Since *The Fires of Spring* focuses on David Harper's growing up in the America of the 1920s and 1930s, the women characters are seen as they play their part in his story. From a feminist perspective, Michener does not go beyond the stereotypical presentation of women characters, in either his descriptions or his dialogue. In this early novel, only his second published work of fiction, he is traditional in his characterizations and trite in his images, but at times admiring in his illustrations.

David's Aunt Reba is the "ugly, unloving witch" (8) of his childhood. For reasons that are never fully explained in the novel, she has become a hate-filled, angry woman. However, Michener does not indicate that her personality and actions are due to her gender; they appear to stem from her character, which causes her to abuse others because of the misfortunes she has suffered.

The image of the elderly women living in the poorhouse is one of courage. Ten-year-old David notices that the women's rooms are prettier than the men's, with pictures from magazines tacked to the walls and knitted pillow covers. The women adapt to life in these surroundings rather than fight it: "No, the women went right on living, fighting, being mean, elbowing for the best seats at supper. It was the men who quit and died" (27).

Along his path to adulthood David meets four young women with whom he falls in love. None of these women is completely authentic as a human being, but each one is important in David's coming-of-age process. The young prostitute Nora at the amusement park haunts his dreams, and he is sure that their relationship is different from those she has with other men. David never completely loses his illusions about Nora, even when she goes to Florida for the winter with another man.

She lives and works as a sexual object, but David will never accept the park cashier's opinion that Nora was doing more harm in the world than good.

Mona Meigs is a singer at the amusement park when she enters David's life, but she is ambitious to be a star with her name in lights. She is the stereotype of the woman who uses her body and other people to advance her career. Mona comes in and out of David's life when she needs his help or money, and he always comes through for her, even after realizing the extent of her self-absorbed nature.

Alison Webster crosses David's path during the Chautauqua tour. She is already self-confident about her ability to write, and once in New York, forges ahead. David can offer nothing that will help her achieve the success she seeks, and so his love is rejected. Yet David learns from his experiences with Alison how important women are to him. Michener never explains why or how this is so; he merely states David's conclusion: "To him that year they were more important than bread" (398).

Marcia Paxson is part of David's life from his childhood. She is shown as a high achiever during their high school years, being elected class president and winning the award for best student. Marcia does well in college, but she must complete her identity through marriage. When David joins the Hargreaves troupe, Marcia marries a man whom she doesn't love in order to forget David. She realizes that what she has done is not fair to her husband and later gets a divorce. Although her ultimate goal is to make something of David, she has enough of a reflective consciousness to realize that he must overcome his cowardice and work toward his dream before their marriage is possible. She will be able finally to return to their hometown with her head held high. Her life will be affirmed in the terms valued by her culture.

In this novel Michener accepts the attitude that "good" women find their identity by sustaining their men. However, women like Nora, Mona, and Alison are not evil; they are part of a man's growing up. Until he is an adult, David wants Marcia's "rich and strong character" alone, seeing her as a safe harbor where he can rest. He does not think of her as "a warm, tremulous girl longing for bed" (337).

In the story of David's coming of age, Michener perpetuates a version of the traditional images men have imposed on women. He does not condemn Nora, Mona, and Alison, but Marcia Paxson is the ideal wife for the hero. Even the older women who encourage David—Miss Adams who encourages his writing and Mom Beckett who supports him during his unemployment—find their emotional realization from their relationship with the men in their lives. Mom Beckett's image of men accepts this situation: "But hell, sister! All men are weaklings. Women marry 'em and make 'em strong" (460). Women may have the strength, but they can realize it only through a man. From a feminist perspective, *The Fires of Spring* continues the portrait of women as the Other. They may be admired or appreciated by the hero, but they are of interest in this novel only as they assist in his coming of age.

4

Hawaii
(1959)

Hawaii, James Michener's first historical, panoramic novel, appeared in November 1959, only a few months after Hawaii became the fiftieth state, and stayed on the best-seller list for some twenty months. The novel is not textbook history but the story of what could have happened as various ethnic groups settled the beautiful islands. Michener traces his fictional characters from their origins through their travels across oceans to their interactions in the islands. Within the more than one thousand pages, these characters let readers into their Hawaii, involving them in their lives.

This chapter will discuss elements of plot construction that enable such a long book to hold the reader's attention, how characters are developed, and the themes that are an integral part of the story. Finally, the critical viewpoint of Marxism will be introduced, and ways in which a Marxist literary critic might look at *Hawaii* will be suggested.

PLOT DEVELOPMENT

The novel opens with a description of how the islands were formed millions of years ago. No people at all appear in this portrait of land emerging "from the boundless deep" (as the chapter is called). Only the islands appear, slowly evolving through the passage of time, waiting for people to settle them, "a paradise in potential, with almost no food available, but with enormous riches waiting to be developed" (17). This introduction sets the scene in a unique way; readers can understand and picture the natural setting in which people will interact and events will take place.

Five sections follow the introduction, bringing four groups of people to settle the islands through time and concluding with how these ethnic groups live together in "present-day" Hawaii, the time just before statehood was granted in 1959. The novel reconstructs several past ages as it moves to the twentieth century. This reconstruction conforms to the historical novel tradition, with a slight modification: Michener's fictional characters participate in events as they could have occurred, and actual historical people are very rare.

The organization of the book into separate sections that focus on different groups in a specific time period helps keep the reader's interest in this long and detailed story of the islands' development. As the story moves toward the present day, Michener uses descendants of characters from the first sections to continue the narration. He also helps his readers keep track of all these people by providing a family tree for each important family as a sort of appendix at the end of the novel.

"From the Sun-Swept Lagoon" brings the Polynesian people northward from Bora Bora in the South Pacific. In Michener's explanation of this migration, the islanders set forth in their large canoe toward an unknown destination to escape the bloody worship of a new god, Oro. The long sea voyage, with its hardships and moments of joy, is an eventual success, and the islanders transplant their material culture to their new home. Teroro, the king's brother, returns to Bora Bora in order to bring to "Hawaii" what had to be left behind the first time: his wise first wife Marama, the goddess Pere of the volcano, and a canoe filled with children and flowers. Now the islanders can feel at home, establish their new lives, and prosper.

Nine centuries after the Polynesian settlement is established, Christian missionaries from New England come to Hawaii. "From the Farm of Bitterness" tells their story. Abner Hale hears the call to convert the heathen after listening to a talk from Keoki Kanaka, an exiled Hawaiian. The mission board accepts Abner with some misgivings—he is not an attractive person and the board members sense his rather rigid view of the Christian faith. But his sincerity convinces them, and after an arranged marriage with Jerusha Bromley, the board chairman's niece, Abner and his new wife join the ten other missionary couples for the long, hard voyage on the ship *Thetis* to the faraway islands.

The trip is a story in itself with all the hardships of seasickness, storms, cramped quarters, and the clash between missionary zeal and the sailors' way of life. The ambiguity of the forces of the universe is underlined when the *Thetis*, with its missionary passengers, takes forty-two days to round Cape Horn while the whaling ship captained by Rafer Hoxworth, Jerusha's former suitor, makes the passage in three days.

Arriving in Hawaii, the Hales meet Keoki's parents; his mother Malama is the *Alii Nui*, a kind of princess-priestess and descendant of Marama and Teroro of the long-ago migrations. Malama, a massive woman, immediately welcomes the missionaries, especially the wives, and requests a dress made like theirs. Malama is interested in learning how to write rather than in becoming Abner Hale's variety of Christian. She respects his sincerity but has difficulty with his sense of righteousness. The two cultures clash over moral standards and customs, with Abner especially adamant against the island girls' habit of swimming out to welcome the incoming whaling ships.

"From the Farm of Bitterness" presents other cultural misunderstandings and attitudes: for example, one of the missionary wives dies in childbirth because the missionaries are unwilling to use native midwives; Abner also refuses ordination to Keoki, who returns to his own cultural ways by marrying his sister Noelani and also burying his mother according to their customs.

But both cultures influence each other, creating a new type of life on the islands. Noelani marries Rafer Hoxworth after Keoki dies of the measles. Dr. John Whipple leaves the mission to join the *Thetis*'s captain in business ventures. Abraham Hewlett, whose wife had died, is condemned for marrying a Hawaiian woman. His comment, when dismissed from the mission, summarizes Abner Hale's basic attitude: "You love the Hawaiians as potential Christians, but you despise them as people" (350). This attitude drives Abner's son Micah from the ministry; Micah, after successful studies at Yale, meets and marries Noelani and Rafer Hoxworth's daughter Malama, but his action is condemned by his father, and Micah goes into business with his father-in-law.

The next cultural group to reach the islands comes "From the Starving Village." Michener creates a certain symmetry in structure by tracing the history of the Chinese immigrants back to the same era of the first Polynesian immigrants to Hawaii. But the Chinese migration first takes place on land, as an entire village population slowly moves south to escape famine and war. This group remains highly disciplined and holds on to its culture as the people farm the highlands of the "Golden Valley." Known as Hakku, they have little friendly contact with the neighboring Punti lowlanders and their more urban culture.

After establishing this background Michener moves to the nineteenth century and tells the story of a Hakku woman, Char Nyuk Tsin, and a Punti man, Kee Mun Ki, descendants of those whose story has been traced in the first part of this section. The two are part of a group of Chinese workers chosen by Dr. John Whipple to work in Hawaiian fields. Dr. Whipple insists that part of the group be Hakku, for he sees a resemblance to his New England heritage in their industrious village. The Punti village allows none of the Punti women to accompany the workers, for the stay in Hawaii is to be temporary. The Hakku have a different attitude, and Nyuk Tsin is part of the Hakku contingent.

She and Kee Mun Ki form a relationship that continues during the hellish trip to Hawaii in Rafer Hoxworth's ship. The Chinese sleep in the hold with no fresh air or sanitary facilities and little food. Whipple obtains some concessions by threatening to publicize Hoxworth's actions all over the world.

Once in Hawaii Char Nyuk Tsin and Kee Mun Ki work for the Whipples, who allow Nyuk Tsin an acre of land on which she can grow vegetables. Because of Kee Mun Ki's official Punti wife in China, Char Nyuk Tsin must be known as the aunt of the children she has with Kee Mun Ki. She is the family's driving force, seeing that the children are educated and always striving to obtain land. Whipple encourages her efforts in spite of the prevailing "establishment" attitude that "the Sonofabitch ought to be horse-whipped" (530).

The Chinese couple suffers a serious setback when Mun Ki develops leprosy and must go to the leper colony on Molokai. Nyuk Tsin finds temporary homes for the four children and accompanies her husband. Once they reach the island colony and discover the inhumane conditions that exist there, for "there was no voice of government, no voice of God, no healing medicine" (597), they work to create their own space of peace and organized living.

After Mun Ki's death, Nyuk Tsin returns to Honolulu and collects her children—all but the fifth child, born on Molokai and sent to Honolulu right after the birth. The Hawaiian foster parents beg her to leave the boy, whom they have loved since birth, with them. Nyuk Tsin consents, and the boy provides a special link between the Hawaiian and Chinese communities. Nyuk Tsin continues her hard work, growing vegetables, acquiring land, and seeing that her sons get an education. When houses in Chinatown are burned by the authorities in an attempt to get rid of bubonic plague and the resulting fire destroys all of the area, Nyuk Tsin is the one who counsels the Chinese to buy land and solidify their place in the Hawaiian economy.

The Kees are the focus of this section, but the missionaries and their descendants also play important roles. Michener is again moving his story along by showing the connections and interactions among the various settlers of Hawaii. Micah Hale is the symbol of power and propriety while his nephew Whipple ("Wild Whip") Hoxforth is known for his escapades with women and property. Yet it is Wild Whip who works to establish the pineapple industry and joins with Micah to thwart Queen Liliuokalani's efforts to end *haole* (white) domination. Hawaii is designated as a U.S. territory on August 12, 1898. Malama Hale, half Hawaiian and half white, identifying with her Hawaiian heritage, recognizes the annexation sorrowfully: "In the end we were pitifully used by a gang of robbers. . . . We poor, generous Hawaiians were abused, lied about, debased in public and defrauded of our nation" (701).

The final group to contribute to the ethnic mix in *Hawaii* comes "From the Inland Sea." Michener does not present the historical roots of the Japanese but begins this section in 1902, tracing the fortunes of Kamejiro Sakagawa, who comes to Hawaii with some 1,850 Japanese to work in the sugarcane fields. He is sent to Wild Whip Hoxworth's plantation on the island of Kauai and starts his career by insisting on building a Japanese-style bathhouse. Along with the majority of the imported workers Kamejiro wants to earn enough money to return to Japan. But each time his earnings from the field work and the bathhouse accumulate, Japanese agencies appeal to his patriotism, and he contributes to the current cause. Finally, in 1915 he sends for the girl he had chosen before leaving Hiroshima. She has long since married, and his mother picks a wife for him. This girl refuses Kamejiro the workman, and he trades brides with Mr. Ishii. Kamejiro gets the better wife, for Yoriko is also a hard worker. Four sons and a daughter are born to the couple who move to Honolulu after the plantation workers' strike for a living wage is broken.

Kamejiro, always willing to work hard even at a menial job if necessary, gets a job emptying human waste from outhouses. He and Yoriko are determined that their five children will receive an education, and all five justify their parents' efforts by their own hard work, even though prejudice keeps them (and other nonwhites) from entering the elite prep school, Punahou. It's athletic talent that finally breaks the barrier when Tadao is recruited on a full scholarship. The daughter Reiko, however, cannot continue to college for her parents contribute to Japan's war against China in the 1930s. Reiko must work in her father's new venture, a Japanese barbershop, where the Japanese girls attract many customers.

Interspersed throughout this section are the various ventures and activities of Whipples and Hales and Kees. The *haoles,* or whites, control the political and economic life of Hawaii during the first part of the twentieth century, but Nyuk Tsin manages her family enterprises so well that the Kees are also a potent force in island life.

"From the Inland Sea" concludes with World War II and the contributions of the Japanese brigade, including the four Sakagawa brothers, under the command of Col. Mark Whipple, which must be "more American" than any other fighting unit. They bear the discrimination at a military camp in Mississippi because of their determination to prove their patriotism. Their culminating act of heroism is the rescue of a trapped battalion of Texans in the Vosges mountains of France. Minoru Sakagawa dies during this battle, joining his brother Tadao killed earlier. Goro has an emotional breakdown, and Shigeo is promoted to lieutenant on the field by Col. Whipple before the latter is killed. The Japanese brigade with its Hawaiians has given its all to the American effort.

"The Golden Men," the novel's concluding section, discusses the new type of man being formed in this group of islands, one who understands the movements around him and has vision for the future. Michener brings the strands of his four groups together in this conclusion, focusing on *haole* Hoxworth Hale, Chinese Hong Kong Kee, Hawaiian Kelolo "Kelly" Kanakoa, and Japanese Shigeo Sakagawa, as well as summarizing the conditions of postwar Hawaii from the sugarcane and shipping strikes to the arrival of mainland chain stores to union organization to antistatehood efforts.

Hale represents the "establishment," known unofficially as the Fort. The businessmen who control the islands' economy are sure they know what is best for Hawaii. Yet Hale is revealed as the narrator in the book's final pages, the one who defines the "Golden Man." Hong Kong Kee continues to advance his family's financial empire with the help of his grandmother Nyuk Tsin's advice. Kelly Kanakoa, a beach boy sleeping his way through a procession of mainland women, is taken in hand by Hong Kong's daughter Judy, who channels Kelly's musical ability into paid performances and recordings and proposes to marry him in spite of her father's objections. Shigeo Sakagawa enters politics after law school and works toward land reform with the help of Hale's daughter. Although Hoxworth Hale worries about his daughter's emotional involvement with Shigeo, he invites Shigeo to become a member of the board of Whipple Oil—after Shigeo introduces his land reform bill in the legislature. Hawaii has now accepted the idea that the cross-fertilization of ideas stimulated by different ethnic and cultural groups enables a civilization to grow and flourish.

In this first of his long, panoramic novels Michener recognizes the difficulty of providing a narrative point of view and doesn't quite solve the problem. A narrator who stands apart from the story might make it less believable as history that could have happened. However, the occasional first-person approach in *Hawaii* doesn't seem necessary. When the "narrator" is revealed as Hoxworth Hale in the final pages, the reader may feel that this identification adds nothing to the unfolding development of the islands.

CHARACTER DEVELOPMENT

In the historical, panoramic novel that covers centuries of time and features hundreds of people, fully developed, three-dimensional characters are not the author's primary focus. Yet Michener presents unforgettable individuals who remain in the reader's memory after the book has been read. These people are seen in action, rarely in thought or reflection.

"From the Sun-Swept Lagoon" the king's brother Teroro leads his companions into the unknown. Headstrong yet courageous, he is the one who has faith that the canoe and its passengers will find land where a new home can be established. His wise wife Marama is interesting as a woman who sees and understands consequences that may come from impulsive actions.

Abner Hale and his wife, Jerusha Bromley Hale, plus John Whipple and Captain Rafer Hoxworth as well as the *Alii Nui*, Malama, enliven the novel's next section, "From the Farm of Bitterness." Abner, sincere and stubborn in the righteousness of his faith, is convinced that he must reform the culture of the islands and give the islanders a sense of sin in order to lead them to the Lord. Jerusha, while supporting her husband in all his endeavors, lives her faith in practical ways, establishing a school for the Hawaiian girls as well as praying for their physical and spiritual health. She gives of herself to all who need her and dies at a relatively young age, worn out by hard work. "Of her bones was Hawaii built" says the inscription on her tomb (427). Jerusha's character is given a dimension beyond that of hard-working missionary wife when she writes to her sister back in New England: "I find myself desiring just once more a dress of my own" (371). This touch of vanity makes Jerusha more believable and human.

John Whipple, with his scientific curiosity and interest in the values and customs of other cultures, represents practical Christianity. He separates himself from the official missionary group when Abraham Hewlett and his Hawaiian wife are expelled, and he joins Captain Janders's business ventures. It's Dr. Whipple who sees how the white man's diseases will decimate the native population and foresees the need and benefits of introducing new ethnic groups. He realizes that his fellow whites do not have his vision and confides his thoughts to his diary: "The best thing I ever did for Hawaii was to import Chinese" (533).

Captain Rafer Hoxworth is a contradictory mixture of characteristics. He is a harsh sea captain, cheering for the sharks when Abner Hale falls into the sea after visiting Hoxworth's ship off Cape Horn. Jerusha's suitor before her marriage to Abner, Hoxworth brings a disassembled New England–style house to be put together for the Hales in Lahina, yet nearly kills Abner when he learns of Jerusha's death three years later. And his brutal treatment of the Chinese coming to Hawaii aboard one of his ships completes the picture of a violent man with few redeeming qualities. Yet his marriage to Noelani is one of love and tenderness. Through this character Michener seems to be showing the paradox of human personality: there may be admirable traits in even the most violent of people.

The reader first sees Malama, the *Alii Nui,* in her canoe coming to greet her returning son and the accompanying missionaries. A gigantic and majestic woman, she is transported in a sling to the ship's deck. And her welcoming of the missionary wives shows both her love and her determination. After weeping over the hardships of their voyage, she commands them to make her a dress like theirs. Malama adopts the Hales as her own *haoles.* It's Jerusha who will teach her to write and Abner who will work for her conversion. Their discussions are debates about opposing values and opposing customs, and Malama slowly accepts the white man's ways that she sees will help her people. As she is dying, she makes one last procession through Lahina, emphasizing that the new laws must be kept, yet instructing her family to follow Hawaiian customs once her Christian burial has been accomplished. Malama is a moving example of a people faced with adaption to other ways in order to survive.

Char Nyuk Tsin is the most memorable character of the Chinese group. She is known always as "Wu Chow's Auntie" by everyone including her own children because, according to Chinese culture, Kee Mun Ki's official wife was the woman he married in his home village before leaving China. But her dogged determination to own land and further her family's interests defines this hard-working woman who starts out as the Whipples' maid for fifty cents a month. Her devotion to her husband and the other lepers on Molokai reveals her loyalty and compassion to her fellow humans. This experience begins a habit that will last until her death the night she achieves American citizenship at age 106: every night she examines her body for signs of leprosy, and when no such signs are found, she can continue on her hardworking way.

"Wild Whip" Hoxworth, Noelani and Rafer's grandson, appears first in "From the Starving Village" and continues into the book's next section, "From the Inland Sea." Exhibiting many of his grandfather's traits, Whip slashes his way through brawls, voyages, and women with exuberance and little compassion. When he returns to Hawaii, he alienates his relatives who control the family businesses, but he finds his own niche in growing pineapple and experimenting with the best ways to make this plant flourish in the soil and climate of the islands. Whip is basically representative of a certain type of adventurer, vividly drawn by his author but not presented in depth.

Kamejiro Sakagawa from Japan is another like Nyuk Tsin, hardworking, family oriented, and determined to prosper in a new land before returning to the "Inland Sea." Never fully assimilated into the new culture, Kamejiro and his wife find in the novel's final section that they cannot adjust to postwar Japan, and the Japanese-style toilets, after their many years creating their life and work in Hawaii. Kamejiro is another representative character, but memorable as a figure who, with his wife's help, withstands the pressures of discrimination to support his family and raise the children, who retain aspects of their parents' original culture while forging their own way in the Hawaii of the twentieth century.

In the final section of *Hawaii*, the characters the reader remembers are those representing the four ethnic strains portrayed in the previous sections: Kelolo Kanakoa and his mother Malama, Hoxworth Hale, Hong Kong Kee, Shigeo Sakagawa.

Treated with kindly contempt by the *haoles*, Kelolo and his mother are the descendants of the *Alii Nui*. Malama lives on an incredibly valuable piece of property but under a trusteeship imposed by the "Fort," those businessmen who control the islands. A graduate of Vassar, Malama returns to the islands after her college years only to be told by members of the Fort that she is incompetent to manage her own affairs. At first insulted, Malama remembers that she had been taught during her high school years that Hawaiians were different; she accepts that assessment from the culture in control of her islands. She relaxes and enjoys her life with her friends and her music. She doesn't appear often in the novel's pages, but her gracious hospitality to the visiting mainlander Elinor Henderson is one of the unforgettable moments in *Hawaii*. Elinor, feeling that the Hawaiians are the dispossessed in their own islands, tries to understand the enjoyment Malama and her friends find in their simple life complete with music.

Her son Kelolo, or Kelly as he is known by all the mainland women who seek him out when their ships dock, lives for the moment. His short-term relationships with the women to whom he gives surfing lessons are interrupted only by his music, which he shares as willingly as he shares his body. His meeting with Elinor Henderson, who is truly interested in the Hawaiians as individuals, shakes his comfortable existence for the moment, and he expresses the underlying bitterness of a people who are not treated as equals: "It's as clear as the mountains at dawn. God loves first white men, then Chinese, then Japanese, and after a long pause He accepts Hawaiians" (1010).

Hong Kong Kee is a worthy descendant of his grandmother Nyuk Tsin. He has her vision and tenacity and is finally accepted by the Fort, who make him one of Malama's trustees. Hong Kong is the representative Chinese of postwar Hawaii; while not a fully developed character, he is shown in action, furthering the family enterprises, and comes alive as a caring father when his daughter Judy considers marriage to Kelly. The proposed marriage outrages his sense of Chinese identity, but he attends the wedding out of respect for Kelly's mother.

Shigeo Sakagawa is the representative "American of Japanese ancestry." Formed by the Japanese culture of his hardworking, peasant parents, he becomes part of the "American way of life" through his athletic abilities during high school and his outstanding service during World War II, fighting in the Japanese-American unit. Shigeo becomes a lawyer and enters politics, demonstrating the upward mobility characteristic of the American Dream. The reader sees him as symbolic yet as a human being who grieves over the deaths of two of his brothers in battle and is both infuriated and saddened when the visiting congressman from Texas refuses to shake his hand because of the color of his skin.

Hoxworth Hale, the revealed narrator of the Hawaiian panorama, has appeared as the symbol of the economic and political clout of white families of the islands. Descended from Abner and Jerusha Hale and also Rafer and Noelani Hoxworth, Hale works consistently and ably for the status quo. Yet even he recognizes in his changing world the need for the ethnic groups to work together, as he invites Hong Kong Kee and finally Shigeo Sakagawa to serve on the boards that run important business ventures. He becomes more human than symbolic when he travels to the South Seas during the war and meets the hospitality of Bora Bora, and when he grieves over the death of his son in a bombing raid over Japan and the failed marriage of his daughter.

THEMATIC CONSIDERATIONS

Hawaii, the first of Michener's historical, panoramic novels, contains one specific theme that will be seen in the subsequent novels of the same type: the misunderstanding and lack of understanding of other ethnic or cultural groups, and the ill treatment, misguided actions, and even atrocities that can result from this fear of and sense of superiority toward the Other, those people who are different, who aren't "us." A related theme in *Hawaii* is the role of migration and adaptation to new situations. Through the novel's various sections Michener develops these ideas with a goal in mind: to show how people of various groups can work together and form a liveable, even democratic society.

The interactions of the missionaries and the Hawaiians demonstrate clearly both the superiority-inferiority point of view and the difficulties that can result. Abraham Hewlett's first wife dies in childbirth because her husband and Abner Hale, trying to help with the birth and ignorant of the process, refuse the help of the Hawaiian midwives. Abner considers the Hawaiians doomed to hell and rejects their help in raising his own children: among their other sins, "They gamble and play games on Sunday, and for their sins God has ordained that they shall be stricken from the face of the earth" (345). John Whipple, aghast at this attitude, knows that the Hawaiians are doomed to die from the white man's diseases and the missionaries' insistance that New England customs of dress be adopted in an entirely different climate. He feels that new groups must be encouraged in the islands in order to save this people and their culture.

Whipple's interest in other peoples and cultures, and the enrichment they can bring to a society, illustrates Michener's premise that different races and ethnic groups can work together. John Whipple is ahead of his time, and his ideas are scorned by his fellow whites, but he works tirelessly to the end of his days to help others and learn from them.

Misunderstandings are not limited to the whites. As the Chinese establish themselves in Hawaii, their customs are tolerated to a certain extent because their economic contributions are valued. Yet they are completely bewildered by Abner Hale's solitary death on Maui, far from his rich and powerful descendants: "He died alone, caring for the graves, but no one cared for him" (539). Abner's children had tried consistently to care for him but were always rebuffed and "in the big houses there was profound, silent grief" (540). Family ties are expressed differently by different cultures, and Michener indicates by the two interpretations of Abner's death how difficult it is to achieve complete understanding of the Other.

Mistreatment of the Other is more prevalent in *Hawaii* at the hands of the whites. The brutal treatment the Chinese workers receive on Rafer Hoxworth's ship is horrifying: kicked and pushed down the ladder to the hold of the ship and kept there for fear of a mutiny, the Chinese have only minimal food and water and little ventilation. For forty-six days they exist or die in these appalling conditions. The sailors marvel that the Chinese can stand the situation, forgetting that the captain gave them no choice. Dr. Whipple is able finally to improve things by reminding Hoxworth that even former missionaries write, and he will send letters all over describing the horror of this voyage. However, it is Hoxworth's version of the "mutiny" that Honolulu hears.

Another example of mistreatment has long-term consequences in the unfolding of Hawaii's development as Michener portrays it. Kamejiro Sakagawa is kicked in the face by a German foreman on the pineapple plantation because the foreman, in a drunken state, thinks Kamejiro is pretending to be sick. This extreme insult requires revenge, which Kamejiro obtains by using his sandal to tap the foreman on the head. The foreman doesn't understand the challenge to his honor, but Kamejiro gains status with his coworkers and the event becomes a legend in Hawaii's Japanese community, a legend which expands the original event. By the time Shigeo uses it in his political campaign to recall to his Japanese audience their mistreatment and discrimination at the hands of the whites, this one event is magnified to a belief that the Japanese workers at the plantations were often whipped by foremen. Shigeo, concerned with the truth, drops the story from his speeches, but notes, "This is the greatest evil that grows out of a wrong act. Somebody always remembers it . . . in an evil way" (1121).

In addition to tracing misunderstandings and mistreatment through the four groups that develop the Hawaiian islands, Michener presents how failure and fortitude mark all efforts of emigration from the old homeland and settlement of the new. He notes that later ages look on those who leave for unknown lands as heroes, but says "no man leaves where he is and seeks a distant place unless he is in some respect a failure" (81). The group of Polynesians from the Sun-Swept Lagoon leaves Bora Bora because the power of the new god at the hands of the priests offers only two choices: submit or depart. The missionaries have more idealistic reasons, for they want to convert the heathen, but the Chinese and the Japanese are seeking a way out of economic hardship. Yet all these groups have fortitude and courage to sustain them in their efforts.

The Polynesians, who become the native Hawaiians, show heroism in their efforts to sail to the unknown and adapt readily to their new environment physically, but they lack the ability to withstand or modify the changes that the next groups bring to their culture. They are finally the observers in their homeland as the others gain the political and economic power.

The missionaries' descendants do adapt to the new conditions, creating new and better economic opportunities for themselves, and the Hales, Whipples, Hoxworths, and Janders are as certain of their "rightness" in matters of the islands' political, social, and economic structure as their ancestors were in questions of the Christian faith. In their minds anyone who disturbs the balance they have achieved in the islands is an enemy and deserves to be shot.

The Chinese and Japanese laborers imported by these *haoles* share in that fortitude and the ability to adapt. The Kee family illustrates the Chinese work ethic, as Kee Mun Ki and Char Nyuk Tsin start with the Whipples as the servants but run gambling games and sell vegetables on the side. Nyuk Tsin has the vision, and seeing the need for education, starts the program that will bring her family to economic prominence in the islands. America Kee, one of her sons, is enrolled in Iolani, the school opened by English Episcopalians. His offspring and their children will all work to see that the most intelligent members of each generation are educated in mainland colleges, and the family will overcome all setbacks whether caused by fire, revolution, or economic conditions.

The Sakagawas demonstrate the same fortitude, aptitude for hard work, and interest in education. They too succeed in spite of prejudice and hardships, adapting their own culture to play their roles in the creation of a genuine multiracial society. The children go to Japanese as well as American schools, but the parents recognize that these children will be Americans, part of the new culture, when Tadao is offered a place at Punahou because of his football ability.

Education, and its power to change people, worked for the determined Chinese and Japanese, but in the school founded for Hawaiian children by Abraham Hewlett's descendants, Hawaiian boys were not told they could be anything they wanted to be. The prevailing philosophy of those running Hewlett Hall was that the fine Hawaiian children should not be educated beyond their natural capacity. The theme of superiority of one group over another prevails, and a Whipple who has tried to change this attitude resigns from the school's board, saying, "With love and money we have condemned these people to perpetual mediocrity" (868).

The sense of superiority also is evident in the way each group looks at intermarriage. One should not marry outside of one's own group. Teroro on Bora Bora should not marry a girl from Hawaiki. Abner Hale looks on Abraham Hewlett's second marriage, to a Hawaiian, as an abomination and breaks all ties with his son Micah when the young man marries Malama Hoxworth, granddaughter of Malama the *alii nui*. Kee Mun Ki, a Punti, should not marry Char Nyuk Tsin, a Hakku. The Sakagawas are horrified when Goro marries a Japanese woman not from Hiroshima and cannot comprehend Shigeo's developing relationship with Noelani Hale Janders. Even Hong Kong Kee and the entire clan are furious at daughter Judy's marriage to Kelolo Kanakoa. Hong Kong attends the wedding out of respect for Kelolo's mother, but he will not escort his daughter down the aisle. Yet Michener points out that none of these people can claim to come from "pure" blood lines.

However, in the novel's conclusion he returns to the idea that racial or cultural intermarriage is not necessary to create a new society. It is only required that "ideas clash on an equal footing and remain free to cross-fertilize and bear new fruit" (1130). Throughout *Hawaii* James Michener has shown a civilization developing from the cross-fertilization of many groups to create an island world that he considers to be better than when it was just a cluster of rocks and sand emerging from the sea and empty of any creative life. As he mingles events and people, showing the ideal that can be created along with the dark side of human behavior that tarnishes ideals, Michener presents his historical panorama so that the reader believes that all this "could have happened." And he continues to share through his fictional characters and their interactions his concern about how prejudice and bias, fear of the Other, can be eliminated from this earth.

A MARXIST READING OF *HAWAII*

Karl Marx is best known for his works dealing with political and economic theory, but as an educated German intellectual, his knowledge of the world's literature was both broad and thorough. His comments on art and literature are scattered throughout his published works and do not form a complete theory of literature. It is his interpretation of history that is most influential in the thinking of Marxist literary critics.

For Marx, history is a process of social evolution in which an economically motivated class struggle determines the way events and institutions develop. In a capitalist society, the wealthy exploit the workers to such an extent that these workers will utimately rebel against the system that deprives them of their humanity. History, then, becomes a drama of classes competing for power, not a record of wars and governments.

Social relations between men are linked to the way they earn their living. In a capitalist system one class works to produce goods and earn wages, but another class profits from the production by being able to purchase and enjoy what has been produced. The workers whose labor is being exploited are blocked from actively relating to others and to nature because they have no control over what they produce and can pursue money only in the form of wages: "In the social production which men carry on they enter into definite relations that are indispensable and independent of their will; these relations of production correspond to a definite stage of development of their material powers of production. . . . The mode of production in material life determines the general character of the social, political and spiritual processes of life" (Marx 1859, 11).

This view of human behavior can provide a basis for literary criticism that is concerned with explaining the reality of the work being considered: "the work is good to the extent that it accurately depicts the clash of class interests, the forces of economic determinism, the dialectic process of history, in brief, the social reality as the critic's particular interpretation of Marxism may conceive it" (Keesey 1994, 192). In other words, the truth of a story can be measured in terms of the larger frame-work of Marxist ideas.

A Marxist reading of *Hawaii*, therefore, will decide the "success" or "truth" of the story of these islands' development based on how well Michener shows the economic relationships among the various groups who settle the islands. The novel lends itself to this type of reading be-cause the people who first come to the islands and find nothing there but sand, plants, and a few birds have the opportunity to establish a "new" society. A Marxist critic has, therefore, the opportunity to follow the development of a society from its beginnings in a well-defined place and trace the exploitation of the working class, or "infrastructure," by the social class that owns or controls the means of economic production (Eagleton 1976, 5).

When the Polynesians from Bora Bora arrive, they bring their slaves to perform the manual labor and continue the social and economic re-lationships of their previous society: first the slaves, then the mass of the population, finally the aristocrats or *Alii Nui.* These patterns do not change with the passing of time, leaving the first island settlers unable to resist the domination of the new ways of the next group: American traders, whalers, and missionaries.

The missionaries are most concerned with saving souls, but the traders and whalers are dominated by the pursuit of wealth. Captain Janders of the *Thetis* persuades Kelolo to use his men to cut down as many san-dalwood trees as possible for sale in China. Janders exploits the islands' resources while Kelolo compels his men to work for his eventual profit. The taro fields and fish ponds go unattended. When Kelolo insists, "They're my men! . . . They'll go where I tell them to go" (272), Abner Hale responds, "Kelolo, God says we must respect all who work" (273). The Marxist would say with the missionary that these men should not be forced to work until they drop from exhaustion, and that the sources of food must not be neglected in order to increase one man's wealth.

The next group to settle in the islands is the Chinese, imported as laborers for the sugarcane fields. John Whipple feels that they will pro-vide needed vitality for the working population. While he is motivated by profit, wealth is not his only goal. He wants to see the islands flourish, and he encourages Nyuk Tsin in her efforts to work for her family's growing prosperity, letting her control what she grows and helping her gain title to land. As discussed in the section on character development, Whipple is often at odds with his fellow whites, for whom the Chinese are in the islands solely to grow sugarcane and earn profits for the plantation owners. Whipple applauds the Chinese use of successful labor to change their status. However, he also thinks that new workers must be imported to work the plantations. The dominant economic structure in his mind is still capitalism, according to a Marxist reading of this part of the story.

The Japanese laborers who arrive in 1902 are greeted with joy by the controlling whites, who are sure that the workers, unlike the Chinese, will return home at the end of their contract. They too are expected to work for wages with no control over their labor and its product. The islands' developing history continues to be based on economic motivation rather than on consideration for human relations. When the Japanese employed at Malama Sugar finally rebel against their working conditions, their spokesperson writes: "The other day a plantation manager said, 'I think of field hands as I do jute bags. Buy them, use them, buy others'" (823). Since the Japanese think of themselves as human beings and members of the human family, they want $1.25 a day for an eight-hour day. In the interests of common humanity, they deserve it. The controlling class breaks the strike, the workers are no better off, exploitation wins. From the Marxist perspective, the strike illustrates the essential nature of class conflict.

The same sort of economic motivation continues to control Hawaii. The Fort rules with "benevolent domination" (842), keeping out labor organizers and mainland stores, promoting tourism, and requiring the Chinese and Japanese to obtain written permission to travel on the mainland. All their actions are directed toward preserving a way of life that is pleasant—especially so for those associated with the Fort.

In post–World War II Hawaii, the situation changes somewhat. A mainland chain builds a series of stores, labor leaders form unions, Democrats even get elected to the legislature, and Chinese and Japanese people obtain more and more positions of economic and political power. But is all this a true change? Michener stops his story on the positive note: Japanese have been elected to the legislature, Chinese are already board members of important organizations and companies, ideas from the islands' ethnic strands are free to mingle on an equal basis. The Marxist reader will feel that Michener's picture of a society's development glorifies upward economic mobility and the virtues of hard work, fortitude, and adaptability to change without dealing with those who are left out. *Hawaii* is a realistic portrayal of a society's history within the limits of its author's system of values; the Marxist critic will not be convinced that it is completely accurate.

5

Centennial
(1974)

Centennial is James Michener's birthday present to the United States, a present that had its beginnings in Michener's teaching experience in Greeley, Colorado, in the 1930s. Exploring Colorado with newspaper editor Floyd Merrill, the author had taken many slides that reminded him through the years of the story that could be written about Colorado, called the Centennial State because it became part of the United States in 1876, the nation's 100th anniversary of the signing of the Declaration of Independence. Once Michener failed to involve Congress in what he considered a well-articulated proposal to celebrate the bicentennial, the novel became his own bicentennial celebration (*About Centennial*, 21–23). For the actual writing Michener set up his headquarters in Denver, where he could do fieldwork and consult experts on the settlement of the West for background details of a story that would begin with the earth's creation and continue to 1974. *Centennial* was published in September 1974, and it would be listed near or at the top of the best-seller lists during the following year.

Plot development will be considered in the critical reading of this novel along with development of characters and thematic considerations. The book will also be looked at from the point of view represented by feminist criticism.

PLOT DEVELOPMENT

As he did with *The Source* (1965), Michener chooses the framework story to bring unity to his immense panorama of prehistoric animals, Indians, trappers, pioneer settlers, cowboys, buffalo hunters, ranchers, sheepmen, homesteaders, dust-bowl farmers, and contemporary Colorado residents. In this novel he uses a college professor, Dr. Lewis Vernor, to be a narrator of sorts. Dr. Vernor is sent to Colorado by a magazine to validate the research done by the publication's reporter on the "Centennial State." Dr. Vernor's reports to the editors following each historical section provide a personal and interpretative touch, and the final chapter represents the impact of the entire historical panorama on both Dr. Vernor and the final important character in his report.

The framework is set up in the first chapter with Dr. Vernor's acceptance of the magazine's commission and his visit to Centennial, Michener's fictional town located north of Denver, at the spot where its residents could look eastward to the prairie and westward to the Rocky Mountains. During the visit Dr. Vernor meets several of the principal local inhabitants who will appear in later chapters. He notes that he has met Caucasians, an African American, a Mexican, but not one Indian: "I considered that symbolic of today's west" (39).

The next two chapters present "The Land" and "The Inhabitants." For readers who want to get right into the story with adventures and people, the nearly one hundred pages of factual explanations are tedious. However, other readers find fascinating the geological description of the formation of the land of Colorado, with special attention paid to the Platte River. The chapter introducing the animal population of this evolving land gives the interested reader a detailed view of the animals, starting with the dinosaurs. Diplodocus is almost a distinct character as Michener describes her physically and tells the story of her life and death. The eohippus, ancestor of the horse, and others such as the bison, whose life cycles will ebb and flow on these plains and in these mountains, are also part of the story. The beaver, the rattlesnake, and the eagle complete the tale of the animals, and the land is ready for the humans. Michener supports the scientific accuracy of his presentation through Dr. Vernor's commentaries following the chapters, in which he explains the choice of dates and interpretations.

The chapter called "The Many Coups of Lame Beaver" introduces the first human inhabitants and tells the story of the Indians, using the life of an Arapaho named Lame Beaver to provide the reader with knowledge about Indian ways of life and their systems of values. His life and interactions with other tribes and later trappers make an engrossing story, and Lame Beaver's bravery throughout his life and his willingness to sacrifice himself for the tribe make him a noble figure. Vernor comments that he has depicted the Arapaho as the noble savage, even while noting such aspects as the primitiveness of his social order and his harsh treatment of women. But was the Indian in complete harmony and balance with nature as the modern-day world would like to believe? Vernor poses this question for himself and his readers as the story of this land and its peoples unfolds, but he never gives a definitive answer.

The next episode, titled "The Yellow Apron," brings the *coureur de bois*, "he who runs in the woods," to the forefront. Pasquinel's origins are unknown and his story—as he roams the mountains, trades with the Indians, sets up one family in St. Louis and another among the Indians—is illustrative of the mountain men of the late eighteenth and early nineteenth centuries. Michener moves the story along with the many adventures of men against nature and against other men, with historical events such as the traders' and trappers' rendezvous. The reader wants to know what happens to Pasquinel, his families, and his sometime-partner Alexander McKeag.

The same wish to know what happens continues for the reader in the next chapter, "The Wagon and the Elephant." This part of the story starts on a farm in Pennsylvania, which Michener describes with his customary attention to detail. The reader learns about the Mennonite faith and how to make scrapple and souse, dishes created from pork. Market day in Lancaster—highlight of the Zendt family's week—ends in disaster for Levi Zendt when he tries to kiss a girl who attracts him. He is to be "shunned"—that is, considered unfit for membership by his church. He buys a wagon and heads west with the orphan girl Elly Zahn, who is even more of an outcast because of her birth and homely appearance. What will their trip be like? Will their dreams be realized? Michener presents the small details that make the journey vivid through dialogue, with description, and through Elly's letters back to a friend from the orphanage. The letters particularly add to the reality of the trip for the reader. After crossing the Continental Divide, the Zendts turn back and settle in Colorado. They have seen the "elephant," the beast that stalks the prairie to frighten travelers, according to the legend told to the immigrants.

Description and dialogue enhance the next chapter, called "The Massacre." The U.S. government wants to establish peace for all time with the plains Indians. Army Captain Maxwell Mercy, introduced in the preceding chapter, is to arrange a peace conference with all the tribes. Levi Zendt is now running a trading post near the area that will become the town of Centennial, and Mercy talks with him about the Indian question. This discussion and later ones with the various tribes highlight the difficulties of co-existence between the two groups. But Michener's description of the conference recreates vividly the scene with its sights, sounds, and smells. The conference cannot and does not solve the problems of the two groups, and Michener takes the reader step by step through the events that lead up to the violent conclusion. This fictional account of factual events is not objective nor is it meant to be. The reader reacts emotionally to the story of atrocities and death, and agrees with Mercy's wife Lisette when she states emphatically to her injured husband who had tried to protect and help both sides, " 'Maxwell, we still did the right thing' " (511).

Settlement by whites is inevitable in this land between the mountains and the prairies, and "The Cowboys" relates the story of the next wave of immigration. In addition to learning about the Homestead Act, the reader vicariously participates in all the dust, heat, and hard work of the authentic cattle drive that Michener recreates. The cowboys bring the cattle from Texas across a nearly waterless desert to the Venneford Ranch, soon to be known as the "Crown Vee" for the shape of its cattle brand. The ranch has been creatively assembled by Oliver Seccombe, the Englishman who was part of the wagon train west with the Zendts. The adventures of the cattle drive are seen chiefly through the eyes of fourteen-year-old Jim Lloyd, and the boy's viewpoint makes them even more vivid and engrossing.

The farmers are next to arrive, to face all the difficulties of establishing a lasting relationship with the land. Hans Brumbaugh, a German who has emigrated from Russia, represents the farmer with vision. He seeks and finds innovative ways of irrigating the desert with water from the Platte River to make it fruitful. Conflicts will arise, for the ranchers want to continue using the open land while the farmers build fences, knowing that "the land must be won, it must be revered, it must be defended" (607). However, the chapter is titled "The Hunters," for men continue to hunt—for gold, for land, for buffalo. Such hunts illustrate how change affects the land and its people, and the representative settlement of Zendt's Farm, Michener's fictional town, becomes the town of Centennial to mark the granting of statehood to Colorado the same year as the centennial of the signing of the Declaration of Independence.

"The Smell of Sheep" is the next episode, and the coming of the sheep to the open range moves the story onward, again by the use of continuing characters and their actions and reactions when faced with new challenges. Brumbaugh works on more elaborate irrigation projects, the ranchers try to exterminate the sheepmen and their animals, and the severe winter of 1886–87 ends forever the gamble of letting cattle range over open land with no reserve food stocks. The reader can live in Michener's authentic world so affected by the violence of men and nature, believing in the events as they unfold and caring what happens to the people who populate this world.

"The Murder" is the one chapter that is not really necessary to the development of the saga but does illustrate the variety of people who settle the frontier. The Wendells, a theatrical family, come to town, and when their possessions are attached for previously unpaid bills, the wife wants to settle in, leaving their wandering, insecure existence. The Wendells kill a businessman passing through town when their effort to blackmail him for allegedly trying to seduce Mrs. Wendell backfires. The episode is interesting in that the reader sees many of the events through the eyes and thoughts of Philip Wendell, the ten-year-old son, a technique which adds to the vividness of the situation. The Wendells' secret is not uncovered, and they are successfully integrated into the life of the town, playing their parts in the following episodes of the story.

"Central Beet" tells the story of how the sugar-beet industry becomes important in Centennial and the surrounding region. Michener gives the clear explanation of the planting, growing, and processing of these beets, a technique which is his trademark when he wishes his readers to learn new information. This chapter veers away from the Centennial story to give the history of Mexicans from the silver mines of the state of Chihuahua, their ill treatment, and the way they arrive in Colorado. Tranquilino Marquez's story is representative, and he becomes involved in Centennial, the beet industry, and the Mexican revolution. The new strand of the story is now interwoven with the beet industry and the cattle ranches.

The next strand adds a new type of farmer, one who attempts to conquer the "Drylands." The new farming method, which includes plowing deep and allowing about 60 percent of one's land to "rest" without a crop each year, is outlined in Michener's usual careful manner, which also indicates that the method has one defect. The chapter will illustrate this defect through the reactions of Hans "Potato" Brumbaugh and Jim Lloyd and by telling what happens to the land and the farmers when nature counterattacks with drought and wind. Michener again uses his characters to make the events real and authentic. The deaths of the Grebe family are symbolic and dreadful. There are always those who help the unfortunate and those who profit from them; Michener's saga presents both types. The chapter also continues the story of the cattle industry and Colorado's treatment of the Mexicans.

To bring all the strands together and portray the Centennial of 1974, Dr. Vernor becomes part of the story in the final chapter, "November Elegy," and searches for a prototype of a Centennial resident. He chooses Paul Garrett and presents Garrett's family tree, showing his Indian and European ancestors. Garrett will also marry Flor Marquez, joining the Mexican heritage to his life. This chapter presents both the hope and the despair of Centennial, Colorado, a very liveable town in economic decline, and planet earth faced with environmental problems. Through the reflections and actions of Garrett as he tours his hometown and state accompanied by Dr. Vernor, the thematic considerations are tied together and the historical panorama draws to a close with a conversation between Garrett and Cisco Calendar about why one would live in Centennial. Michener's technique is effective and leaves the reader with questions to ponder about what is important for humans and their environment.

CHARACTER DEVELOPMENT

With the type of historical panorama or saga that Michener presents in *Centennial,* he does not have the time or space to focus on the full development of many characters. He does create memorable figures to whom the reader relates and reacts as the story progresses, however. These characters are people of action but also of reflection as they enact their part of the story.

Lame Beaver of the Arapaho is the most finely drawn of the Indians. Michener shows him in relationship to the land, the animals, and the people with which he lives. The man of many coups, or courageous acts, Lame Beaver makes the ultimate sacrifice for his tribe by staking himself in one place near the enemy camp and saving his ammunition for the enemy chief. The gripping scene of battle ends in inevitable death for Lame Beaver, but in triumph for the tribe. His going-away song sums up his life with these opening words, "Only the rocks endure forever" (202).

The *coureur de bois* Pasquinel and his fellow trapper Alexander McKeag are unforgettable examples of fortitude. Pasquinel wants the freedom to roam, and he leaves each family he establishes to return to his life in the mountains. He and McKeag fight side by side and save each other's lives, yet they break over the hate Pasquinel's son, with his Indian wife, feels for McKeag. Pasquinel never reflects about the consequences of any action, and it is the introspective McKeag who sums up his only friend's character: although courageous in physical battle, Pasquinel was a coward in moral values, always running away from something. "He had called it freedom, but it was flight" (289). McKeag flees into solitude himself, but he cannot forget or deny a need for companionship. He accepts union with Clay Basket, Pasquinel's Indian wife, after finding the trapper killed and continues to show moral fortitude the rest of his life, caring for her and her daughter Lucinda and treating Indians and whites with fairness at his trading post.

Levi and Elly Zendt, the young pioneer couple, also illustrate fortitude as they undertake the difficult journey toward Oregon. Michener gives their background—Elly the unknown orphan and Levi, shunned by his family and church community—which increases the reader's sympathy for these seekers of a new life. Elly's letters recounting the happenings of the journey give her an added dimension, as she is seen in thought as well as action. Her compassion for others, her love for Levi, her courage in facing the unknown make her one of the novel's most sympathetic characters. Levi's fortitude wavers when Elly dies, and as he works through his grief and self-blame, he is a believable human being, more than a representative pioneer.

Army officer Maxwell Mercy is another unforgettable member of the cast of *Centennial*. Married to Pasquinel's daughter by his St. Louis wife, Mercy accepts his Indian in-laws with delight, making sure Lucinda McKeag has a wonderful time in St. Louis. His honest and sincere efforts to establish lasting peace with the Indian tribes are doomed to failure because he cannot convince other whites that Indians are human beings. Yet he never gives up trying to find that balance between obtaining justice for the Indians and meeting the needs of incoming settlers. Mercy's anguish as he tries to carry out his government's orders and finds that promises made to the Indians won't be kept is made real by Michener's portrayal of the army officer's actions and reactions, those of a man of honor and courage.

R. J. Poteet is a character who appeals to the reader's imagination as he leads the cattle drive from Texas to Colorado. His ability to handle both men and cattle is brought out through all the adventures, and the reader accepts with no difficulty the courage and reliability of this man. He is both buyer and seller as he collects the cattle for the drive north, a situation acceptable to all concerned, "for if you couldn't trust R. J. Poteet, you couldn't trust anybody" (531). The reader understands Poteet by what he does and is not concerned with having no insight into what has made him the man he is. He is suitable for his episode and gives authenticity to an epic event.

Jim Lloyd comes through as a more complex character because the reader shares in his thoughts as well as his actions. He plays a part in the story from age fourteen to his death at the age of seventy. It's Jim who thinks as best a boy can about the events of the cattle drive. And as he matures, it's Jim who understands the land and how it must be treated. He notices and appreciates the animals, from the engaging birds to his beloved white-faced Herefords. He cherishes a hopeless love for Clemma Zendt, who refuses any emotional commitment. In spite of his grief, he continues to fulfill his responsibilities to the Crown Vee Ranch, its land and its cattle. When Clemma leaves town for the final time, Jim summarizes his philosophy and his relationship to the land: "You work. That's what you do. . . . And after a few short years they bury you in the earth, and what has happened in between doesn't matter a hell of a lot. Just so long as you keep close to the earth" (753–54).

Another sympathetic character is Charlotte Buckland, the young Englishwoman enthralled with the West. She comes to America with her father, a relation of the English nobleman who originally finances the Crown Vee Ranch. Michener gives her believable individuality by showing her love for new experiences and her appreciation for the land and its people. Extravagant in establishing her castle at the Crown Vee Ranch and stubborn in developing the Hereford breed as show animals, Charlotte is moved to action when she learns that the Mexicans aren't allowed their cantina. With her requests denied by the court, she buys the shacks where the Mexicans live and rents one for the cantina, at $1 per year. In her last years, her enthusiasm still alive, she helps the Grebe family, whose dryland farm has been so affected by the weather, and sponsors a seminar for the farmers that will explain how to plow in order to protect the land from drought and winds. Her motives and feelings are not explored, but her actions make her a memorable part of this land and its story.

Hans "Potato" Brumbaugh is another character whose relationship with the land makes him memorable. He illustrates the contributions of a man who has vision and works to accomplish his goals. His dream to irrigate the land is realized because he refuses to worry about cost or what seems impossible. Brumbaugh is one of the characters whose reflections are presented to the reader. He is seen in thought as well as in action, considering the overall system of the Platte River as well as defending his farm against armed attackers. The "tireless old fighter" continues pondering the water problem even after suffering a stroke and dies peacefully, still considering how it all works.

Three families represent the human interest of the story's last chapters: the Wendells, the Marquezes, and the Grebes. Mervin Wendell and his wife and son begin their path to respectability with a crime. The Wendells are able to impress the townsfolk by their singing and their civic contributions, but their fortune is solidified on the misfortunes of others. Mervin and then Philip encourage land purchases and buy back land of failed farms, only to resell it at a profit. Michener reserves his scorn for such people, yet he makes them human and believable in describing how they behave in the various situations they face.

The Marquez family illustrates the Mexicans whose work is considered necessary, but who are treated as expendable. The reader follows Tranquilino from the silver mines of Mexico until he arrives at Brumbaugh's farm. His adventures during the Mexican revolution are presented with the panoramic detail at which Michener excels. Tranquilino, his wife Serafina, their son Trunfador, and their daughter Soledad illustrate this group of people in a certain time and place, and Michener makes us care about what happens to them.

The Grebe family is representative of the hardworking people who are faced with more than their fair share of adversity. Alice Grebe is especially well drawn as she supports her husband wholeheartedly and sacrifices herself for her family. Her breakdown after years of struggle against the wind, the dust, and the hard times is horrifying in its graphic detail yet believable and poignant in its sadness.

Because of Michener's ability to make his characters believable, they remain unforgettable parts of the story. Those discussed here are representative of their time, place, and situation, but also are individualized, and the reader appreciates them for making history more authentic because it happens to "real" people.

THEMATIC CONSIDERATIONS

The themes in *Centennial* are similar to those developed in *Hawaii*— the problems caused by the lack of understanding among ethnic groups and the role of migration and adaptation to new situations—with an added concern for the environment and the state of modern American society. In addition to interweaving these themes throughout the novel, Michener uses the final chapter, "November Elegy," to summarize the themes through the life of Paul Garrett, the character he creates to symbolize the history of the West.

The stark contrast between fear or acceptance of the Other—those from different racial, ethnic groups—is evident in the land once people begin to live between the mountains and the prairie. The various Indian groups detest and are afraid of each other. Lame Beaver's father Gray Wolf initiates him into the world of adults on his ninth birthday: " 'You must always remember that Our People are surrounded by enemies" (149). The Dakota are fearful warriors, the Utes are unspeakable, the Comanche have horses, the Pawnee are always lurking, always clever.

The Indian-white relationship is also governed more by fear than by acceptance. Pasquinel's point of view that one should avoid fighting with the Indian and instead "bring him to you by faithfulness" (242) is contradicted by the army officer who feels that the only reasonable way to handle an Indian is to kill him. Captain Mercy tries to counter this attitude, but reason cannot prevail when starving Indians rebel and kill and mutilate children. Through such characters as Maxwell and Lisette Mercy, and the commentaries of Dr. Vernor, Michener deplores the lack of tolerance that ends in atrocities on both sides. Yet he does not offer any easy explanations of why the Indian-white interactions were especially catastrophic, indicating through the words of Dr. Vernor what his intent is: "I conceive of my job as placing the confused data of history in some kind of formal order, as interestingly as possible, and allowing the user to deduce for himself whatever misleading and glittering generalities he prefers" (513–14).

The Mexican-white relationship is also characterized by intolerant and uncomprehending attitudes. The silver miners in Mexico are brutalized by the rich and powerful, including American engineers who consider Mexicans nothing but animals. The irony in the statement that workers who labor fourteen hours a day, seven days a week, don't need any extra time off for "all they do is run to their huts and womanize" (823) is evident to the reader, if not to the engineers. The Mexican workers who winter in Denver are also misunderstood by the local residents, who can't comprehend their food, their language, or their way of settling quarrels. There's something shameful about using a knife on your foe in a face-to-face struggle; shooting him six times at sixty paces shows courage. Henry Garrett, who falls in love with Soledad Marquez, is the first Anglo to catch a glimmer of the stable patterns of Mexican society. "Off to a wretched corner by themselves, living in hovels, these quiet people arranged a world that gave them dignity and a kind of rude repose" (979). Michener sees in the Mexican pattern of life a happiness with nature unknown to the Anglo, and the commentary indicates sorrow that no Anglo could or would see a possible symbiosis of the two cultures to the benefit of both (979). There is some hope for understanding, as Vernor's end notes to "Drylands" show: when the state president of the Patriotic Order of the Women of the West refuses the group's All-American Citizenship award for high school seniors to Jesus Melendez of Centennial because as a Mexican, probably an illegal immigrant, he can't possibly illustrate "true American ideals" (992), even the most conservative citizens react against her statement. And the students pass a resolution stating that no other student in the school is half as worthy of the award as Jesus.

Environmental concerns relating to animals and land are evident throughout *Centennial*. First the beaver begin to disappear. Their food supply diminishes as the trees they feed on are cut to make winter refuges for the trappers. This increasing number of trappers, greedy for more and more pelts, kill more and more families of beavers, dooming the species to virtual extinction. Through another irony of history, the disappearance of the beaver coincides with a change of fashion: men in London start preferring French silk for their hats. A way of life on the American plains is over.

The disappearance of the buffalo has more far-reaching consequences. It leads to a near extermination of the Indian tribes and a pitiful existence for those remaining, herded onto reservations. The waste involved when white men kill the buffalo bothers thrifty, careful people like Levi Zendt, but guide Sam Purchas expresses the complete unawareness and unconcern about such indiscriminate killing characteristic of most hunters,

comparing the buffalo to ants, and nobody cares about stepping on ants.
The Indians do not understand how the whites can kill for only hides
and tallow, leaving meat to rot when others are starving. But the objective of certain whites is to kill the buffalo in order to "solve" the Indian
problem. It's a brutal but effective solution that is made vivid through
descriptions of such hunts as Jake Calendar's stand, when he destroyed
eighty-nine buffalo before the remainder of the herd ran. A remnant of
the Arapaho finds the eighty-nine rotting carcasses after two long weeks
of unsuccessful hunting for the buffalo. The leader realizes the tribe must
make the final submission and leave its ancestral territory for a reservation in Dakota: "Through hunger the Great White Father has made us
submit to his command" (634).

In "November Elegy" the concern for the animals, the water, the air,
the people—everything that constitutes the environment—is illustrated
through the activities and thoughts of Paul Garrett. His family tree, presented at the beginning of the chapter, may seem a bit contrived, as he
is a descendant of all the important strands of Colorado settlers, yet it
is a logical progression and the technique is effective. All parts of the
past form his heritage, but his thoughts and actions are of the present
and for the future. Named head of the committee responsible for the
celebration of Colorado's centennial, Garrett has the opportunity to visit
all parts of his state and consider its assets and liabilities.

Concern for what people are rather than what group they belong to
is part of Garrett. He marries a Mexican woman in spite of disapproval
voiced by his children and her father, and his decision is accepted by
fellow ranchers. Is there hope for more acceptance of other groups? Perhaps not, for the brother of Garrett's new wife insists on recognition of
the demands of his La Raza group: Anglos must give back control of
most of the Southwest to the rightful heirs of the land, the Chicanos.
Garrett's new brother-in-law wants no compromise, and understanding
is still not possible.

Garrett is also proud of his Indian heritage, but a visit to the western
Wyoming reservations where his Arapaho relatives live always depresses him. The problems are so overwhelming with the lack of opportunities for the young people, the reliance on alcohol and the suffering
it causes, and the continuing discord between the Arapaho and the Sho-
shone—eternal enemies placed on the same reservation. Garrett feels that
certain Indian values must be recaptured if the white man is to continue
to thrive on the prairies: respect for the land, the animals, the seasons.
He advises closing reservations, encouraging those Indians who wish to

live communally and letting the rest enter the mainstream culture, to sink or swim. "Many good things will be lost, but the best will persist—in legend, in remembered ways of doing things, in our attitude toward the land" (1076).

Two contrasting attitudes toward animals are evident in the trial where Paul Garrett testifies against Floyd Calendar, descendant of buffalo hunter Jake Calendar. The charges against Calendar are two: killing bears, an endangered species, in a cruel and unusual manner and shooting bald eagles from a plane. The prosecution's witnesses draw a portrait of a man for whom killing became an end in itself. He placed radio transmitters on the bears he captured so that once he let them loose, he could make sure all the hunters he guided could bag their animals. He even guided hunters onto Garrett's land so that they could pick off a few wild turkeys from the protected colony there. Since Garrett has just been named deputy to the Commissioner of Resources and Priorities, the defense attorney makes much of his opposition to a sportsman-hunter. Calendar is acquitted on all charges except that of keeping a zoo without a license—those captured bears had been in cages for up to thirty days. Garrett is furious but will continue to protect the turkeys and the prairie dog colony he has encouraged on his land. As he tells his foreman, who is concerned about the horse who broke his leg in a prairie dog burrow, "You preserve nothing without encountering some disadvantages. . . . The trick is to preserve the balance and pay whatever price it costs" (1018).

Air quality and an adequate supply of water are two more environmental concerns for the new deputy commissioner. As he drives across the land he will be protecting in his new post, he laments the thick smog that veils the mountains and settles over Denver most days. Knowing that much of the air pollution is caused by auto emissions, he vows to drive more slowly and get a smaller car. Garrett comments that the West had surrendered to the automobile, if not to the Indian, and that deaths from auto accidents in one year outnumber all the settlers ever killed by Indians.

The aquifer, an underground source of water, is also in trouble with increasing demands from industry, agriculture, and the residential population. Garrett attends a meeting with the Water Board and sees a visual demonstration, complete with a working model of how water is drawn from the rivers and the aquifer as well. Sobered by the complexities of the environmental problems, Garrett reflects that next he will have to worry about the soil to till: "This nation is running out of everything.

We forgot the fact that we've always existed in a precarious balance, and now if we don't protect all the components, we'll collapse" (1042). He realizes the need to return to the sense of responsibility toward the earth that people like his great-grandfather, Jim Lloyd, had shown.

During a flight over the Platte River, which runs free and pure in the uninhabited mountains but is abused by pollution once it reaches inhabited land, Garrett sees the stream of cars heading for the Colorado-Nebraska football game, and he muses about the high priority given to football in educational institutions—imported players exploited for prestige of the state and then discarded. Although he knows his fellow citizens won't believe it, he finds the river more exciting than football.

The changes are difficult to contemplate for Garrett. In order to make his ranch economically feasible, he must purchase another breed of cattle to revitalize his herefords. Central Beet is closing down, and the Centennial feed lots will be moved to other states. The Railway Arms Hotel will be gone in another year, and Centennial as a flourishing town appears to be disappearing. One evening, Vernor and Cisco Calendar, the singer, find Garrett drunk and take him off to his father-in-law's restaurant, where he asks Cisco to sing all the favorite songs of the West. As Cisco puts it, a man needs roots. The two agree that Centennial just might be the best remaining spot on the earth.

But is it a spot doomed to oblivion? The question is not answered. But in "November Elegy," Michener poses the question indirectly, through his reflections on Centennial's problems—itself a microcosm of our planet. As one critic notes, Michener's novels "show a past that is heroic, yet in their last episodes—those dealing with recent or contemporary events—they show a present that is confused, divisive, without coherent purpose or system of values" (Becker 1983, 177). *Centennial*, published in 1974, was written during a time when the United States was confronting Watergate and the end to war in Vietnam. Society at large was facing an uncertain future, and James Michener, in evoking a stirring past, calls attention to qualities and values that helped many realize the American dream. His birthday present to America may end on a somber note, as it refuses to ignore the real problems facing humans and the world in which they live, but it also captures the sense of human capacity to solve these problems if goodwill, tolerance, hard work, and unfailing will are permitted to overcome complacency and inertia. As a former teacher, Michener does not ignore the need to educate as he presents his historical panorama of the American West. The reflective reader appreciates *Centennial* as a fascinating story and a lesson to be studied.

A FEMINIST READING OF *CENTENNIAL*

One of the most important considerations in the feminist perspective on literature as outlined in Chapter 3 is the image of women that a work presents through its female characters. In *Centennial,* with its focus on human responses to the conditions encountered in settling the frontier, the women characters present part of that response. The specific cultural and historical context of the novel must be kept in mind while reading it from a feminist perspective.

In the chapter presenting Indian life, the reader learns how lives are regulated by tribal customs and about the low status granted women without a husband. When Lame Beaver sacrifices himself to save his people, his wife Blue Leaf accepts the fact that his death means her death as well. Without a husband, she has no right to food or shelter. Her possessions are available for the other women to fight over. While her daughter is taken in by an uncle, Blue Leaf is expendable because she is elderly, with no man to care for her. Dr. Vernor makes special mention of the harsh treatment Indian women received; this image is authentic in terms of its culture and time period.

The daughter, Clay Basket, marries the trapper Pasquinel according to Indian ritual and promises always to help him. She needs a man to have any status in her culture—as does Pasquinel's wife in St. Louis, Lise Bockweiss. Both women adjust with dignity to having a husband who is absent for months and even years at a time. When Pasquinel is killed, Clay Basket lives as Alexander McKeag's wife, raising her daughter and trying to reconcile the Indian and white worlds. She succeeds with her daughter, who marries the grieving Levi Zendt, saving them both from useless existences alone. Lise Bockweiss makes her life in St. Louis, playing her role as social leader and raising her children to be productive citizens. Lise and Clay Basket are "traditional" women but also are examples of human beings whose care and concern for others makes them more than stereotypes. They respond with moral courage to the difficulties they face, which a feminist critic would accept as authentic human action.

In the same general time period, Elly Zahn and Lucinda McKeag also must find their places through their relationships with the men in their lives, but nineteenth-century culture on the frontier or in the city offers no other real opportunities for women. Elly has as much fortitude as her husband Levi Zendt in facing the challenges of frontier settlement; they are partners in this venture. Lucinda, as Levi's second wife, chooses to stay with the freedom of the prairies and the mountains rather than accept the city life of St. Louis on a permanent basis. It's a choice based on the love of a man and a place. The lives of Elly and Lucinda are both affirmed through their courageous responses to life on the frontier, making them characters that a feminist would recognize as realistic women in their historical setting.

Charlotte Buckland, the young English woman who chooses the freedom of the prairies over life in England, must marry in order to act on her choice. She selects Oliver Seccombe, manager of the Crown Vee, since as his wife she can be part of this new world. It's a world she doesn't completely understand during her happy marriage to Oliver, but after his death, Charlotte must decide if she wants to spend the rest of her life in this world. Her major problem is how to pick another husband. She realizes the worth of Jim Lloyd, and although they come from different backgrounds, they will build something worthwhile together. Charlotte needs a husband in this frontier society, but as she matures, she becomes a more authentic person, using her capabilities and her money to make conditions better for others.

Maude Wendell directs her energies and abilities to make life better for her family. Tired of the roaming life of theatrical performances in town after town, she wants to settle in Centennial. Maude has the steadfastness and fortitude her husband lacks. She is the authentic half of this couple, in the sense that her goals for a house and stable existence are what drive the family's life, rather than any projects of her husband. Maude trades on her gender, her sex appeal, to get what she wants, but once she gets it, she is a model wife and mother according to the stereotype of the nineteenth century.

As the story moves into the twentieth century, the feminist critic notes that the women characters in *Centennial* are still seen in relation to men. Alice Grebe is the supportive farm wife, a partner in her husband's decision to move to Colorado where he can have his own land. Michener portrays her as one of the admirable American women who insist on the touches like libraries and churches that will civilize whatever frontier they settle, a positive yet stereotypical image. She accepts the challenges of the family's western venture with determination to improve her home and her community. Her eventual breakdown is poignant and tragic. The economic environment of farming in the 1930s and the physical environment of dust and wind storms are too much to overcome.

The three Marquez women—Serafina, her daughter Soledad, and her granddaughter Flor—are realistic examples of women whose main role is to relate to men and their needs. Serafina keeps the family together while her husband works in another country or fights with the Mexican revolutionaries, and she is "Potato" Brumbaugh's compassionate house-keeper in his last years. Soledad teaches Henry Garrett what love means, but she is whisked away by her brother, who won't accept her love affair with an Anglo. Flor decides to marry Paul Garrett because they both feel like better people in each other's company. These women are more traditional than authentic, but they are believable human beings in their cultural context, if not role models from a feminist perspective.

Only one woman in the entire novel is shown with a profession, Carol Endermann, the magazine's researcher whose work Vernor is supposed to verify. She has all the academic credentials, but Vernor still has a problem playing second fiddle to a beginning scholar, and a girl at that. Her character hints at a more self-realized woman, but once Vernor has accepted the magazine's offer, she is offstage for the rest of the narrative.

The images of women in this novel affirm their lives as partners in the settling of this frontier. Their responses are as varied and as courageous as the men's. From the cultural and historical environment that frames the story, the images are realistic. From the feminist perspective, Michener has gone beyond the standard stereotypes to create women who are believable human beings but none whose activities provide opportunities for authentic self-realization.

6

Chesapeake
(1978)

In his 1978 novel *Chesapeake,* James Michener presents the maritime world of the Chesapeake Bay on the Atlantic coast of the United States. His story of fictional characters interacting in an imaginary locale on Maryland's Eastern Shore attempts to recreate the historic past of this area of the bay from the sixteenth century to the present. The writer starts with a disclaimer that the book is not history but a work of fiction, yet historical events and people are part of the panorama that involves the fictional people. And the wonders of the natural world—the river, the birds, the forests, the marshes, the bay—are as integral a part of the panorama as the people and the events.

In this chapter the discussion will focus first on the story's structure and narrative progression. The presentation and development of the characters will be considered, as will the themes that are interwoven with the story. In conclusion, *Chesapeake* will be examined from the viewpoint of a Marxist critic.

PLOT ORGANIZATION AND DEVELOPMENT

Michener uses an omniscient third-person narrator point of view in this novel, which is a relatively efficient means of presenting much descriptive information. To emphasize the maritime nature of this world and provide an organized structure for his historical panorama, Michener begins each of the novel's fourteen episodes with a voyage involving at least some transportation by water. The voyages introduce a character or a situation at a specific time and place, and they are followed by a titled narrative that develops the events and people during the same time period. As in the other historical, panoramic novels, the characters and their families are followed through the centuries; their interwoven lives give continuity to the evolving story.

The first voyage takes place in 1583, when Pentaquod, a Susquehannock Indian, realizes he is about to be expelled from his tribe for not believing that it is necessary to go to war every year to prove one's manhood. His voyage down the Susquehanna River leads him to the Chesapeake Bay. Since he has heard that the more peaceful Indian tribes live toward the east, he heads in that direction, to "the opening of a broad and congenial river" (27).

"The River" portion of the story introduces the reader to Pentaquod and the eastern shores of the Chesapeake Bay. Pentaquod first visits the island at the river's mouth. Even though he is impressed with the plants and animals found on the island, a summer storm shows Pentaquod the danger: the island's western shore is constantly undercut by wave action. He spends some time living on a cliff overlooking the bay, then finds a river beyond the marsh. Now he is impressed by the numbers of great, noisy birds; he has met the geese. Next come the people. Those Indians who winter along this part of the shore belong to the Nanticoke, but they are a timid, peace-loving group who vacate their shelters when more aggressive Indians confront them. Pentaquod joins forces with the group, and when Nanticokes from the north invade, Pentaquod scares these Indians into flight because of his great size. Becoming his group's leader, he must learn the tribal legend about the big canoe that had visited years before, carrying men with white skins. Although life is satisfying for Pentaquod and his family for several years, he fears the changes to come to this small group of people living in peace and harmony with themselves and their world.

The people with white skins arrive in "Voyage Two: 1608." Captain John Smith of Pocahontas fame leads a small ship on an exploratory voyage from Jamestown. Edmund Steed is part of the company and has the task of writing the chronicle of Smith's exploits. Steed is attracted by the island Pentaquod had explored and then left.

Since Steed and his descendants will be one essential strand in the development of the Chesapeake story, Michener presents Edmund's family history in "The Island." The background is necessary to appreciate fully Edmund's Catholic faith, which will also be important to future Steeds. Michener gives the reader a history lesson about the Protestant Reformation of sixteenth-century England at the time of Henry VIII, making the lesson more vivid by showing the events as they affect one Catholic family over the years, until Edmund decides to leave for Jamestown to avoid the restrictions on Roman Catholics in early seventeenth-century England.

Settling on the island at the mouth of what will be called the Choptank River, Edmund names it Devon, after the part of England he had known as home. The narrative moves through Edmund's hard work at developing the island, his basically friendly relationship with Pentaquod and his Indians, and his efforts to find a wife who shares his faith. He finally marries Martha Keene, who is sent from England by Edmund's father. Michener moves the story along by showing how the relationship with the Indians deteriorates because of a difference in values. Why do the white men insist on burning acres of forest every year just to plant tobacco? He also makes the religious question a continuing part of the story as Ralph Steed, Edmund's son, cannot marry as he chooses because he is a Catholic. He becomes a priest. Michener also develops ideas about governance through Steed's participation in the assembly that considers this matter for the new colony of Maryland. His point of view that the colony's laws should be determined by the settlers who know the land prevails, but Edmund dies as he returns home. His part of the story is ended, but his family is well established on Devon.

During "Voyage Three: 1636," another family strand starts on its way to play a role in the evolving society of the Eastern Shore. Timothy Turlock is a petty criminal in London who is banished to Virginia. The reader gets to know the unsavory details of Turlock's character and career through Michener's customary attention to creating a life and a background for his characters. When Turlock arrives in Virginia, he is purchased as an indentured servant by Simon Janney. Turlock finally attacks Janney, steals some tools and other goods, and flees to the Eastern Shore marshes in a stolen boat.

Turlock's fortunes and those of the Indians in the area are intertwined in the narrative following the third voyage. The chapter is called "The Marsh," and the four Indians who find Turlock after his flight give him a survival course for living in the wilderness. He concludes an agreement with the Indians that makes him the owner of four hundred acres of marsh and eight hundred acres of the more solid land behind the streams

and bogs of the marsh. Turlock makes an effort to help the Indians resolve the problems with the encroaching white hunters and settlers who
kill any Indians in their way. Pentaquod, elderly now, is saddened, and
when his daughter Tciblento follows Turlock back to the marsh, accepting the inevitable loss of her people and culture, Pentaquod soon dies.

The religious struggle is still part of the developing story. When Edmund's son Ralph returns from Rome in 1648, ordained as a priest, he
brings word of the civil war in England between royalists under Catholic
king Charles I and the Protestants of Parliament with Cromwell as their
leader. Although most of the planters are royalists, there are enough anti-
Catholics to attack Devon. Turlock helps repulse the attack, but the
chapel is burned. Ralph will spend the rest of his life ministering to those
living in the wilderness of the Eastern Shore.

"The Marsh" concludes by describing Timothy Turlock's existence in
these waterways and byways, the Steeds' increasing prosperity, and the
elimination of the Indians, even the peaceful Choptanks. Turlock has a
growing family of children with different women, hunts wolves for the
bounty paid, and ignores rules and regulations as much as possible. The
Steeds add to their holdings and carefully manage their assets. The Indians are targets for any white hunter, and when Tciblento dies, attended
by Martha Steed and her sons, the final Indian presence is removed from
the marsh.

"Voyage Four: 1661" is the spiritual and physical voyage of Edward
Paxmore. The colony of Massachusetts will tolerate no deviation from
the religious beliefs of the established church and imprisons Edward
Paxmore, a carpenter, along with Thomas Kenworthy, a man condemned
to be whipped and then hanged for his faith, which deviates from the
established church. Their discussion solidifies Paxmore's religious beliefs, and he prays for the courage to endure his own punishment—to
be whipped in four different towns and finally expelled to Rhode Island,
"where heretics abide" (229). Along the way he meets Ruth Brinton, who
is enduring the same type of punishment for her convictions. Paxmore
returns to Massachusetts and refuses to keep silent about his faith. The
judge who condemns him to be hanged has doubts, and Michener uses
dramatic dialogues between the two men to present the ideas of the
Quakers and the fears of the Puritans for the tranquillity of their colony.
The judge decides that having Paxmore hanged is not right, so he has
him put on a ship to Maryland, where people are more tolerant. Paxmore
eventually arrives at Patamoke Landing, where the Steeds have estab-

lished a warehouse and where he encounters Ruth Brinton, gravely ill from the whippings she has endured.

Another major strand of the story is now in place, and "The Cliff" sets up the Quaker role in the narrative of the Chesapeake. The Quakers will be a moral as well as an economic force in the region. After Edward and Ruth marry, they build a home that they call "Peace Cliff" on the headland beyond the marshes. Edward tries to build his first boat, and the process is described with Michener's usual care for detail. When the Steeds want Edward to build an actual ship, the reader participates in his problem solving as he encounters the difficulties of ship construction.

The ongoing question of religious belief continues when Father Ralph Steed and Ruth Brinton Paxmore discuss their ideas about faith. And slavery becomes an important moral question in this section. Edward receives nine slaves from a man in Barbados as payment for work he had done while there. Since he can use workers in the boatyard, he is pleased, but Ruth is appalled at his equating slaves with indentured servants. This event is the opening of the long debate in *Chesapeake* concerning the morality of slavery. Ruth's efforts to persuade Edward to free the slaves cause a transfer of the Paxmore slaves to the Steeds in exchange for tools, books, and a permanent site for the boatyard. Yet the moral dilemma is not so easily solved, for Ruth's attempt to do the right thing results in the eventual death of the slaves after pirates raid Devon. The storm tormenting the bay at the end of the chapter reflects Ruth's troubled spirit as she thinks about the deaths she feels are on her soul.

"Voyage Five: 1701" is a short trip. Rosalind Janney, an intelligent woman of no beauty, is to leave her family's plantation on the Rappahannock River in Virginia to marry Fitzhugh Steed of Devon. She has trained herself to be an excellent plantation manager, but she feels the humiliation of her father's long efforts to find her a husband. This short trip to a new life feels like exile to Rosalind; her husband to be is a Catholic, and exchanging the civilization of Virginia for the unknown wilderness of Maryland is challenging her courage.

In "Rosalind's Revenge" the story chronicles Rosalind's activities on Devon and the way she brings order to the plantation. She wants to create a beautiful house and gardens, but when she visits the Paxmore home, she learns more than how a house is designed. Ruth Paxmore, now sixty-nine but as concerned with moral questions as ever, brings up the question of freeing slaves and Fitzhugh Steed's liaison with Nelly Turlock of the marshes. Rosalind will follow Ruth's comment that "life consists of sending everything forward" (327) and continues organizing the Steed enterprises until her stepson Mark returns from his studies in France. When pirates raid Devon one winter, Rosalind's daughter Rachel and Mark are among the dead. Rosalind wants revenge and badgers Fitzhugh until he joins the expedition sent after the pirates. She wants revenge to tidy up the world, not to even things out. Rosalind will also not tolerate the whippings poor women receive from the town authorities for alleged misdeeds. She and Ruth Paxmore join the latest victim and bare their own backs for the lash; no more women are ever whipped in Patamoke. Rosalind continues to support the unfortunate, taking in the local judge's abused servant girl. Although she is condemned by the court, under the same judge, Rosalind is able to make his actions part of the public record. She receives a ducking as ordered, but it is brief and public opinion is on Rosalind's side. All through the years of combating pirates and injustices, Rosalind continues the work on her house, until at last the design is both pleasing and functional. "Rosalind's Revenge," as the house has always been known, is now complete.

"Voyage Six: 1773" is another short trip. The Church of England rector of Wrentham, Jonathan Wilock, is transported by his boat to Patamoke to testify against three defendants who have failed to deliver the yearly tax of tobacco to the rector. The three accused are Simon Steed, Levin Paxmore, and Teach Turlock. One of the justices notes after the trial that the condemnation has created an alliance among three unlikely candidates; new ideas are being heard in the land.

"Three Patriots" brings the American Revolution to this corner of the Chesapeake. Simon Steed, afraid of the ugly spirit coming, wants ships from the Paxmore yard to maintain his ties with England. Levin Paxmore accepts little by little the idea that he is building a warship. Teach Turlock, furious at losing part of his land for not paying the tax to the rector, uses a Paxmore built boat to prey on English shipping. When war breaks out, Steed's wife returns to England with their baby on the Paxmore-built ship *Whisper,* captained by Teach Turlock. Baby Penelope is looked after in part by seven-year-old Matt Turlock, an able child who is the first Turlock to learn to read: "prospects unlimited lay ahead" (460) for both Matt and the new colonies.

Michener uses the chapter to give the reader a personalized mini-history of the American Revolution by involving the three families in actual events. Steed, now supporting the colonies' cause, is sent to France to help solicit French aid. Ben Franklin becomes part of the story momentarily, and convinces Steed that the Americans will win the war. The

French naval engagement with the British fleet off the entrance to Chesapeake Bay is observed by Turlock and his crew on their way home from a run to the Caribbean. Steed's profits through commerce running the blockades and speculation with paper currency increase the family wealth, but they keep him from a role in the new U.S. government at war's end, as he learns in a meeting with George Washington. Turlock does get the return of his land authorized by Washington, and Paxmore is paid for the cost he incurred building ships for the American cause.

"Voyage Seven: 1811" is a digression but illustrates Michener's interest in the causes and interrelationships of things, even the origin of Chesapeake Bay. Thomas Applegarth, a Steed employee, has borrowed a book on geography from Elizabeth Paxmore. Noting the way the Pennsylvania mountains seem to drift from the northeast to the southwest, he is intrigued: why and how did this happen? His speculations lead him to consider the effect of an Ice Age on the earth, and he decides to make a voyage to the source of the Susquehanna River. Applegarth's voyage enables him to experience the Susquehanna River system as a whole, and the digression serves as a reminder that the earth is an ecological entity.

With "The Duel" the story moves to the War of 1812. The British are treating the Chesapeake as their own lake, and their goal is to capture the *Whisper*, the Paxmore-built ship captained now by Matthew Turlock. The ship is hidden in the marsh, but a spy reveals its presence to the British. Turlock loses a hand in the fight, and his wife is killed in the British shelling. His duel with Captain Gatch is under way. Paxmore's boatyard is not destroyed, and the shipbuilder will start a new ship for Turlock. While waiting his chance to reenter the blockaded Chesapeake, Turlock decides to join the illegal slave trade—for just one trip. Turlock is finally victorious in the duel because of his tactics. The sailing scenes are described with Michener's usual attention to detail, making the reader feel part of the action.

"Voyage Eight: 1822" could be seen as another digression. This trip is the long migratory voyage of the geese that have been appearing in the story since Pentaquod's arrival on the Eastern Shore. One family of geese is the focal point of the voyage, and Michener lays out for the reader information about the feeding, mating, and migratory habits of geese, through the story of Onk-or and his mate and goslings. Their journey south ends in the Turlock marshes, where Lafe Turlock and his sons are after enough birds to fill the icehouse. In spite of the mate's wound, Onk-or and his family are able to rejoin the migration back to the Arctic.

Michener makes the geese almost human in their reasoning in order to bring the reader into their world. This technique bothers some readers, but animal lovers will appreciate the reality of the voyage and the mysterious passage of the geese on a moonlit night.

"Widow's Walk" is the soap opera section of the story, emphasizing the affair between Susan Steed and Matt Turlock. While Paul Steed, Susan's husband and current master of Devon, ignores the situation by both beating and sleeping with the slave Eden, the plantation suffers from lack of attention. A Steed relative displaces Paul as estate administrator. Inserted amid the passages describing Susan and Matt's sexual relationship is a dialogue between Matt and Elizabeth Paxmore about his use of the *Ariel* for slave trading; the problem of slavery is never far from the forefront of the Eastern Shore story. Michener uses this chapter to make the slave Eden part of the narrative, and the Steeds' relationship and actions show what can happen when people are self-indulgent. However, the description of the Steed-Turlock affair and the emphasis on the phallic imagery of the ship masts seen from the widow's walk on the roof of the Steed mansion are melodramatic and overdone.

The slavery question will be of primary importance in the following two voyages and chapters. "Voyage Nine: 1832" tells the tale of Cudjo's voyage from his African village to Devon. The horrors of this representative voyage are told soberly, with each stage in the journey showing that this commerce is dealing with human beings who have the same capacities to feel and think and act as human beings of other colors. After a takeover organized by Cudjo during the voyage on Matt Turlock's ship *Ariel*, the slaves are captured by a French ship after a voyage of some weeks and judged guilty of mutiny on the high seas by an English court. Cudjo is slipped into America by a slave dealer.

"The Slave-Breakers" begins with a discussion of how various nations have handled slavery. From the general aspects Michener moves the story to the particular, almost trivial, situation of slavery on the Steed holdings. All the Steeds pride themselves on being good masters, and they are sure that it is their destiny and inherent superiority that give them power over their human property. They are horrified that Elizabeth Paxmore is teaching blacks how to read, and slaves who study with her are "sold south" when the overseers learn about their actions. Cudjo's adjustment to slavery, his determination to learn, and the time spent with the slave-breaker illustrate how the system affects one man. When he joins with Eden in plans to gain freedom, they are representative of all those who seek to be free. They are not forced to use violence to achieve their goal because Susan and Paul Steed free Eden, and they say that Cudjo can purchase his freedom with the money Eden will earn by working for the Steeds. But Eden will keep the weapons they have so carefully accumulated.

In "Voyage Ten: 1837" Bartley Paxmore enters a new world when he travels in his small sloop to propose to Rachel Starbuck. Rachel's family has taken the opposition to slavery one step further; they help runaway slaves. Bartley becomes involved while staying with the Starbucks, and his life is changed.

"The Railroad" continues the story to the Civil War. The Steeds of Devon furnish a framework for Michener to present the prevailing thinking on slavery, property rights, and the attitudes of whites regarding the abilities of blacks. Since Paul Steed wants to obtain construction of a railroad line to the Eastern Shore, he opens Devon to entertain important personages. Three well-known historical figures of the 1830s to the 1850s come to Devon to discuss the issues of the day: Henry Clay, Daniel Webster, and John Calhoun. Through these visits, Paul Steed's writings, and discussions with the Paxmores, the various opinions regarding slavery are aired in the narrative. Although the state of Maryland stays in the Union, many residents fight for the southern cause. At the war's end Paul Steed is alone at Devon; his wife is dead, his son has been killed, and his slaves are gone. Lafe Turlock, who has been one of those chasing runaway slaves, is interested now only in the return of the geese. He gets his food supply.

Michener concentrates again on the maritime world of the Eastern Shore in "Voyage Eleven: 1886" and its following chapter, "The Watermen." This voyage relates what happens when untoward quantities of fresh water hit the Chesapeake as the result of a storm and decrease the salinity of the bay, harming marine life. Michener the teacher gives his readers the information needed to understand these effects and focuses specifically on Jimmy the crab, who lives on a ledge near Devon. Jimmy's efforts to both molt and escape the fresh water are descriptive, although it is hard to imagine a crab having a personality. Between the fresh water and the sewage that inundate the bay because of this storm, the fishing industry is prostrated for two years. The interconnectedness of the human and the natural world cannot be ignored.

"The Watermen" focuses on life on the water, so the Turlock clan is the important group of characters. Jake Turlock and Tim Caveny, son of the Irish immigrant sponsored by Paul Steed, compete over the relative merits of the Labrador and the Chesapeake Retriever as hunting dogs. The reader learns all about hunting and oyster dredging, but the relationships between Turlock and Caveny and their dogs keep the reader involved. The competition between Maryland and Virginia skipjacks, the oyster boats, is also part of the story. The black residents participate with whites to some extent in life on the water but not on shore, where they are a race apart. An amendment proposed in the legislature and aimed at taking away the right of black citizens to vote is defeated, thanks to the untiring efforts of Emily Paxmore. The peaceful sail home of the Turlock-Caveny skipjack at the chapter's end marks the calm before the twentieth-century storms.

In "Voyage Twelve: 1938" Woolman Paxmore tries to avert one of those storms by traveling to Germany. He makes a direct appeal to Hitler to end persecution of the Jews. He is allowed to help 40,000 Jews leave Germany upon payment to the authorities, but only 25,000 are saved because no country will take the Jews. Again, Michener's fictional characters are involved in a historical event.

"Ordeal by Fire" is a somewhat scattered chapter as Michener moves back and forth between the various characters and episodes. He wants to show the complexities that confront the Eastern Shore residents, but the continuity of the story suffers. The reader learns about discrimination against blacks through the lives of Jeb and Julia Cater and their children. In between the Caters' ongoing struggles are John Turlock's transformation to J. Ruthven Turlock, real estate broker and developer of the marshes; Amos Turlock's confrontation with the game warden over the long gun, a virtual cannon which decimates the wildlife population; and Jefferson Steed's conversion of his fields from tomatoes to corn. Black anger against poor living conditions and lack of educational and economic opportunities surfaces during a church festival in the late 1960s, and buildings in the black section of town are burned, but the wind carries the fire to the Paxmore boatyard. Pusey Paxmore, home from his government post in Washington, D.C., is horror-struck at the destruction of his family's way of life.

In "Voyage Thirteen: 1976" Pusey returns from prison after his involvement in Watergate. His wife Amanda goes to the prison to bring him home after his release, traveling by boat to Annapolis. "Refuge" brings Paxmore and Owen Steed back to the Choptank area, and gives Michener a chance to present ideas about moral choices, ethical dilemmas, and ecological problems through his characters' discussions. The story is coming to a stopping point with concerns for the future voiced through the decisions made by the characters. "Voyage Fourteen: 1978" concludes the narrative of this maritime world. Pusey Paxmore has committed suicide and his body is transported by water to its final resting place. Steeds, Paxmores, Turlocks, Caters, and Cavenys come to pay their respects. Forced to spend the night at Peace Cliff because of a storm, they note the next morning that the island of Devon, crumbling through the years, has disappeared, a victim of nature's relentless forces. Erosion takes over all existence.

CHARACTER DEVELOPMENT

The story is the most important element in Michener's explanations of history through fiction. In novels like *Chesapeake*, which cover several centuries of events, the characters are developed to fit the demands of the narrative. The principal families of the novel illustrate first how new settlers cope with a new land and then, in later parts of the story, how they react and adapt to the conditions of each historical period. Each family represents a different approach to life, with certain members living up to the family values or traditions better than others and standing out in the reader's memory from the total cast of characters.

The first Steed to reach the Eastern Shore, Edmund, is a straightforward man who wishes to be open about his Catholic faith. His courage at tackling an unknown wilderness and carving out a life for himself and then a family is described as his story unfolds. Edmund establishes friendly relationships with Pentaquod and his Choptanks, even paying the Indians for their land. However, he cannot accept them as his equals and refuses to marry Pentaquod's daughter. Once Martha Keene joins him, Edmund takes firm hold on Devon. With his wife working with the same tenacity and effort, he clears fields for tobacco, makes tools, teaches his children and servants, upholds his faith, and contributes to Maryland's form of government.

Another memorable Steed marries into the family. Rosalind Janney comes from Virginia in 1701 to marry Fitzhugh Steed, whose administration of the estate has been half-hearted at best. She has been born into a society and time when a woman must be married to have status, and as an unattractive woman, she lacks suitors. Her father arranges her marriage. But Rosalind has spunk. Deciding that if she is not beautiful, she is intelligent, she trains herself to manage a plantation. The reader sees Rosalind in action as she administers the estate, supervises the construction of her house and gardens, raises her children, but also realizes her human side as her thoughts and reflections are part of the descriptive narrative. She is outspoken and confident, but also human enough to regret that her husband never realizes a loving woman exists behind the unattractive face and form.

Simon Steed, who heads the Steed clan during the American Revolution, is individualized enough by his situation to be remembered. A man of forty-three when he marries Jane Fithian of London, Simon is made human by this happy relationship. Simon is desolated when Jane's contempt for the colonies and their Revolution drives her back to London, but he carries out his duties to the estate and his fellow Americans. Shrewd enough to profit from his commercial ventures during the war, human enough to mourn the loss of his family and honor, Steed of Devon exemplifies the courage of the Steed tradition and the concerns of a thoughtful man faced with a changing world.

Paul Steed in the nineteenth century, vacillating and refusing to accept responsibilities, illustrates the danger when families become self-satisfied and don't challenge their children with exposure to new ideas. His motivations and feelings are presented in his relationship with his wife Susan, but are never fully explored. In her boredom with Paul and her life, Susan becomes obsessed with her sexual fantasies, throwing herself into the affair with Matt Turlock. Michener uses this couple as an example of what happens when people drift away from the values that have been important to them for generations. He does give Paul and Susan a chance for redemption after their confrontation over her affair. After fourteen more years of ignoring the estate's administration, they finally take control, firing the harsh overseer, retiring Uncle Herbert, and freeing Eden. What has enabled this change of purpose is not clear, for they are characters presented by what they do and what happens to them, rather than by analysis of their thoughts and motives. Their purpose remains steadfast for the rest of their lives, and they are sure that everyone under their enlightened management, including the slaves, is free and happy. Paul is the representative southern planter convinced of the rightness of his position, with Susan supporting his ideas.

Owen Steed in the novel's final chapters brings the family's story full circle. He and his wife move to the Eastern Shore after Owen's career in the Oklahoma oil business. The reader learns little about Owen's life prior to his return to the Choptank, but his reactions to returning to his family's roots illustrate thematic concerns of the story's modern-day phase and give some insight into the person. He becomes involved in feeding the birds, takes up hunting again, participates in a skipjack race, waxes indignant about abuse of the land and water systems, and discusses the ethics and values that motivated those caught up in the Watergate affair. He has returned in an effort to rediscover the courage and values that the best members of his family have upheld.

The Paxmores represent physical and especially moral courage. Edward and Ruth Brinton Paxmore must physically suffer for their Quaker beliefs, and Ruth's abiding conviction that slavery is morally wrong gives depth to her unique personality. She never deviates from declaring slavery to be wrong, but her anguish over the fate of the slaves transferred to the Steeds is also real and believable. Edward is not as vivid a character as his wife, but his pragmatism and pride in his work as a carpenter and then boat builder outline his individuality. The couple's disagreements concerning the morality of slavery are shown realistically, as is the love that supports their marriage. They set the standard for future Paxmores to follow.

The subsequent Paxmores for several generations do adhere to the standards set by Edward and Ruth, and it is not easy to distinguish between them. The Paxmore husbands tend to business at the boatyard while acknowledging the justice of the Paxmore wives' stand on slavery. Levin during the Revolutionary era must face the fact that he is constructing ships for a war he sees as deplorable yet inescapable, while his wife Ellen presses him to join her public testimony against slavery at Quaker services. In the nineteenth century, Elizabeth Paxmore teaches the slaves to read, and she and her husband George speak to Matt Turlock about the immorality of his slave trading. Their son and daughter-in-law, Bartley and Rachel Paxmore, carry the moral concerns of the parents to the next step by actively helping runaway slaves. As the twentieth century begins, the Paxmore character is exemplified by Emily Paxmore, who lobbies against a proposed Maryland law with the unstated purpose of depriving blacks of their right to vote. As written, the law could be applied to other immigrants, and Miss Emily hammers that point home. The law is defeated, and Emily regrets her tactics, but she would use them again if faced with a similar wrong: "Because each soul on this earth faces one Armageddon . . . if thee runs away or fails to fight with vigor, thy life is forever diminished" (887). The situations that prompt these characters' moral positions individualize them to a certain extent, and they all illustrate moral courage and the dilemmas that such courage can create.

Pusey Paxmore is the only member of the family shown as not living up to this courage. His conversations with Owen Steed and his introspection before his suicide reveal Michener's attitudes about moral values as much as they portray the essence of Pusey himself. He was loyal to his president and served his prison term without revealing the whole truth of what he knew about Watergate and the events surrounding it. He explains to the Steeds that the entire event was "a failure of moral intelligence" (1050), and that he, too, had been seduced by the power of the presidency, refusing to believe that criminal behavior could stem from that power. Nothing can save him from the disintegration he has brought upon himself. Again, it is the Paxmore wife who upholds the family's moral strength. Amanda Paxmore has given Pusey her unfailing love while warning him of the dangers he faced and never telling him "I told you so" when the worst happens.

With the Turlock clan it is the men who remain in the reader's memory. The men who adapt to the marsh, refusing the standards of the Steeds and certainly those of the Paxmores, represent the courage of resiliency and survival and an instinctive connection with nature. Not always admirable in character, they aren't clear-cut villains, either. Timothy is seen in action as he uses every tactic possible to survive in his new world. Inarticulate but joyous in his watery kingdom, Timothy can almost be appreciated as he welcomes the returning geese each October.

Matt, a few generations later and the first Turlock to learn to read, is the wandering sea captain who becomes a slave trader almost in spite of himself. Michener presents Matt in action, from early voyages with his father to his duel with the British captain to his affair with Susan Steed. He refuses to accept the Paxmores' disapproval of his slave trading or his open liaison with Mrs. Steed, thinking of the Paxmore women as "some of the sharpest-tongued busybodies God ever put on earth" (607). Yet he does return to sea, to his wandering, leaving Susan behind and advising her that it is time for both of them to begin again. Matt's death at the hands of the slaves taking over his ship ends a violent life, but his adventures are a lively part of the story, leaving him in the reader's memory as much more than a cardboard character.

Jake Turlock, the skipjack captain and hunter in the late nineteenth and early twentieth centuries, is another Turlock with a unique personality. Michener portrays him through his relationship with Tim Caveny and his actions as a hunter and waterman. Although not a complex character, Jake shows the inconsistencies that are part of being human. He hates blacks, like all Turlocks since ancestor Lafe hunted down runaway slaves and since cousin Matt was killed, yet he hires Big Jimbo Cater, a black, as cook of the skipjack and appreciates his work. Jake is not a caricature; instead, he comes across as a vivid representative of his time and place.

Amos Turlock in the twentieth century carries on the family tradition of thumbing his nose at rules and regulations. Amos hunts the geese with the outlawed long gun, a weapon which can decimate a flock with one shot. He and the game warden carry on a running feud over the gun, and Amos prevails against authority as the Turlocks have always done. A true Turlock, he is a contented man when his grandson shows promise at hunting and keeping the secret of the gun's hiding place.

The Caters enter the story in the nineteenth century; this family started by the two freed slaves Eden and Cudjo illustrates dignity and hard work. As he tells their story, showing these characters through their actions and thoughts, Michener has a point to make: the slaves and later their free descendants are in no way an inferior group of people; they are human beings with all the virtues and faults of their species. Cudjo has the intelligence to sail the captured ship by figuring out the compass and how the sails should be handled. On the Eastern Shore he is able to repair tools and create machines that work. Eden is a compassionate person in her care of crippled Susan Steed, yet she is determined to gain freedom at whatever cost. Both are courageous in helping runaway slaves, and Eden's account of these experiences underscores the white and black differences of the slave era: "Even when we did travel with the noble Quakers we followed two different roads. If they were caught, they were fined or placed in jail for a few months. If we were caught, we were hauled back to slavery or hanged" (982–83).

Jeb and Julia Cater in the twentieth century are vivid examples of people living and coping with second-class status. Their story is told by showing them in their everyday lives, at work in whatever low-paying jobs they can find, with their children, involved in their church. They are individuals doing the best they can to get along in their world.

Hiram is the one of their children who comes across as an individual. Hiram spends time in prison as does his sister Luta Mae, but his path through service in Korea, involvement in Patamoke's one fiery riot, and many conversations with both whites and blacks concerned with the situation causes him to think seriously about the complications of race relations. He attends Pusey Paxmore's funeral, remembering the family tradition that the Paxmores can be counted on in time of trouble.

Four families, four paths through the novel, and all four have members who come alive through Michener's ability to develop a story. *Chesapeake* is also populated by secondary characters who add to the reality of the narration, such as the Cavenys, originally from Ireland, and the Pflaums, who come from Germany. They are portrayed anecdotally: for example, Tim Caveny and Otto Pflaum are part of the life of the watermen; Father Caveny plays the clarinet at a black church festival; Hugo Pflaum, the game warden, and his son Chris debate ways to save the environment. *Chesapeake* is a good example of how in Michener's historical, panoramic novels, all of his characters reflect the diversity and richness of American culture through their ethnic and religious backgrounds and their contribution to the life of the land they occupy.

THEMATIC CONSIDERATIONS

Human tolerance is an essential value in James Michener's historical, panoramic novels, as has been seen in the discussion of *Hawaii* and *Centennial*. Discrimination against human beings because of their race, religion, or place of origin leads to a diminished use of human potential and skill and a society that is impoverished through underutilization of its resources. In *Chesapeake* Michener illustrates this point of view through the story of the elimination of the Eastern Shore Indians and the treatment of the slaves and then the freed blacks.

At the novel's beginning, tribes of Indians prey on other groups, and then the new white settlers shoot the Indians as if they were game animals. The Indian must abdicate wherever the white wants land, and it is impossible to share with those judged inferior.

The Indians are killed before they can become property, but the black slaves are considered a possession similar to a ship or a wagon. They must be well treated, says Edward Paxmore, but his wife Ruth states with passion during many First Day meetings that slavery must end: "I see a day when the members of any Christian church will be ashamed to hold another man or woman in bondage" (277). This conviction will be stated in similar words by generations of Paxmore women until the blacks obtain freedom.

However, freedom does not mean equality. Blacks are still inferior beings in white eyes. Even the evidence of Jimbo Cater's contributions to the success of his skipjack doesn't change Jake Turlock's conviction that blacks are vengeful, stupid, and irresponsible. If the blacks stay in their allotted place, life will be peaceful and orderly along the Eastern Shore, think those who support the law to keep the blacks from voting. After Jeb Cater's son is born, the discrimination his family lives with becomes even more evident to him. Baby Hiram has to be treated in a basement ward, separate from white children in the hospital. Julia must have her teeth extracted because there is no regular dental care available for blacks. The Cater children attend schools with inadequate facilities, books, supplies, and teachers. Michener uses abundant examples from the ongoing story of generations of the Cater family to show the dignity and worth of the so-called inferior race.

Tolerance of different religious beliefs is another repeated value in the *Chesapeake* story. Edmund Steed faces discrimination in England and Virginia because of his faith, but he does not suffer the physical cruelty that Edward Paxmore undergoes at the hands of Massachusetts Puritans. Edward wonders why people so attached to God would punish others equally attached but who express their attachment in a different manner. The later generations will save their cruelty for slaves who run away or refuse to submit, young women servants who don't conform to conventional morality or are sexually abused by their masters, and crew members hired by force to dredge for oysters. Cruelty and prejudice are not easy to eliminate, as Michener's tales show, but his stronger characters will struggle against it, whether by standing up with the woman to be whipped, like Rosalind Steed, or burning down the inadequate school building, like Hiram Cater.

The second major thematic consideration in *Chesapeake* is the issue of the environment. From the first burning of the forests by Edmund Steed to create fields for growing tobacco, the reader is aware that the land will suffer from wrongful use. Pentaquod tells Edmund that by burning the trees, driving the animals from their homes, and singeing the birds' feathers, he has destroyed the paradise he shared with the Indians. That land recovers over the years, but the earth is always threatened by man's encroachments. The geese disappear when they are hunted in great numbers, yet they return when most of the long guns are confiscated and the Steed tomato fields are converted to growing corn.

J. Ruthven Turlock sees the chance for "economic development" and makes the marsh into a landfill for garbage and then a subdivision of waterfront homes. Chris Pflaum is infuriated at the destruction of the natural balance of water and land, plant and animal life, but his father reminds him of the laws passed to prohibit more cementing of the marshes and protect the wetlands. Chris has trouble persuading anyone but the Owen Steeds of the impact of beer cans and other litter tossed in ditches and along roads, and a meeting on the subject depresses everyone attending. The speaker at the meeting points out over lunch the problems facing the entire bay from industrial and human pollution. Michener even brings in the ecological question of excess population, as his speaker talks about the oil spills being the conspicuous disasters but the large accumulations of human beings in clusters as the permanent one. If left alone the earth can possibly renew itself as well as destroy itself. The island of Devon has been losing ground since the opening of the story, and it disappears completely during the storm that closes the story. Those who treasure this pleasant place can only hope that enough like-minded souls will work in harmony with the land to share rather than plunder its fruits. Michener has recreated lovingly and carefully a world that has been a special part of the United States. He suggests its future by indicating what it should value—its natural and human resources—but gives no assurances that these values will be upheld. He can only hope that human beings will learn from their history.

A MARXIST READING OF *CHESAPEAKE*

Like *Hawaii*, *Chesapeake* is the story of people settling a new land, and it lends itself to a reading from the Marxist perspective presented in Chapter 4. By tracing the development of the society the settlers form, the Marxist reader has an opportunity to look at the relationship between the producing and the controlling classes.

When Edmund Steed starts planting tobacco on Devon, he employs the Indians to clear the fields—more and more fields. The Indians refuse to labor any more, saying the land is being destroyed. From a Marxist standpoint, Steed has exploited his workers to the point that they rebel. They can no longer relate to the white men because their relationship to nature is being altered by the controlling class. The Indians withdraw rather than pursue payment in useless trinkets for their work.

Simon Janey, with his arrogant attitude toward the indentured servants who replace the Indians, graphically illustrates the exploitation of workers: "Secret is, buy them cheap, work them to the bone. And when their seven years are up, kiss them goodbye" (146). His treatment of Timothy Turlock causes this worker to openly revolt and flee, proving the point that a worker like Turlock will eventually rebel against a system that treats him as expendable.

At the beginning of the settlement of the new land, the controlling class works as hard as the laboring group. Edmund Steed and his wife toil fifteen and sixteen hours a day to create a plantation. However, this type of effort changes as the plantations become more established and slave labor replaces the owner in the fields. In slavery the workers become the owner's property; what they receive for their labor is subject to the owner's complete control. Slavery is the ultimate exploitation. One week's holiday at Christmas with a set of new working clothes does not compensate for fifty-one weeks of endless toil for food, poor housing, no education, and no recognition of the worker as a human being: "Generation after generation they were judged to be alike: treated alike . . . dressed alike . . . ignored alike . . . and buried alike" (661). Slaves who struggle against the system are sold or sent to a slave-breaker, who works them relentlessly with inadequate food and abusive treatment as their wage. The only way to rebel is to run away; as the nineteenth century continues, more and more slaves try to head north. The history of slavery is one of the powerful trying to maintain its control over the powerless.

The Marxist critic would note with interest the attitude of the various classes of white citizens toward this system of production:

> It was as if the Steeds had used witchcraft to persuade the slaveless farmers to defend a system which benefited not them but the rich, and when George Paxmore tried to argue that the economic life of the river would be enhanced if black men were set free to work for wages, he was considered an irresponsible fool . . . especially by the Turlocks . . . whose relatively low position was caused primarily by the region's insistence upon slave labor. (662)

This system of production has conditioned the social and political life of the region in a way a Marxist critic would recognize. When Paul Steed compares the working conditions of his slaves to those of factory workers in the northern states, he is sure that his system is the better one because his slaves are treated well and are happier than they would be if set free. "Everyone believed this, that is, except the slaves themselves" (723), notes the third-person narrator. From the Marxist perspective both slaves and factory workers are held in bondage, since the systems in which they labor favor the pleasant life of the wealthy over the deprived life of the workers. Michener focuses more on the immorality of treating another human being as personal property than on the forces of economic determinism, but his portrayal of slavery in *Chesapeake* can be seen as illustrative of the class struggles of this time and place.

After the Civil War the freed slaves are still the underclass, the workers who get jobs after everyone else is employed. The Turlocks and the Cavenys continue to regard the blacks as inferior beings except for the occasional exception, like Big Jimbo Cater who is a wonderful cook and fine crew member of an oyster dredger. The whites on the lower end of the economic scale fear being displaced by the blacks. Yet Jake Turlock is reluctantly admiring when Jimbo is able to buy his own boat; on the water a man is judged by his skills and not his color. In Michener's portrait of this Chesapeake world, hard work and fortitude bring success. The Marxist critic, however, would see how even the independent oystermen are dependant on the prices offered by the buyers. It's the wealthy restaurant patrons who profit from their catch. The oystermen are able to earn only enough to repeat their labor the following day.

The continued exploitation of black workers is illustrated through the experiences of Jeb and Julia Cater during the decades of the twentieth century. Julia holds three jobs, and Jeb does any work he can get however physically demanding it is: "but on and on he worked, a machine that was employed at slight cost and would be discarded at the first sign of slowing down" (910). Michener views this situation as tragic from the human point of view and nonproductive from the economic standpoint, since taxes could have been kept lower if black incomes had been allowed to rise. In addition, black energies could have made almost every enterprise from which they were excluded more productive. The Marxist critic would agree and extend the comment to cover all those who produce goods without having any control over the means of production.

Some of the Patamoke blacks do rebel against the system in the 1960s. During a church festival, Hiram Cater's frustration at his own lack of employment opportunities and the drudgery of his parents' lives boils over: the whites' presence at the black festival is seen as condescending charity. The blacks burn down the school, the church, and other buildings in the black area, not for revenge against the whites but in anger at the intolerable conditions in which the "system" forces them to live. From the Marxist perspective the fire shows that people will revolt ultimately against what destroys their humanity; in this situation the inadequate buildings symbolize the people's lack of power in a system that pits one class against another.

The forces of economic determinism are also involved in exploitation of the environment. In this situation it is the struggle for profit that dominates. J. Ruthven Turlock does not care about upsetting the balance between humans and the land they occupy. His only interest is in selling lots created by filling in the marsh with garbage. The local authorities worry only about the burden of a bottle deposit for the merchant, not the litter along the roadside. In addition, Norman Turlock has just built a canning factory for beer and soft drinks and must be allowed to profit from his investment. Throwing bottles and cans along the road, however, is another form of rebellion by those who think themselves disadvantaged by society, according to a local ecologist.

Michener presents in *Chesapeake* the dangers that exist when all human and natural resources are not valued. The Marxist critic sees in the history of this place many examples of the clash of class interests and the dangers to humanity when people are blocked by their economic situation from relating to others and to nature.

7

The Covenant
(1980)

Some fifteen thousand years of history are spread out before the reader in *The Covenant*, James Michener's 1980 novel telling the story of South Africa and its people. The panoramic history traces the experiences of three families over several generations. The black Nxumalos, the Afrikaner Van Doorns, and the English Saltwoods represent the three main groups figuring in the development of South Africa. Their stories unfold against the factual background of historical events and people plus the other groups such as the Bushmen, the Hottentots, the Indians, and the mixed-race Coloureds who play their own role in the saga. Michener's greatest contribution with this book is the clarity with which he makes the history of this troubled land understandable and believable. The reader can follow how the Afrikaners' belief in their covenant came about and how this conviction led to the isolated, fractured society of the late 1970s. The actual changes that have occurred in the South Africa of the 1990s are predicted as a possibility by some of the characters, and Michener must be cautiously optimistic about the country's future.

This discussion of the novel will center on the plot and character development along with the thematic considerations. The chapter will conclude with a consideration of the book from the point of view of a Marxist critic.

PLOT DEVELOPMENT

The reader sees the unfolding story of *The Covenant* from the point of view of the third-person narrator, and continuity is provided by the use of ongoing families of characters. Maps and genealogical charts included at the end of the book help situate the land and its people.

Chapter I is the "Prologue," introducing the land through its first inhabitants, the Bushmen. Drought is forcing Gumsto, leader of a clan of twenty-five, to consider moving in search of water. Michener depicts the way of life of these hunters and gatherers through the story of their migration. And he highlights the art they leave behind on the walls of caves: portraits of the animals the hunters have killed. The rhinoceros drawn by Gumsto's son Gao was "an animal that throbbed with life" (37). Carbon dating makes it possible to determine that the rhinoceros had been on the cave wall since 13,000 years before the present era, say experts of the 1980s, so the human story of this land has begun far back in the past. The sense of place and the relationship of humans with the land and the animals have been established.

The story moves to the fifteenth century of the present era in Chapter II, "Zimbabwe." Old Seeker, a black who roams the continent looking for new gold mines and goods to trade, persuades Nxumalo, a young black man he meets, to hunt the rhinoceros horn he wants to bring to the Arab traders on the coast. He feels Nxumalo should seek to test himself in the world beyond his miserable village on the shores of a lake in southern Africa. Michener brings in the history of Nxumalo's people in order to portray this black culture unknown and unimagined by the European world. On the trip with Old Seeker, Nxumalo sees the natural wonders of Africa and then is impressed with the massive city of Zimbabwe. The reader learns about the government of this capital city and the interactions of its traders with their counterparts from the Middle East and the Far East. In Europe at this time Prince Henry of Portugal is urging his sea captains to find that Biblical city of Ophir, built, he believes, by Phoenicians or maybe by Old Testament Jews. The fact that blacks are capable of constructing cities, working gold mines, and governing territories never occurs to him.

The black strand is in place; the white strands are introduced in Chapter III, "A Hedge of Bitter Almond." The historical framework is provided with the summary of the Portuguese conquests and control of the spice trade. The Dutch and the English are also becoming active, and ships stop for repairs at the Cape of Good Hope, the southern tip of Africa, so a record of the native inhabitants with their language of clicking sounds is established.

The English Saltwoods enter the story in 1637, when Nicholas Saltwood starts a trading venture with the Spice Islands. At the Cape, he takes on board one of the little brown men whom the sailors call Jack because they cannot pronounce his name. Eventually Saltwood's ship reaches Java, and the Van Doorns are introduced. The widow Van Doorn has two sons, Karel and Willem. These sons must return to Holland to have a future with the Jan Compagnie, the firm that has an iron control on its employees' lives as well as the spice trade. Michener moves the story through the Dutch-Portuguese battles to Willem's first visit to the Cape, where he is captivated by the new land. Jack, back with his people, offers to work with the Dutch, but he is turned down, for the Dutch feel the Cape is worth nothing. However, Willem has a different opinion. In the Bible, he finds the first reference to the Promised Land and God's covenant with his chosen people. The story has many turnings before Willem can act on his new certainty that God has chosen him to settle this land. The severe treatment handed out to the Hottentots, the black slaves brought to the Cape, and those who go against the Compagnie's rules sets patterns that will be continued throughout the saga. And a hedge of bitter almond is planted around the small Dutch settlement to cut it off from the rest of Africa. When Willem receives land to the east of the settlement in 1664, he cuts through the hedge and sets off for these more spacious lands with his Bible, his tools, the crock for pudding, and his wife and son.

French Protestants come to the Cape in Chapter IV, "The Huguenots." Michener recounts the adventures of Paul De Pré, a Huguenot and a wine maker from southern France, who must leave his country in the late seventeenth century to escape religious persecution. Paul and his family go to Amsterdam, which has become a place of refuge for those seeking religious freedom. With his usual attention to creating a sense of place, Michener describes vividly the bustling commerce of this port and the weigh-house where the riches of the Baltic Sea are handled. Paul works at the weigh-house before moving to take care of the gardens belonging to the Widows Bosbeecq. He also works for Karel van Doorn, Willem's brother, now an important Jan Compagnie official in Amsterdam who persuades him to get vine stock from France and move to the Cape to improve the wine that Willem has been making.

The sea voyage to the Cape with its difficulties is another vivid description, showing the fortitude that must characterize those moving to a new frontier. Paul's interactions with the Van Doorns and his efforts to merge his farm with theirs are part of the narrative of this frontier development. Attacks by the Bushmen and questions about arming the Coloured servants move the story onward. Another ongoing problem is the difficulty of finding wives for single men. Willem's wife came from Holland, as did his son's. Paul is now a widower, and he too should have a wife. When Willem's son is killed by a Bushman's poisoned arrow, Paul immediately proposes to the widow. His goal of uniting the two farms has been reached, but he cannot survive the smallpox epidemic that hits in 1713. Sarel, one of Paul's stepsons, will run the farm with the help of his wife and mother-in-law. Hendrik, the other stepson, has already left for the lands beyond the mountains; a new frontier beckons.

Life on the frontier is seen from the perspective of Hendrik van Doorn and his descendants in Chapter V, "The Trekboers." *Trekboers* are the wandering farmers who move slowly from place to place when the land wears out or the drought comes. Hendrik's son Adriaan is the true wanderer of this episode, traveling with his Hottentot friend Dikkop. The two meet two black youths, the first meeting of a white with an African black in this area. The two youths belong to a group called the Xhosa, which has been wandering toward the Cape as the Trekboers wander away from it; confrontation is inevitable. The reader observes the Xhosa way of life through the perspective of Sotopo, one of the young blacks Adriaan meets, as he watches his brother participate in the ritual of becoming a man and notes how the tribe's witch doctor is focusing on his family as the cause of tribal misfortunes. Sotopo follows his brother and a few others as they leave the tribe, expelled because of pressure generated by the witch doctor. The narrator indicates that the Xhosa and the Dutch Trekboers resemble each other. Each group loves its cattle and measures a man's importance by his herds. Each wants unlimited grazing and knows that any pasture it finds belongs to it by "divine right." The scene is set for violent conflict.

Returning to the Van Doorns, the narrative brings in Adriaan's son Lodevicus and his wish to put down roots. As he becomes an adult, Lodevicus is more and more convinced of the truth of the Old Testament as it applies to the Trekboers: they are the Chosen People for this new land. Lodevicus the Hammer, or "God's Right Arm," is summoned always when trouble threatens with the Bushmen or the Xhosa, or his own people who do not live up to God's commands as Lodevicus and his wife Rebecca see them. Adriaan and Dikkop escape for one last trek, and their adventures form an intriguing part of the story, where the reader participates in their exploration of the natural beauty of land and animal in balance. The increasing violence between the Boers and Xhosa causes Adriaan's death shortly after his return and later also Rebecca's. Lodevicus realizes God's plan takes time to put into effect, but he never wavers, even when the English take over the colony. His son Tjaart will follow his father's example, building his life on the principle that the Dutch way of life must be defended against the English enemy.

The Saltwoods return to the story in Chapter VI, "The Missionary." Their family history since the return of Captain Nicholas to Plymouth is summarized to set the scene for Hilary Saltwood's decision to go to South Africa as a missionary. The efforts of officials to change the way the Boers treat their black workers affect Hilary's relationship with Lodevicus and the other Boers plus the progress of his mission work. With his usual technique of relating historical happenings through the direct involvement of his characters, Michener brings out the growing grievances of the Boers toward English rule. Yet the two white groups will unite against the Xhosa when those warriors threaten white settlements.

Hilary's brother Richard gets a government appointment to South Africa, but the prospective wife for Hilary, whom Richard escorts on the trip from England, will marry another. Hilary is left alone to contemplate a vision of a South Africa where all God's children will work and live together. Neither he nor his vision will be understood, and when he marries the black Emma, his isolation from both the Boers and the English is nearly complete. Hilary and Emma move their mission to the north, and they illustrate by their lives and actions the New Testament message of social justice, equality, and brotherhood. This couple is killed by unknown murderers, and the missionary's hope for South Africa is not realized.

During the same time period—the first part of the nineteenth century—the Nxumalo strand of the story becomes involved in the black struggles against the encroaching whites. In Chapter VII, "The Mfecane," Nxumalo of iziCwe's experiences with Shaka, known as "the lion," present the historical Zulu leader who unites the blacks. Shaka reorganizes the black method of fighting and sets up a regime directed toward war. Nxumalo, although benefiting from Shaka's favor, sees that the continual killing must end. After the assassination of Shaka, Nxumalo flees with his family. Crossing the land devastated by the black troops of a leader called Mzilikazi, Nxumalo reaches that lake between the two hills whose beauty Adriaan had noted and where the cave has a painting of a rhinoceros. The narrator explains the meaning of the Mfecane, the sad migration of bands of blacks. One group displaces another, which then moves on, and the cycle continues, with both the people and the land suffering. Yet Shaka's vision of a united people remains as an imaginative force for the Nxumalo clan and others like them.

The events and forces that lead Tjaart van Doorn to move to the north are narrated in Chapter VIII, called "The Voortrekkers." The picture of the Boers' faith and way of life becomes clearer at the beginning of the chapter, as Tjaart takes his family to the Nachtmaal, the Holy Communion of the Dutch Reformed Church celebrated four times a year. Like the Van Doorns, most Boer families live too far from a church to go regularly to this celebration; when they can make the pilgrimage, the event is one of special fellowship with those who share similar experiences on the frontier. The details of the trip and the Nachtmaal itself highlight the human side of the Van Doorns and their friends.

After returning home, the Van Doorns learn that English law is setting all slaves free. Tjaart's wife Jakoba understands the radical change the new law will make, and she reminds the men that God has ordered the Boers to follow a different path: the whites are to be the masters of the blacks. If the English cannot accept this truth, the Boers must go north and form a new country. Richard Saltwood will buy De Kraal, the Van Doorn farm, and obtain payment from London for Tjaart for the freed slaves.

Men, women, children, Coloured and black servants, oxen, other cattle, sheep, horses—the procession starts slowly north. The trek will take over three years. The Voortrekkers will fight Xhosa and Zulu, young Paulus de Groot's parents will be killed and he will join the Van Doorns, the mountains will be nearly impossible to cross, but the wagons and their occupants will persevere. When the Zulu kill many Boers, including Tjaart's wife and daughter, Tjaart and the survivors try to understand why God has punished them. Deciding that they have been lax in their attention to worship and the keeping of the commandments, they vow to demand retribution. The final battle against the Zulu at Blood River is an overwhelming victory for the Boers, who thank God. They are convinced that He has offered them a covenant because of their faithfulness to Him. The narrator notes that instead, the Boers have offered the covenant to God, who is not obligated to accept it, "especially not if their unilateral terms contravened His basic teachings to the detriment of another race whom He loved equally" (694). The Boers will create a theocracy—a government based on the recognition of God as the supreme ruler.

Yet Tjaart's personal story must continue. When the horses and oxen die north of the Limpopo River, Tjaart and his companions move south, following the sable antelope to that lake between the two hills. They live in peace with Nxumalo and his group at the place they will call Vrymeer. Assessing the new situation in light of the past, Tjaart is sure that he has never been at fault in the deaths of the blacks he has killed in battle. He is equally sure that while many blacks will be his friends and trusted associates, no black is capable of attaining the cultural or moral level achieved by an ordinary white man. The Voortrekkers have conquered their frontier, and all their experiences have served to strengthen their conviction that they are following the path that God has set before them.

The English come back into focus in Chapter IX, "The Englishmen." The story moves on with the tale of what happens when a young black girl sees visions in a pool and her uncle, interpreting the visions for his own purposes, tells the people to kill their cattle and burn their grain. He says the Russians will come over the sea to help them defeat the Boers and the English. It is 1856 and fragments of news about the Crimean War between Russia and England have reached the blacks of Africa. The people believe in this hope; animals by the thousands and food supplies are destroyed as the story spreads. Richard Saltwood, seeing the death and destruction, realizes the scope of the disaster and organizes what food supplies he can for the starving people.

Richard's grandson Frank is the next Saltwood to play a role in South Africa. As an employee of Cecil Rhodes, an actual historical figure, Frank participates in Rhodes's dreams to extend the British Empire in Africa. The reader learns about the diamond mines through Frank's letter to his parents and about President Paulus Krueger of the Orange Free State when Frank approaches him on Rhodes's behalf. He also reports to Rhodes after visiting the Van Doorns of Vrymeer that the Boers are determined to hold on to their freedoms and way of life. Paulus de Groot and Jakob van Doorn are ready at any moment to reform a commando, a collection of fellow Boers armed and ready to back up their convictions with force. Again on behalf of Mr. Rhodes, in 1895 Frank travels to the ruins of that city called Zimbabwe with orders to prove that blacks could not have been responsible for its construction. Rhodes's venture against the Orange Free State is a disaster, and Frank narrowly escapes execution as a spy. The conclusion of Rhodes's story is seen through Frank's eyes as he observes the intrigue of Princess Radziwill, who pursues Rhodes in an effort to marry him. The attempt fails, and Rhodes dies at the age of forty-nine, in the midst of the war between the Boers and the English, with his dream of extending the British Empire from Cape Town to Cairo unrealized.

The story of the Boer War—that conflict between the Boers and the English—is seen in Chapter X, "The Venloo Commando," through the actions of Jakob van Doorn and Paulus de Groot as they ride and fight with this commando. Michener's fictional characters play important roles in this historical event, participating in the real battles and observing the stupidities, the bravery, the death, and the destruction that are the actual results of war. Frank Saltwood is an aide to the English general, Redvers Buller, who finally relieves the besieged town of Ladysmith.

The remaining Boers refuse to surrender, and the Venloo Commando engages in guerilla tactics, earning a heroic reputation as the group evades capture. Yet finally the war ends. Because of the scorched-earth policy of the English, Frank Saltwood must be involved in the burning of Vrymeer. The surviving Van Doorns and Paulus de Groot's wife Sybilla are herded into camps with other Boer women and children where food is scarce, sanitation is nonexistent, and disease runs wild. Frank Saltwood's wife Maud visits the camps and makes public the deplorable conditions. When the final Boer surrender comes, new grievances will be part of their history. Paulus de Groot, surveying the desolation of Vrymeer, sums up the situation: "We lost the battles. We lost the war. Now we must win in other ways" (900).

These other ways are the focus of Chapter XI, "Education of a Puritan." Micah Nxumalo and what is left of his family return to Vrymeer to help rebuild the farm. They too have suffered in the internment camps, and how many black and Coloured people have died will be left unrecorded. Detlev van Doorn and his older sister Johanna, Jakob's two surviving children, represent the hope for the future. When the English start a school in Venloo, Detlev must attend to learn what the English know, says Paulus de Groot: "Books. Figures. Big Ideas" (906). Then the Boers of Detlev's generation can retake control of what they see as their land. Detlev does well in school except when he forgets that he must speak English. He also does well with the new sport of rugby.

The story continues by showing the ongoing conflicts regarding the governing of the country. The Boers are outraged at the importation of Chinese workers for the mines. Micah Nxumalo, attending meetings of the African National Congress in Johannesburg, shares the group's concern over the new laws restricting the right of both blacks and Coloureds to vote and to live in certain areas. And Johanna's new husband, Piet Krause, encourages the belief in the rise of the Afrikaner Volk, the whites who trace their heritage from the Dutch but who have developed their own language, Afrikaans, and their own way of looking at the different races. Detlev even changes the spelling of his name to reflect his distinct language. He is now Detleef.

With the approach of war between England and Germany, many Afrikaners want to fight with Germany. The Venloo Commando will ride once more, although there is no support from the church. General Paulus de Groot, now in his seventies, rides at the commando's head but dies one night after a tiring ride across the veld, the Afrikaner name for the grasslands. There will be no union with the Germans coming from their African colonies, and Jakob van Doorn is killed in the last battle with the government troops. Detleef must return to De Groot's original plan of victory for the Afrikaners through education. He attends the university at Stellenbosch, where he combines his studies with rugby. The experience solidifies his belief in the Afrikaner Volk and the separateness of the races as he sees it ordained in the Old Testament. He becomes a South African Springbok, an athlete entitled to wear the green blazer with the springbok antelope emblem, when he is chosen for the national rugby team that will tour New Zealand. His education is complete.

The Afrikaners win control of South Africa in Chapter XII, "Achievement of a Puritan." Detleef observes and also takes part in the changes that transform the country. He becomes a member of the Broedersbond, the brotherhood whose program promotes the supremacy of the Afrikaners through establishing them in minor administrative positions from which they can be promoted to positions of real control. At the same time Micah Nxumalo sees what is happening and encourages his son Moses to follow the dream of learning. Moses's experiences in Johannesburg bring to life the violence and uncertainty of life for the poor and the dispossessed.

The ideas of Nazi Germany influence some Afrikaners, including Detleef's brother-in-law Piet Krause, but Detleef refuses to join Piet in any uprising against the government. After World War II, Detleef becomes a member of the Commission on Racial Affairs and is ready to reorganize South Africa once the Afrikaners win a majority in the elections of 1948. In discussions with his wife Maria and his sister Johanna, Detleef clarifies his thoughts on the separation of the races: no intermarriage and certainly no sexual relations will be tolerated; all public services will be separated along with areas of towns and parts of the country as a whole;

laws will suppress communism; all citizens of South Africa will be classified according to race; since the Coloured are children of sin, their right
to vote will be rescinded. As a counterpoint to these laws, a group of
concerned Afrikaner and English women form an organization called the
Black Sash to oppose the restrictive and unlawful proposals of their government. Laura Saltwood, Frank and Maud's daughter-in-law, is the
president and follows her mother-in-law's pattern of direct speech and
timely intervention against injustices. Detleef and Laura illustrate the
two currents of white South African thought and make the troubled nation's story vivid to the reader.

Chapter XIII, "Apartheid," is organized to show how the policy of
"apartness" affects all stages of life in South Africa. At birth, a baby is
classified by racial designation and will always be evaluated on that
basis. Heather Botha, whose identification card shows that she is Coloured, is encouraged to emigrate to Canada, where her indifference to
outworn custom and acceptance of all people will be valued. At school,
the same racial distinction must be upheld. Petra Albertyn, age nine, is
accused of being Coloured and has no right therefore to attend the white
girls' school at Venloo. The investigation does show that her father is
descended from that Van Doorn daughter of the seventeenth century
who married a Coloured slave. The Albertyns lose their home and business. At home, the blacks have no right to areas where they have always
lived if whites want the neighborhood. Two shopkeepers whose parents
came from India watch the bulldozers and fear that their homes will be
next. At work, blacks and whites have separate job categories. Jonathan
Nxumalo, Moses's son, has papers for work in the gold mine, so he is
not allowed to work anywhere else and must do only those tasks assigned to him. Even at death, the rights of blacks are constrained by
apartheid: the widow of a black working in the city has no right to stay
there. Laura Saltwood tries to help one widow who is being sent to a
black homeland she has never seen, but there is no recourse to the law.
Michener shows the blacks' hope for a resurrection from the system
through the Nxumalo brothers' dream to be free. Daniel goes to the black
college at Fort Hare and learns the history of blacks in other lands. Jonathan, in trouble with the police, must flee to Moçambique. The explanation of apartheid ends with Detleef's collapse shortly after dedicating
new housing at Sophiatown where the black homes had been bulldozed.
He sees a triumph in the new housing and never considers that the
triumph was at the expense of other human beings, not poverty and
slums.

The story of South Africa comes to a stopping point in Chapter XIV, "Diamonds," as Michener evokes the country's situation in 1979 and sets forth possible scenarios for the future. By bringing in a new character from the outside who has connections inside, Michener gives an objectivity to the observations as well as personalizing them through the character's reactions. Philip Saltwood, an employee of Amalgamated Mines and descendant of a Saltwood who went to America instead of South Africa, comes to check out the diamond find made along the Swartstroom, a stream north of Vrymeer. He meets and falls in love with Sannie van Doorn, Detleef's granddaughter. He encounters Daniel Nxumalo and learns about black homelands and the conditions in the township of Soweto. He even visits Laura Saltwood after she has been banned—that is, sentenced to remain alone in her home, never seeing more than one person at a time. Through these contacts he learns possible scenarios for the future. Jonathan Nxumalo sees revolution while Daniel hopes for orderly change. Sannie chooses to marry Fikkie Troxel, who is as convinced as she that Afrikaners will fight to keep the control over the land and its people. Laura still has hope because sensible people in South Africa know that changes have to be made in the apartheid system: "There is enormous wisdom in this land, and one prays it will be granted the necessary time to manifest itself" (1203). The various points of view are summarized by Philip in a letter to a former professor, but he himself is "desolate of spirit" for Sannie has married another, he has found no diamonds, and the future is unclear. However, Michener does not stop the story quite yet. Philip finds new signs indicating diamonds near Vrymeer's beautiful lake. The lake at Vrymeer will look quite different after Philip brings in men and equipment to drill deep into the earth. Perhaps when the flamingos return to the lake the next year, the face of South Africa will also look different—and, one hopes, better.

CHARACTER DEVELOPMENT

The three families whose stories are traced in *The Covenant* represent the three main ethnic and cultural strands in the novel, and as such they illustrate certain ideas as well as ways of life. The Van Doorns exhibit steadfast courage as they settle the frontier lands and steadfast purpose as they develop a country according to the word of God, as they see it. The Saltwoods also face the frontier with courage, maintain their own way of life, yet also show concern for the sufferings and misfortunes of other groups. The Nxumalos become second-class citizens in their own land by the nineteenth century, but they show care and compassion for their employers or masters and seek the ways and means that will allow them to live as human beings of worth. Various members of the three families loom large in their particular parts of the story and remain in the reader's memory because of their important roles in the unfolding story or the way they reflect ideas or concerns that illuminate the narrative.

Among the Van Doorns, Willem, the first to make South Africa his home, is also the first to see a connection between himself and the Biblical Israelites who are sent by Moses to look over the land of the Canaanites. He, too, should be part of the majestic land he sees from the top of Table Mountain. Willem has not yet developed the sense of superiority that will characterize his descendants. He befriends Jack the Hottentot and wants to see his people as allies. He cares deeply about Deborah, the Malay slave girl, and lists his two children by her in the Bible he rescued from a wrecked ship. The company officials will not permit a marriage, but Willem continues to help Deborah after her marriage to the slave Jango and his own to Katje, the young woman sent out from Holland to be his wife. His love for the new land and his concern for others make him a sympathetic character.

Willem's grandson Adriaan is another Van Doorn who stands out because of his love for the frontier his family is settling. Through his trips of exploration he knows the land, its trees, its birds, its animals, and is called "Mad Adriaan" by those who don't understand what he has learned in his wanderings. During Adriaan's last long trip, he tames a hyena, whom he calls Swarts. Their relationship and the description of what Adriaan and his Hottentot friend Dikkop see make this part of the story memorable for its sense of place and freedom.

Lodevicus, Adriaan's son, is completely different in personality but larger than life as he lives up to his informal title, "the Hammer." Convinced that he is to bring order to shapeless lives, Lodevicus marries Rebecca, as determined as himself to do God's will as they know it. His commando exterminates the Bushmen and fights the Xhosa for control of the land. His mother describes him as limestone hardening into granite, and his father says he will be too stiff and too unforgiving. Lodevicus is two-dimensional but believable in his single-minded passion to do what he is sure the Lord requires of him.

Tjaart, as single-minded as his father Lodevicus, is less exuberant but equally steadfast as he runs his farm, fights the advancing Xhosa, and maintains his way of life against English laws. Tjaart is seen more often with his family, and his concern for daughter Minna's future happiness brings out his human side. Encouraged by his wife Jakoba, Tjaart finally decides that the family must make the Great Trek to the north in order to remain true to their beliefs: they cannot surrender to a government that, as he writes to his English neighbors,

> has tried to alter the natural relationship between the races, exalting the savage and debasing the Christian. . . . God has said that there shall be master and servant, and that each shall keep his proper place, and we propose to form a new nation in obedience to that law, one in which people of all color shall have their proper place, under the guidance of those whom God has elected to lead them. (639)

Tjaart is individualized by his situation, symbolic of his time and his people.

Paulus de Groot, although not a Van Doorn, is raised by Tjaart when his parents are killed, and he grows up to be another of the hard-hewn men of the veld. He is most memorable as a man in his sixties leading the Venloo Commando and refusing to give up the struggle against the English. The picture of the old man in his frock coat with the silver buttons and his tall black top hat riding cross country to dynamite the railroad in three different places on three different nights is an unforgettable one. He is a vivid part of the universe Michener has created to illustrate the development of a conviction that directs the unfolding of a country's story.

Detleef van Doorn is the member of this family tradition who is seen in the greatest detail. He is the courageous small boy of the internment camp who will never forget the horrors of his stay. He is the schoolboy being trained to defeat the English through education. He is the young man seeing in the separated colors of a gelatin dessert the image that must determine the organization of a society. He is the adult formulating the rules and regulations for this organization. He is the elderly man never understanding that the separateness created by his rules has condemned the majority of his country's people to economic, intellectual, and personal stagnation. Yet Detleef is drawn with a skill that makes him more than a mouthpiece for apartheid. He is believable when he remembers that Maud Saltwood saved his life in the camp by bringing in food and when he is so pleased to see Micah Nxumalo at his bedside as he lies dying. And he is as convincing when he finds justification for his convictions in the Old Testament and when he exhorts his listeners to resist any onslaught from those who would keep them from doing the work God has placed them in South Africa to do.

The Van Doorn women resemble their men for the most part—steadfast, courageous, and convinced of how God wants them to live. It's Lodevicus's wife Rebecca who is positive that she and her husband are ordained to bring order to a pagan land. It's Tjaart's wife Jakoba who articulates the need to start the Great Trek north in order to preserve their freedom. It's Tjaart's granddaughter Sybilla whose courage never flags as she accompanies her husband Paulus de Groot when he leads the Venloo Commando during the Boer War. It's Detleef's sister Johanna and his wife Maria who help him devise the laws that will set up apartheid. And it's Detleef's granddaughter Sannie who summarizes the argument that has led all these women: "Philip, we're a small group of white people on the edge of a hostile black continent. God placed us here for a specific purpose and gave us a commission. I assure you that we will all perish before we prove false to that obligation" (1176). Yet Michener is able to give the women a sympathetic side as the reader sees them with their families or suffering over the loss of loved ones or appreciating the natural beauties of the land.

The Saltwoods don't put down any roots in South Africa until the nineteenth century, when first Hilary as a missionary and then his brother Richard as a government official come to this new frontier. Hilary is shown with the Boers, the Hottentots, the blacks, preaching and living the New Testament message of love and justice for all. He will fight against the Xhosa attacking Grahamstown because he realizes the frontier must be pacified for missionary work to proceed, but he will grieve over the slaughter of human beings. He is a memorable figure as with his wife Emma, a former slave, he carries "the soaring promises of the New Testament" to the lonely wilderness of South Africa's northern frontier, treating all humans as children of God, equal in His sight.

Although he is not so fully defined as Hilary, Richard Saltwood is portrayed as the caring Englishman, sincerely sorry to see men he respects like Tjaart van Doorn treated unjustly by the government. He buys De Kraal, Tjaart's farm, when the family starts on the Great Trek and makes sure that Tjaart receives the promised compensation when his slaves are freed. He also remains in the reader's memory when he tries desperately to save the Xhosa dying of starvation. He represents the best of English actions on this frontier, doing his duty while expressing his concern for the injustices affecting people.

Frank Saltwood is not particularly individualized but is memorable because of his involvement in the historical events of his time period. It's through his eyes that the reader sees Cecil Rhodes's contribution to African history. Frank is also part of the Boer War, serving as General Buller's aide and the participant who interprets historical action. His horror at the conditions of the Chrissiesmeer internment camp is expressed in a letter to his wife, in which he urges her to do what she can to alleviate the deplorable conditions, and he leaves his duties with the army to help, hoping to save future relations between Englishman and Boer.

Two Saltwood wives are individualized by their actions, Frank's wife Maud and her daughter-in-law Laura. Maud's sincere and lively interest in everything she sees in South Africa makes her stand out among the cast of characters. In addition, her efforts to help the dying at the camps with supplies and her refusal to keep quiet about what she sees reveal her compassion for others and her concern for injustice. Laura learns from Maud how to speak directly against injustices, and her courage never fails as she works against the restrictions of apartheid. Her last appearance with the Lady Anne Barnard lawn bowling team before her banning and her matter-of-fact description of her own restricted life as she serves tea to Philip Saltwood from her five silver pots add to the humanity of this determined woman, one of the most admirable Michener has created.

The Nxumalos appear early in the story as the Nxumalo of Zimbabwe in the fifteenth century presents the black civilization of that era by his experiences with the traders, builders, and gold mines of Great Zimbabwe. He is portrayed as a man of intelligence, curious about new sights, places, and people, with the skill and courage to adapt to the land he explores. He is interesting because of what he illustrates about his people.

Some 350 years later Nxumalo of iziCwe is the fictional character whose adventures with Shaka, the historical leader of the Zulu, teach the reader about the society organized by that warrior-king. He is made more than merely representative by the presentation of his relationship to Shaka, his feelings for his wives, and his growing wish to end the killing required by Shaka's military dictatorship.

Micah Nxumalo is another humanized figure whose participation in the historical panorama illustrates the contradictions of the human condition. He fights with the Venloo Commando because of his emotional attachment to the people of Vrymeer, especially Paulus de Groot. But he notes during the battles of the Boer War that the next struggles will be white against black and foresees the need for his son to be educated in order to confront the increasing oppression of the black majority. Moses won't be going to college because Micah can't accumulate sufficient funds by working at Vrymeer, but Moses's son Daniel will become a professor, hoping for orderly change. His other son Jonathan will join the black South Africans who have fled across the border into Moçambique, believing that only armed force will give blacks their rights. All three will be individualized enough to make them more than mere representatives of an oppressed people. They are real human beings who suffer physically when stabbed or beaten and emotionally when forbidden opportunities for work or education because of their skin color.

THEMATIC CONSIDERATIONS

The value of human tolerance underlies the thematic considerations of *The Covenant.* As one critic expresses it, "If there is discrimination against other human beings because of race, color, or place of origin, then there is diminished use of human potential, of human skill, and the result is not merely diminished well-being for those discriminated against but a diminution for the whole society of which they are an unsufficiently utilized part" (Becker 1983, 179).

The discrimination against those who are the Other ranges from outright violence to ill treatment to neglect throughout the narrative. As the black ancestors of Nxumalo of Zimbabwe migrate southward, the little brown people are being eliminated. These little brown people fit nicely into the underground gold mines run by the blacks; the fact that life in the mines kills them within a few years is of no concern to those in charge. The Arab traders Nxumalo meets make slaves of any black foolhardy enough to go on an Arab ship.

The first Dutch at the Cape kill the Hottentots who won't trade their cattle, and one Jan Compagnie commander carries out a policy of mutilating runaway slaves. The violence of black tribe against black tribe; of Boer against Bushmen; of Boers, English, and blacks against each other is vividly described throughout the novel. The ill treatment and neglect of those who are different and therefore inferior are also well documented in the story.

Why and how does intolerance come about? Religious bigotry and arrogance are not exclusive to the Afrikaners, but their illustration in the narrative takes on a particular perspective with the belief in a special covenant with God. However, a brief comment from the narrator indicates the error inherent in the Afrikaner belief: they have forgotten the message of freedom and love of the New Testament in their eagerness to attain the order they see laid out in the Old Testament (972).

Another aspect of the theme of intolerance is the arrogance and misunderstanding of the other's culture. The whites arriving at the Cape consider the brown people uncivilized. The Dutch from Holland see those born in South Africa as uncouth. The English and the Boers feel that each other's way of waging war is dishonorable. The English use bayonets, the Boers kill horses; the English play cricket during the Sunday truces, the Boers hold religious services. And once the Afrikaners control the South African government, they become completely intolerant of those who do not accept their point of view, banning people such as Laura Saltwood and convicting blacks such as Daniel Nxumalo of treason for supporting a national day of mourning for blacks killed by South African police. The comment from a disappointed rugby player when New Zealand refuses to allow his team into the country expresses the bewilderment he feels about the world's opinion. Why should the world protest when all the Afrikaners want is to maintain an orderly society?

The role of language as it expresses a people's culture is an interesting thread of this novel's thematic considerations as it illustrates concern for identity. When the French Huguenots arrive in South Africa at the end of the seventeenth century, they are scattered by the authorities in order to be more easily assimilated into the prevailing Dutch culture. Paul De Pré is determined to resist the effort to eliminate his language, writing to his fellow Huguenots, "The most sacred possession a man can have, after his Bible, is his native tongue. To steal this is to steal his soul" (265). However, his children will speak Dutch.

When the English take over the colony, the Dutch spoken by the Boers has evolved from the language spoken in Holland, with new words and different pronunciations. Criticism from mother country officials only strengthens the Boer determination to speak Dutch the way they want it to sound. These settlers will also resist the English effort to erase their language, but after the Boer War, Paulus de Groot recognizes the need to learn the English language in order to use it as a weapon against the victors: "Accept English in your mind, but keep Dutch in your heart. For if a conqueror once makes you accept his language, he makes you his slave" (909).

By the time of World War I, the Dutch spoken by the Afrikaners is truly "Afrikaans," a precise language with clear, direct syntax. Its supporters say that it is the means to unite the Afrikaners and inspire them to gain control of the country. But Afrikaans also limits them to their own world, which is not open to the new ideas that make a country flourish. Laura Saltwood's speech on language summarizes the handicap that faces a monolingual society: "The edict that makes me learn a language spoken by only a few people puts me in a cage" (1170). Daniel Nxumalo also sees the dilemma of the language question for South Africa. Saying that Afrikaans is a "splendid, functional language," he notes that it is impossible for blacks to discuss freedom in it because of the system this language represents. And, as he tells the court trying him for treason, he is a citizen of the world as well as of South Africa. Because he wants to share ideas with the total human race, he advocates learning English. Both English and Afrikaans are necessary for South Africa's future—one to open the cage of this closed society and the other to enable it to function within.

The relation of human beings to their environment is another thematic consideration in *The Covenant*. South Africa is a promised land to Willem van Doorn, whose report to the Jan Compagnie officials in Java informs them of the amazing fruits and vegetables that can be grown there. Hard work and fortitude will enable the Trekboers to prosper until drought and depleted soil force them to move their flocks and families onward. Game will be plentiful until enough people with guns deplete the abundant herds, or until hundreds of animals are killed in a hunt organized to entertain an English prince. Yet the Van Doorns and Nxumalos at Vrymeer live in harmony with a group of antelope they have encouraged to live at their lake. The references to the diminishing numbers of animals or the droughts that drive farmers to seek work in the cities are interspersed throughout the story, but Michener's focus is on the human resources in this narrative. He only touches on concerns about depletions of the land and the animals, without suggesting concrete solutions.

This focus on human resources supports a very readable narrative that presents the historical panorama of a complex country with a rich, exciting, and often appalling history. In telling this story Michener has managed to remain matter-of-fact and show the human face of all the participants in this history. When readers reach the story's stopping point, they have a deeper understanding of South Africa, its policies, its potential, and its people.

A MARXIST READING OF *THE COVENANT*

Michener focuses on human resources in this novel, but a Marxist critic, working from the perspective outlined in Chapter 4, would concentrate on these human resources as they are affected by the way they earn their living. Since the history related in *The Covenant* takes place over several hundred years, the Marxist critic would be also interested in how the social and economic relations between classes evolve over time.

In the fifteenth century the relations between the black people and the brown people are determined by the desire of the former for the gold that the latter extracts from the underground mines. Gaining profit through trade with the Arabs is the motivation behind this exploitation of the little brown people. The mine workers earn no wages at all; they eat what is thrown down to them and stay in the mine until they die. Yet the emphasis on the profits to be earned from the mines dooms the city of Great Zimbabwe to extinction. It had been a place where all enjoyed a modest well-being and a few were greatly enriched. But it had spent its energy searching for gold and its income on ostentation. The precious goods carried to the city by long lines of slaves had done nothing to nourish the real city. In this society there has been no real class struggle, but the economic system with its exploitation of the productive workers eventually collapses.

The social history of South Africa develops along the lines of Zimbabwe, according to the Marxist perspective. Those who have the power look on the profits they can extract from the land and its peoples as more important than the welfare of those who produce what earns the profits. The first Dutch arrivals expect the Hottentots to work for them, not with them. The Jan Compagnie officials don't care what restrictions they place on their employees as long as the company receives the fruits of their labors.

The same type of treatment of employees continues as the Dutch begin the agricultural development of the land. Like the first plantation owners in *Chesapeake*, however, they labor as hard as their workers, and the Jan Compagnie still controls the way the land is distributed and settled. In

its concern for profits, the Jan Compagnie ignores the needs of its employees. Schools are few and of poor quality; no publication of books or
newspapers is allowed for nearly 150 years after the first settlers arrive.
With a chance to set up a new society in an area where no established
one exists, the Jan Compagnie perpetuates a system of exploitation that
is refined by the incoming white settlers.

The Dutch settlers justify the system they impose on other races as
ordained by the commandments of God. A Marxist critic would say that
this type of justification is only another way of explaining the goal of
the group in power to control wealth and maintain its privileged position. The end result is alienation of the producing classes from each
other; all they can do is attempt to earn enough to survive. For example,
the blacks see themselves as separate from the Coloureds, who are always looking to move "up to whitehood" (996), and the Coloureds look
on the blacks as inferior beings. This type of class struggle hampers both
groups.

From the Marxist perspective, the discussion of some of the novel's
black characters about the inequities of employment in South Africa
shows a glimmer of understanding about how an exploitative economic
system is harmful to all participants: "The worst thing a nation can do
to itself is to cultivate and maintain a supply of cheap labor. When sal-
aries are kept down, money stops circulating, taxes bring in diminished
funds, and everybody loses" (995). From this point of view, a more equal
distribution will increase the available wealth for all.

Apartheid sets into law the customs that have governed the relationships between the controlling class and all others. The work rules restrict
blacks to certain jobs; for example, in the mines no black can have a
position where he would give orders to a white. And once a black is
trained for a certain job, he is not allowed to change assignments. Mine
workers can leave at the end of their contract, but other opportunities
are rare. The home rules mean that blacks working in a city like Johannesburg must leave at the end of the working day for places like Soweto,
a dormitory-like settlement which officially doesn't exist. The blacks are
not allowed to live in a city. If, as the Marxist states, labor of all sorts
proves humanity's ability to produce, its results should be enjoyed by
all humanity. In the South Africa portrayed in *The Covenant*, the blacks
are dehumanized by the apartheid system. It may be based on what its
supporters see as a religious principle, but from the Marxist perspective,
the controlling group wants to keep economic as well as political and
social power.

The history of South Africa as told in the novel can be viewed from the Marxist perspective, therefore, as a dramatic one of class conflicts. The classes are determined in large part by race; the "haves" are sure that their wealth, status, and power are God-given and fail to accept the reality that their system is dehumanizing the "have-nots." Will the latter rebel? Is revolution the next phase of the story? Michener does not answer directly, for the story continues after the novel stops. The dangers of the type of exploitation illustrated in this novel are evident to the Marxist critic—and all thoughtful readers.

8

Space
(1982)

Space, the story of America's space program, was published by James Michener in 1982. While its historical period is much shorter than Michener's historical panoramas discussed in this volume, the novel is still panoramic in scope. Starting with the end of World War II and continuing to 1982, Michener tells the story of space exploration from the rocket experiments in wartime Germany to the first shuttle flight. The story's episodes proceed in orderly, chronological fashion, involving an invented set of characters who are part of the political and scientific aspects of space activity.

In addition to his usual thorough research on any subject he chooses for a novel, Michener gained specialized knowledge on space through his service as a member of the NASA Advisory Council. He was appointed to the council in the spring of 1979, and for four years he was able to participate in the life of NASA, the National Aeronautics and Space Administration, talking to experts, visiting laboratories, and studying procedures.

This chapter will consider the organization and development of the space story, the presentation of the characters and their roles, and thematic considerations that support the panorama. In addition, *Space* will be looked at from the viewpoint of a feminist critic.

PLOT ORGANIZATION AND DEVELOPMENT

With this novel the reader enters directly into the story on a specific date, October 24, 1944. The section "Four Men" introduces each of the four main male characters with his actions of that day. Stanley Mott is in London, having been sent by American officials to persuade English and American military personnel that the bombing of the German rocket research center at Peenemünde must avoid the living quarters of the German rocket scientists, for the United States needs their expertise once Germany is defeated. Norman Grant, a U.S. Navy lieutenant commander from the fictional western state of Fremont, is involved in a major naval battle against the Japanese in the Pacific Ocean. When his ship breaks apart, he spends a heroic forty-eight hours on a raft and in the sea, doing his utmost to save as many men as possible. Back in the town of Clay, in the state of Fremont, a high school student is preparing to participate in the big football game of the season. John Pope, a serious young man and fine student, wins the game with his excellent running but remembers the date primarily because of being able to look at the stars for the first time through binoculars and then through a telescope at the local observatory. His future path will follow astronomy in some way. The fourth member of the quartet is Dieter Kolff, a rocket technician in the German army. Dieter has little formal education but a brilliant mechanical mind; he makes those rockets work. The chapter ends with Dieter and Stanley Mott making contact as the Russians push into Germany from the east and the Americans from the west.

The progression of these four men into the next phase of their lives is portrayed in the context of the "Four Women" in the next chapter. Elinor Stidham Grant, an intelligent college student, loves her husband and is proud of his heroism in the war. However, she cannot cope with his drive toward political office and the tactics it takes to get elected. Rachel Lindquist Mott comes from a Boston family who feels that Stanley can't be all that brillant because he attended Georgia Tech! She spends the war years alone, not knowing what her husband is doing or even if he is alive. She rejoins him in late 1945, when he arrives in Texas accompanying the German scientists. Rachel gets involved teaching English to the Germans and is concerned about when the German wives will be allowed to join their husbands. Stanley continues his top-secret work, and once the U.S. government realizes how badly the scientists are needed, it's Rachel who solves the problem of how the Germans can appear to have entered the country legally. From El Paso they go into Mexico with officials looking the other way and reenter the United States on visitors' visas. Liesl Koenig Kolff has more difficulty coming to the United States. Because she and Dieter were never legally married, she has no papers and spends months doing menial jobs before Stanley Mott intervenes. She adapts to life at Fort Bliss as a supportive, hard-working wife. The lives of the Motts and Kolffs continue to be wrapped up in the rocket experiments, and the team of scientists and technicians is sent to Alabama, where the U.S. Army intends that serious experiments will take place. Penny Hardesty, the fourth woman, has been John Pope's girlfriend in high school. Now in college she becomes involved in Norman Grant's campaign for senator. When he wins the election, Penny goes along as an office assistant and finishes her degree at Georgetown University. When John receives the appointment to the naval academy, she visits him in Annapolis, appreciating the charm and beauty of the old town. Penny is scathing about the inability of Elinor Grant to appreciate the work her husband is doing and encourages Senator Grant to "get off dead center" and identify a cause to champion. Penny marries John after his graduation from the academy and they both commit to aviation, Penny by joining the staff of Senator Glancey who heads the Senate aviation committee and John in advanced fighter training for the navy. Senator Grant becomes a member of Glancey's committee. The four men and the four women are now all involved in some way in aviation and space.

The next episodes in the unfolding tale of space exploration take place during the Korean conflict. The chapter titled "Korea" begins with John Pope as a navy pilot assigned to fly at night to knock out the enemy's small plane, Slow Boy, which is causing havoc with its bombing of American ammunition dumps. The detailed descriptive passages of John's night flights practically put the reader in the pilot's seat as the plane soars through the empty night air, searching for enemy activity, especially for their supply trains. Michener spent considerable time in military aircraft during the Korean fighting, experiencing what he would depict so authentically in *The Bridges at Toko-Ri* and now in *Space*.

During one flight John does destroy a locomotive by first dropping bombs at the mouths of two tunnels, cutting off the engine's safe haven. His success is confirmed by the photos Randy Claggett takes. Randy is a marine captain and a braggart who lives up to his statements with his accomplishments. He is a new type for John Pope, who doesn't understand Randy's values but respects his ability as a flier. The two of them apply for a new test-pilot situation to seek new challenges.

"Korea" also presents Penny Pope returning to work for Senator Grant's reelection campaign and the Motts and Kolffs traveling by car caravan with other German scientists to Alabama. During the car trip the vision of these scientists is evident in their discussions of the potential of space exploration. Scientific information is presented with Michener's usual thoroughness through conversation between Mott and the German scientists. Rivalry between the army, navy, and air force and the political dealings for funds are also part of the story of space exploration, and "Korea" lets the reader be part of negotiations, progress, and setbacks. When Mott is let go by the army because his job with the German scientists is completed, Kolff supports his employment by the National Advisory Committee for Aero-nautics, NACA. This group is hiring the best and brightest engineers and theoreticians to study flight. He works on the problems posed by potential space travel, and again the reader is part of the thought processes, the questions, the answers, as these men of vision, drive, and intelligence seek solutions to the difficulties travel in space would involve.

Senator Grant, because of his work on the aviation committee, visits the NACA-sponsored center often, but his wife refuses to be involved at all in his work. Instead she accepts the statements and publications of a con artist, Dr. Leopold Strabismus, who promotes the idea that visitors from outer space are about to take over the United States. Dr. Strabismus's past is shadowed, but his abilities are extensive, and he convinces Mrs. Grant of the truth of his remarks. The lines are beginning to be drawn between those who are excited by the possibilities of scientific study and explorations and those who fear what they do not understand.

In the chapter "Pax River" the story moves on with more training for those who will be directly involved in space. Now John Pope enters a Ph.D. program in engineering and astronomy, finding in the challenges another series of the "best days of his life." For Pope, "life was providing a series of graded adventures, each appropriate to its moment" (262). Pope is also accepted into the navy's test-pilot program along with Randy Claggett, and the accomplishments and the tragedies of this select group are portrayed in the authentic Michener manner—through explanation and conversation. Dieter Kolff is not as satisfied with his work, for the army is ordered to stop work on any rockets with an anticipated range of more than 200 miles. Grant is involved in the congressional discussions and negotiations about the space program while his wife continues to support Strabismus's campaigns regarding visitors from outer space. In spite of her daughter's tawdry affair with Strabismus, Elinor will not be swayed from her conviction that the United States is in danger from the "visitors." Hearing the news that the Russians have launched the first *Sputnik*, she is sure that Strabismus's predictions have come true.

The United States response to the Russian accomplishment is the essential part of the story in the next chapter, "Intellectual Decisions." The questions about who is going to organize and control the U.S. space effort are engrossing, and Michener gives his readers insight into the political process with the description of the creation by Congress of the National Aeronautics and Space Administration. Penny Pope, back in her role as administrative director of the Senate aviation committee after helping with Grant's reelection campaign, is instrumental in writing the bill that establishes NASA. Michener is able to give the facts of a historic event an authentic, human aspect by using a fictional character's involvement as their framework. The personal concerns of the main characters continue to be part of the story: Senator Grant is despairing over his daughter's ongoing participation in Strabismus's schemes; Rachel Mott worries about her sons' development; Liesl Kolff regrets how developers are taking over the green space she has nurtured near their home; and Dieter refuses to allow their son to profane his musical talent by participating in the University of Alabama marching band. Dieter is also despondent about the U.S. government's lack of understanding of what he and his fellow scientists and technicians have been doing with their research. As the space program progresses, Michener makes the debate about its direction more real by having his characters an integral part of the discussion. Kolff sees chiefly the scientific aspects of the program and deplores the decision to have a manned flight to the moon, since such a flight will take funds from the research projects he feels are necessary to increase human knowledge of space in general. When Mott supports his ideas, both men are told the political realities: the taxpayers are the ones who must be listened to, and they have no emotional attachment to machines. Mott realizes the social implications and accepts the new policy: "Man was the measure of all things, and although it was correct that machines could perform miracles, they could not enlist the emotional support of the public" (383–84). The Michener technique of presenting his readers with the knowledge necessary for understanding, at least partly, the questions under consideration is again evident as believable people talk about the ways and means of making the manned moon flight. Dialogue and description develop the story and the ideas. The chapter concludes with John Pope's decision to apply for a spot in the next group of astronauts and German scientists in Alabama watching a fictionalized version of Wernher von Braun's life that does not reflect reality as they see it.

"Twins" follows the six new astronauts, including John Pope and Randy Claggett, through their training. An interesting angle to the story is the public relations attitude about the six new trainees and their wives and families. They must be human but conform to the public's stereotype regarding their behavior. On launch day the wives must be shown at home, behind the white picket fence with the children's toys scattered neatly in the living room. Penny Pope and Debby Dee Claggett don't quite fit the picture. The former has an administrative career and the latter's language and looks don't fit the "All-American" image. The Motts become involved with the new group, Stanley inducting them into the workings of NASA and Rachel overseeing the presentation of the wives. The *Gemini* phase of the space program, with its "twin" or two pilots for each launch, is featured in this part of the story. Pope and Claggett are to be the pilots for the last flight in this phase, and the reader participates in the training exercises as well as the actual space flight. Space travel becomes real in this novel, but the human element from political maneuvers to life-style choices is as much a part of the saga as flight simulators and jungle training.

In "The Moon" the four families whose stories help frame *Space* come together in a suburb of Houston to watch the televised first landing on the moon. It's a triumph for Mott the engineer and Grant the politician. Dieter Kolff, on the other hand, is disappointed, for he realizes American energies will veer away from exploration of the life history of the universe.

Kolff is right as the next segment reveals. "Real Time" presents the scale-back of NASA programs, but funding for a fictitious *Apollo 18* mission to the other side of the moon is engineered through Congress by Penny Pope. John Pope and Randy Claggett with Dr. Paul Linley, the first black astronaut, are to fly this mission, and their training is a major part of the chapter. But the personal lives of the characters are also important; the troubles of the Motts' son Christopher with the police and Randy Claggett's relationship with the Korean journalist Rhee Soon-Ka, or Cynthia Rhee as she is known in the United States, provide part of the human drama. Dr. Strabismus's ventures are also an ongoing part of the story as he now sees the potential in television evangelism.

"Dark Side of the Moon" is one of the most gripping sections of the space story. Michener provides a detailed description of the *Apollo 18* equipment and its movement to the launch site. But the mission itself has an unforeseen result when sunspot radiation causes Claggett and Linley, walking on the moon, to be too weak to manage a complete take-off in the lunar module. The terse yet emotional narrative is one of Michener's best as Pope verifies the fate of the module and its occupants and then brings the spacecraft safely back to earth.

With the close of the *Apollo* program the story too begins to wind down. Yet there are still questions about the universe to explore, and Stanley Mott thinks about them. John Pope makes a world tour and discusses his feelings about space with Cindy Rhee for three days in Australia. But on the political front Senator Grant backs away from NASA, and Mott wonders how to retain a basic capacity for space exploration with all the cutbacks. Pope becomes a professor of applied astronomy in his home state. Strabismus sharpens his campaign against scientific explanations of the universe and attacks the theory of evolution. But the *Viking* probe lands on Mars: "Man had reached the planets. He stood challenging the entire solar system to reveal its secrets. . . . Where this vast adventure into space would end, no man could predict" (713).

The shuttle program and the *Voyager 2* fly-by of the planet Saturn involve Mott as he nears retirement. But the questions of science and religion brought out in the concluding chapters, of new ideas and change, remain to challenge human beings. A conference between scientists and religious leaders is chaired by Mott in the novel's final chapter, "The Rings of Saturn." Mott tries to calm the passions by recognizing the need for both science and religion to consider and discuss together the origin, design, and governance of the universe. Yet the eternal debate will continue. This story can come to a stopping point, but it is never ending.

CHARACTER DEVELOPMENT

To a storyteller like James Michener, thorough development of a novel's characters is not the most important consideration. But in the story of space exploration and adventure he chooses to tell the tale through selected characters, thereby letting in his readers more fully to these lives. Michener makes the four families ordinary with their relationships, their concerns about their children, their marriages. However, they are also exceptional people involved in exceptional events, and all except Elinor Grant, and at times Norman Grant, illustrate the value Michener places on endurance, hard work, and the capacity to rise to the occasion when tested.

Stanley and Rachel Mott are perhaps the best examples of exceptional people rising to the occasion. Stanley is first seen in London, a twenty-six-year-old civilian engineer directing the way bombs should be dropped on the German rocket installation. Rachel is back in the States, taking care of their first child, working in a day-care center, and organizing as always the space she occupies in the least cluttered, most efficient manner. Rachel recognizes that owing to the top-secret nature of Stanley's work, their worlds are in danger of drifting apart, to the detriment of their marriage. Michener doesn't really deal with how they resolve this problem other than to show them sharing pleasure in music, art, literature, and each other when time permits. They continue to support each other through Stanley's various roles in the space program, becoming representative of families in which the wife must assume basic responsibility for the children while the husband is involved in his work. Although the Motts are developed to explain the space program and certain of Michener's ideas, they are still more than cardboard figures. Rachel is a no-nonsense, sensible elder sister to the wives of the six astronauts, and the grief of both parents over the death of their younger son in a drug-related plane crash is human and natural. Stanley's frustration is also believable when the politicians and the magazine writer prefer manned space flights to true scientific exploration because such flights are the only way to get public support for the enormous expense involved: "To Stanley Mott, ideas were the noble manifestations of mankind, and he felt that in this room his ideas were not being accorded the dignity they deserved" (382).

John and Penny Pope are the other couple whose marriage is portrayed in some detail and whose personalities and characters are somewhat more than representative of a certain type of person. John is called a "straight arrow" at numerous points in the novel. He is focused on his passion for astronomy, for flying, and for Penny. He doesn't drink or smoke, and he jogs to keep in shape. Yet John Pope comes across as a real human being—intense, yes, but sensitive and sincere. As he brings the spacecraft back to earth alone after the *Apollo 18* voyage, he notes that the hours are long and heavy. Those few words say volumes about his sadness at the loss of his companions in this mission.

Penny is another focused individual. She is presented as the small-town girl who wants to achieve something better for herself. Her education, marriage, and developing career in politics are outside the "normal" range of activities for a woman of the fifties and sixties, and Penny is the despair of the magazine writer assigned to tell the story of the "Solid Six" astronauts. She won't fit into his box of the home with the white picket fence and the children's toys. John and Penny thrive on their intense lives that come together at odd moments, and it's during cross-country trips by car, when John is going to a new training site or a meeting and Penny has some time off, that they have the conversations that help bring them alive to the reader. During a trip near the end of *Space*, Penny fails to persuade John to run for Grant's Senate seat and then informs him of her decision that she must therefore declare her own candidacy. John ponders how to respond as he is honor-bound to support Grant. His reply shows the balance the two have worked out in their lives: "Penny, when I flew *Gemini* with Claggett, I sat in the right-hand seat. I can do so again" (766).

Dieter and Liesl Kolff are more types than individuals. They are from Germany and are shown as hard-working, diligent people, small in size (although Liesl does gain weight in middle age) but large in determination. Dieter is completely devoted to his rockets and not shy about supporting his point of view. He deplores the American decision to put a man on the moon, and even when rejoicing that the moon landing has been made, he feels that the whole effort ignores the necessity of knowing everything possible about the universe. They are the most vivid when they make their difficult journey across Germany in the last days of the war. Dieter is an eloquent spokesperson for his ideas and vision, but the reader knows very little about him. Liesl is presented as being concerned about her husband's work, her home, and her son's education. She is likeable when she appears in the story, but she is never seen apart from her role as a German housewife adapting to life in America.

The Grants are a couple for whom the early promise of their marriage is not realized. Norman Grant has his heroic moments when his ship is sunk during World War II and when he champions America's space effort in the Senate. However, he has to be pushed in his Senate career to devote himself to the "big" causes. Penny Pope finds him honest but with limited horizons and eventually "a soggy, pathetic politician. . . . He stood for nothing. He represented no vital force. He had no vision of the future" (688). But the reader is not told how or why he became that way. He is real enough within his role as a Senator on the committee dealing with budgets and directions for the space program, but the development of Norman as a character goes no further. Elinor Grant seems to have been created to show what happens when a person has no lasting courage or drive. Her withdrawal from Norman's life starts with his first campaign for a Senate seat. She refuses to make any effort to understand the space program, preferring instead to send money to Dr. Strabismus and believe in his promise to protect the United States from extraterrestrial invaders. Elinor's hold on reality lessens as the story is told, until she is finally hospitalized. She illustrates Michener's belief that part of humanity will always refuse to face the challenges of their world; she has intentionally drawn in the limits of her world to make it easier to understand and control. These two characters are memorable only within the context of the unfolding story.

If Michener does not concentrate on analyzing and developing his characters, he is able even with the secondary members of his cast to create personalities to remember. Randy Claggett is one such person. Randy first enters the story in Korea, where he is an outstanding pilot and his rambunctious life-style contrasts with the approach of calm, intense John Pope. The reader can't forget Randy's direct and inelegant language when he has a comment on a subject such as doing reconnaissance work in Korea: "Y'all know that when I go up there, I got no guns, no bombs, no nothin'? Takin' pitchers like some clown at a carnival" (187). He is a flamboyant, exuberant test-pilot–astronaut and one of the most vital cast members Michener has ever created.

In addition the reader won't forget Cynthia Rhee or Leopold Strabismus. Cynthia, a Korean journalist, wants to tell the true story of the astronauts and is able to ask the questions that bring forth solid answers. Like a Korean potter who allows the clay "to work out its own destiny" (489), she works with her data so that they will portray the story honestly for future generations to understand fully. She is an interesting personality, a Korean brought up in Japan where Koreans are treated as second-class citizens, and she feels her heritage has given her a special compulsive force to follow her story wherever it leads, as she explains in a conversation with Rachel Mott.

Strabismus's origins are brought out through the descriptive part of the narrative. He is almost a caricature as a con artist who devises original ways to separate the gullible from their money and who enjoys the young girls who clamor to share his bed. His United Space Association is directed toward the fear of UFOs and his University of Space and Aviation sells degrees. With his United Salvation Alliance he sees his chance to be a powerful part of the American cultural swing against science and intellectualism and toward the nostalgia for the "good old days." He decides that if society is rotten, he will manipulate it, and joins the crusade to outlaw the teaching of evolution in the state of Fremont. Piece by piece, the reader begins to understand what motivates Strabismus, realizing that this strange person is representative of those who further their own power at the expense of others.

THEMATIC CONSIDERATIONS

Space becomes more than a chronicle of the U.S. adventure in space exploration, with the theme of how society challenges the new explosion of knowledge—and how this knowledge challenges society. The head-on confrontation between the two sides occurs late in the book, but as early as Chapter 3 Elinor Grant's belief in Dr. Strabismus's United Space Association is an example of a refusal to face the potential of new ideas. Stanley Mott cannot understand how an intelligent, college-educated woman can ignore evidence. She is, according to Strabismus, one of the common people who must not be confused and can be used because they want to be used.

As the time period of the novel takes the reader into the early 1980s, the struggle between those who want absolute answers to complex questions and those who search to expand the possible answers and pose new questions takes many forms. Park rangers talking about geology are challenged by those who believe that the earth was created in 4004 B.C. In the state of Fremont, a campaign to prohibit all teaching of evolution is effective, in large part because of the efforts of Strabismus, a man of no religious convictions who is driven by a desire for power and revenge on the academic establishment, which had not accepted him on his own terms. All textbooks must be purged of positive references to Charles Darwin, dinosaurs, and geology, and there is no shortage of volunteers for the task. John Pope comes to teach applied astronomy at the state university about the same time, and his old professor will give the welcoming address. His point of reference is a supernova that occurred in the constellation Taurus in 1054 A.D. and was noted by observers in many parts of the world. There is no mention of this event in any European written record. Professor Anderssen says that an age is called "dark" because people refuse to see the light that is shining.

Michener avoids a moralistic tone in his presentation of such issues by voicing them through such characters as Stanley Mott, a thoughtful, reflective scientist. Mott, meeting with Strabismus in the Grants' home, thinks that perhaps he has been fighting the wrong battle. He realizes that Dieter Kolff, with his support of the bigger and bigger rockets, failed to understand the frightened people who wouldn't see the need or the value of the big enough rocket that could do anything. Mott even wonders if Strabismus could be right: "Keep the citizens ignorant. . . . Convince them that the truth lies elsewhere than in the questing human mind" (760). But in a conversation with his wife, Mott says that while science doesn't serve in the role of deciding what is right or wrong, one must hope that those like Strabismus will pass quickly without doing too much damage. He recognizes, too, that Strabismus's appeal may be because of men like himself "who had blindly pursued their own narrowly defined interests while ignoring the vast, sloppy, stumbling universe of people who could not keep pace with the discoveries" (774). And he is sure that humankind stands at the threshold of vast new horizons of knowledge that will need new interpretations.

While chairing a meeting between scientists and religious leaders concerning the possibility of life elsewhere in the universe, Mott must diffuse the passions that arise, and he does so in a reasoned speech. He notes the need for an ethical system to judge the good and evil of a proposed act; the ethical systems on earth have been given the name of "religion." He applauds the role of religion in structuring society. But as a scientist, he cannot ignore the evidence accumulated by space explorations regarding the nature of other planets such as Saturn. Mott refers to the problems facing humanity, such as how to handle atomic energy and genetic engineering. Unity is essential to bring order to a threatened Earth; both sides must work together in exploring the structure of matter, the working of the human mind, the chances of society's survival. The implication is that the pendulum may be swinging toward simplistic answers, but the debate has been going on since human life began. It will continue a thousand years from now on another planet orbiting some other star in another galaxy.

Since in this novel Michener is dealing with a social and cultural context covering more than four decades, other contemporary thematic considerations become part of the story; family life, women's roles, life-style choices, popular culture, the Vietnam War, and opportunities available for African Americans are threads of the main confrontation.

Michener treats the problems of family life and raising children through the lives of the four families. The Motts have two children, both problems, and Rachel bears the direct responsibility for their upbringing. She feels that Stanley's involvement is necessary to get the boys on the right track, but this involvement is sporadic as his work is so absorbing. Yet what is the answer to the older son's homosexuality and the younger's eventual jail term for drug running? Marcia Grant makes a life for herself with Strabismus, far away from the values represented by her confused mother and patriotic father. Magnus Kolff, with his musical talent, is the only "normal" achiever of these children. Michener does not provide direct answers to the questions of how to raise one's children to be useful, productive citizens, but he gives some indications through the characters. Grant notes that when he was a boy in Clay, Fremont, every element of society was supportive—police, Sunday School teachers, coaches, even the town loafers who discouraged him from exploring the pool hall. Liesl Kolff remarks that sometimes a parent must take the hammer and smash the trumpet, as Dieter had done when Magnus wanted to be part of the university marching band. Yet the Kolffs bought another trumpet, and Magnus established an outstanding career. The Motts come to terms with Millard's life-style and grieve over Christopher. There are no easy answers.

Women's roles and abilities are highlighted through Penny Pope. She has the same type of drive and capacity for hard work as do the astronauts, and when she looks around the Congress, she is appalled at the number of incompetent men in government and the number of outstanding women in the role of assistant. She reflects on the outstanding male officials she has worked with, but she knows that there are an equal number of outstanding females who have not been allowed to participate in power. Penny realizes that compressing men and women into specific categories is damaging to both sexes and society in general. When Tucker Thompson's last picture of the "Solid Six" depicts Penny as the wife helping her husband campaign for Senator Grant, she is infuriated with the reversal of the truth. Penny Pope will run for the Senate on her own merits and record.

Since tolerance is an enduring Michener value, it is not surprising that Millard Mott's choice of a homosexual life-style is treated sympathetically. From their initial shock and grief Rachel and Stanley come to appreciate their son's work and committed relationship. When the Strabismus campaign against homosexuals in political life targets Millard as the elected mayor of his fictional Colorado ski town, Stanley is there to remind those attacking his son that the Biblical text they are quoting goes on to condemn also those who curse their fathers, commit adultery, and appear to be witches. The referendum to recall Millard fails. This one time at least a "decent public life of service and the good report of one's neighbors" (776) count more than an arbitrary condemnation.

Popular culture is not a particularly evident theme in *Space*, but references occur occasionally. The trial of Christopher Mott provides the framework for an indictment of a permissive, fragmented society. His mother thinks that songs, clothes, television programs idealizing disruptive behavior, and peer pressure had conspired to put her son on trial. Parents preoccupied with society's business could not combat such destructive influences. The counterpart to the negative image of popular culture is a discussion of the best of science fiction, when Randy Claggett brings a selection of books to a hospitalized Stanley Mott. The best authors have tackled visionary ideas and problems with innovative solutions—and kept the spirit of fun that Randy Claggett feels the space program should have.

Since the U.S. involvement in Vietnam is part of the time period of the novel, it becomes part of the discussion occasionally. Millard Mott goes to Canada to avoid the draft. During the conversation of the four families as they wait for the moon landing, the contrasting viewpoints of Americans are brought out. Rachel relates Millard's point that Congress has not declared a formal war in Vietnam, and Senator Grant is shocked that young people don't recognize the validity of their elders' judgment. His attitude is that citizens must follow the plans of the president and Congress. The opinions are a reflection of society in general, but they are tangential to the focus of the main story.

Also apart from the novel's central ideas are the issues facing African Americans during the more than four decades covered in *Space*. Every time Gawain Butler, whose life Grant had saved in the Pacific during the war, appears as a supporter in the Senator's election campaigns, he calls attention to the wider social problems that Grant ignores. In 1952, the questions of employment practices and education, especially in the urban areas, are Butler's concern. In 1964, it's the lack of African-American participants in the space program. Why, asks Butler, is this group cut off from the best parts of the national life? Penny Pope organizes a tour to five excellent universities, but her committee finds that the brightest African-American students are not choosing the hard science courses that would qualify them to be astronauts or part of Mission Control, preferring to make their mark in the business world. However, Butler's challenge does get the attention of those in charge, and little by little black faces are added to the white faces in the pictures of NASA employees.

James Michener is most interested in telling the story of the U.S. space program in this novel called *Space,* and he does so thoroughly and in an engrossing manner, bringing out the factual information through the actions and reactions of the fictional characters he creates. His focus is on intellectual ideas and problems, but he does not put aside social issues. He brings them into the story as they affect the lives of his characters. The reader is left with the sense of having participated in an exciting adventure and of having been stimulated with ideas and issues.

A FEMINIST READING OF *SPACE*

Although the male characters in *Space* are the ones most directly involved in space research and exploration, the female characters are an important part of the story. A feminist reading of the novel according to the criteria outlined in Chapter 3 will concentrate on an analysis of the authenticity of the principal women in the narrative, with attention also to the culture and time in which they live as well as their potential as role models.

At first glance, Rachel Mott appears to be the stereotypic supportive wife, finding her identity through her husband's work. Yet her talent in working with people is recognized when she is asked to help the German scientists and their families, and later the astronaut families, adapt to new situations. The work with the astronaut families is even paid. She is authentic as a human being operating within the culture of a certain time frame, the 1940s to the 1970s. Treated by her husband as a person whose opinions he respects and whose abilities he appreciates, Rachel is more than an object who supports the goals of the man in her life. She is a realistic self in the context of the novel.

Elinor Grant is difficult to classify. She withdraws completely from her husband's work and is described as "fragile" and "vulnerable." The idea of space exploration and travel frightens her; as Stanley Mott puts it, "she had intentionally contracted the perimeters of her world, making it ever smaller and easier to control" (759). However, she is not the stereotypic Other who is seen only in relationship to men; her role goes

beyond gender and illustrates Michener's wider concern about how society should face the challenges of science. It is not just women who
retreat from these challenges. Dr. Strabismus tells Stanley Mott that half
the members of Universal Space Associates are men: "Some are men just
like yourself who are sick and tired of the pretensions of established
science" (257). Elinor can be considered as representative of a certain
type of human being—a negative image for those who accept what is
valued in this novel but not primarily because she is a woman.

Liesl Kolff is the traditional housewife and mother, finding the land
for the Kolff home, supervising her son's homework, preparing her husband's favorite food. However, she extends the boundaries of the supportive wife stereotype with her interest in preserving a greenbelt from
overdevelopment. Liesl is obviously representative of her culture and
time period, and she does not present a new role model for women's
activities. But Michener is telling a story, portraying a society as it was,
and Liesl is a realistic part of that society.

It's Penny Pope who branches out, who finds activities that encourage
her self-realization as a person. She earns a law degree, works on a Senator's staff, and gains more status and responsibility as a top-ranking
staff member of a Senate committee. With the passage of time she has
her own consciousness-raising experience when she mentally surveys the
U.S. Congress and realizes how many highly competent women are limited to supporting roles in government. She has been too busy to realize
that feminist concerns about "traditional women's roles" are hers also:
"it was quite clear to her now that America produced an equal number
of good women who were held contemptuously down" (672). Penny
tries to persuade her husband John to run for Grant's Senate seat because
of John's intelligence and reputation as an American hero, but when he
refuses, she is ready to be the candidate. She is a role model as a professional woman. The Popes' marriage is one of mutual support and
encouragement but not traditional as their work keeps them in different
places. Yet Michener presents such an arrangement as perfectly valid
when the two people involved are in agreement. From a feminist perspective, the writer has affirmed two human lives and presented a female
character whose life is associated with men but not defined by them.

Marcia Grant, on the other hand, decides to associate with Dr. Strabismus in all his dubious enterprises. Since Marcia is a secondary character, her motivation for staying with this man is not developed in the
novel. But from the feminist standpoint, she appears to find her identity
through the man's activities. She doesn't protest when Strabismus pro-

poses marriage as part of his venture into religion and wants to profit from her position as Senator Grant's daughter. Marcia makes no objection to being used; she merely helps her husband refine and carry out his plans. A feminist has difficulty accepting this image of a woman character, and yet she is not a helpless victim. She deliberately chooses her path.

Cynthia Rhee, the Korean journalist, is another type of woman, one "without sham or pretense who wanted to delve into problems of intense mutual concern" (488). The six astronauts are her story, one she wants to write truthfully and not for public relations purposes. When Rachel Mott confronts her about her alleged intent to sleep with all six, she laughs, "Surely you must know that men always spread such rumors when they feel challenged by women who are brighter than they are" (445). Her personal involvement with Randy Claggett is interrupted by his death during *Apollo 18,* and Randy's widow plus the remaining astronauts recognize Cindy's right to mourn with them, in spite of concerns about damage to the public image of the astronauts. Cindy's models are three women journalists of the post World War II period who died in the line of duty but whose example gave women new definitions of what they could do. Cindy does not intend to be a lesser woman than these three.

Michener has presented women characters who go beyond stereotypes in this novel, but he is well aware that stereotypes exist, as the episodes with magazine writer Tucker Thompson illustrate. Thompson's publication, with NASA's blessing, is to present the six astronauts and their families to the American public. The wives must be beautiful, not too intelligent, devoted to their families. They play the game by the rules in public, but Thompson is horrified on one launch day to find four of them playing cards and ignoring the television in the corner. The wives clear away the cards and greet the reporters with graciousness. American society as a whole is not ready to accept women as human, and these wives understand their role, playing it with wry amusement.

A feminist reading of *Space* finds basically authentic women characters, considered in relationship to men but not necessarily defined by them. Penny Pope and Cindy Rhee provide role models for activities that go beyond the boundaries while the other women are more traditional in their choices. The four decades of space exploration presented in this narrative are seen against the changing American culture, and the women who are part of the story reflect the changes in realistic and individual ways.

9

Texas
(1985)

With a fascinating combination of fact and fiction James Michener presents the sweeping panorama of the history of the state of Texas in his 1985 novel of the same name. Beginning with the age of the conquistadores, those Spanish adventurers, and continuing to the wheeler-dealers of the twentieth-century economic booms and busts, Michener tells the story of a challenging land and the people who settled it.

This chapter will look at the construction of the novel and consider how the author has put together his saga, drawing his readers with him through the migrations, wars, and interactions of diverse peoples. It will also discuss the perspectives offered by the various characters, most imaginary but some actual historical figures, and the themes that play an important part in the development of a land and its citizens. In addition, the discussion of this novel will suggest how a feminist critic might read *Texas*.

PLOT DEVELOPMENT

Texas is organized as a framework story, resembling *Centennial* and *The Source* somewhat in its structure. The historical sections are presented within the framework of a Governor's Task Force composed of five citizens who are to make recommendations on how to instill a love for the uniqueness of Texas in the state's children. These citizens represent certain groups who came to Texas at different points in its history. The narrator of the pages dealing with the work of the task force is Professor Travis Barlow, whose ancestor arrived in Texas three days before the siege of the Alamo. His fellow members include Ransom Rusk, a Texas billionaire and descendant of a Quaker Indian agent; Lorenzo Quimper, "the prototypical Texas wheeler-dealer" (5), whose ancestors came from Tennessee in 1822; and Miss Lorena Cobb, the descendant of plantation owners who established themselves in the Texas of the 1840s. The final task force member is Professor Efraín Garza, who amazes the group with the announcement that his ancestor started exploring the area in 1539. The historical saga starts then with the story of Spanish-led explorations given from the point of view of an eleven-year-old mule driver, son of an Indian mother and a Spanish soldier.

The framework story continues after each historical section as the task force discusses the interpretation of the history it has just studied. The entire panorama is tied together by tracing the families of the task force members, a technique which keeps the reader's interest in the people as well as the events. As the novel moves into the present day, the task force participants become actors as well as reactors in the story.

Like the previous historical, panoramic novels *Texas* is divided into sections, each one telling the story of a particular time and people involved in the story. Before the narrative begins, Michener indicates in a few pages which characters and events are substantiated in history and which are invented to make his "honest blend of fiction and historical fact" (xiii). "Land of Many Lands" takes the young mule driver from Mexico up into the land that will be known as Texas, with all its variety of climate and terrain. Actual historical expeditions such as those in search of the Seven Cities of Gold are presented in the Michener manner—an interpretation of the events by the fictional character, in this case Garcilaçao, the young mule driver of mixed Spanish and Indian heritage, a *mestizo*. The reader sees the Spanish explorations through Garcilaçao's eyes, learning about honor and courage in the face of disappointments and death.

The following section presents the contributions of the Spanish in spreading Christianity into "Tejas." "The Mission" features the Franciscan order and two missionaries invented by Michener, Fray Damián de Saldaña and Fray Domingo Pacheco. The time period is the early 1700s and these Franciscan brothers serve their order, traveling all over the territory, building missions, and illustrating the humility of their faith.

Simón Garza, descendant of Garcilaçao, also is involved in this section, thereby maintaining continuity between the historical periods portrayed. Garza is a wood worker whose building talents are much appreciated by the Franciscans. And Fray Damián's brother Alvaro also comes to Tejas to serve as commander of the military detachment at Béxar, the settlement which will become San Antonio. The story of the two Franciscans' mission-building efforts is a poignant one, punctuated with violence and hardship as both brothers are killed by Apaches. But there are also some successes in furthering Christianity.

With an interlude devoted to the task force's studying the lasting legacy of the missions, the story moves onward to "El Camino Real." The time is now the late 1700s, and the Spanish influence is being modified by newcomers. Descendants of the de Saldañas carry the concern for the purity of Spanish blood, and Alvaro's son Don Ramón worries about finding a true Spaniard to be his granddaughter Trinidad's husband. His friend Don Lázaro Veramendi is more adaptable to the changes time brings. Don Lázaro notes that Spain cannot support its colonies, and new people and ideas will come to Tejas down El Camino Real from the new United States and the French territory of Louisiana rather than up from Mexico. And "El Camino Real" traces the interactions of the Spanish and the new groups. Don Rámon remains true to his ideals, dying in a duel with an American trader. Trinidad adapts to the changing scene by writing to Domingo Garza. Domingo, exiled to land near the Rio Grande with his family by Don Rámon some years before, returns to marry Trinidad, who thereby brings her Spanish heritage to a family already marked by courage, hard work, and artistic talent.

In "The Settlers" Michener brings in the Americans, through the story of Mattie and Jubal Quimper, who come from Tennessee with their son Yancey to escape bankruptcy. Since Catholic Mexico controls Tejas in the 1820s and decrees that only Catholics may own land, Father Clooney, an Irish priest who likes to drink, serves the needs of Protestants like the Quimpers by "converting" them so that they can obtain land in Tejas. Two actual historical figures make their appearance: Stephen Austin, who leads American settlers into Tejas to establish a colony, and Sam Houston, who plays an important military and later political role in this territory. The settlers face all the hardships of newcomers; for example, the Quimpers struggle to have enough to eat as they run a ferry and an inn of sorts. It's Mattie's courage and determination that give them their foothold in the new land and she will continue to pole the ferry across the river even after Jubal dies of cholera.

To continue his historical panorama Michener adds new ingredients to the mix in "The Trace." Finlay Macnab's wanderings lead him from Scotland to northern Ireland, the United States, and finally to Texas with his son Otto. The new American ingredient joins forces with the Hispanic when Benito Garza, son of Domingo and Trinidad, arranges marriages for his two sisters. One marries Finlay Macnab, and Otto has a mother to replace the one left in Baltimore. But the differences in cultural values—between the more relaxed Mexicans and the new, tense "Texicans"—perplex young Otto, giving him an ambivalent attitude for the rest of his life toward the group that has lived in Texas for more than a century.

Actual historical events play an important role in the section "Three Men, Three Battles," but the fictional characters continue to be essential in Michener's tracing of the development of Texas. Benito Garza is faced with his ties to his *Norteamericano* in-laws and his connections with Mexico, but he rides off to join Santa Anna's army, for "we can't rule side by side. We cannot be treated justly by men who hold us in contempt" (423–24). Michener portrays the events leading up to the siege of the Alamo, complete with the actions of Sam Houston, Davy Crockett, Jim Bowie, and General Santa Anna, and keeps the reader's interest in his fictional people by describing the battle from varying viewpoints. The Alamo is taken, the Texicans lose at Goliad, but Santa Anna is captured at San Jacinto. Tejas is now forever "Texas," its Spanish spelling replaced along with its leaders.

The story of Texas's development enters its next phase in "The Texicans," which presents the republic of Texas. The new nation finds it hard to establish a stable government in this land inhabited by individualistic citizens and faced with ongoing poverty. Michener keeps the reader's attention by including the adventures of his fictional characters like Yancey Quimper and Otto Macnab. Violence is also part of the republic's development as the goals of the North American settlers are to kill Mexicans and expel Indians; Otto and Benito Garza meet for the last time at the graves of Benito's two sisters, killed by the Comanches. In this section the author brings in another group that influences the development of Texas: Germans fleeing hunger and governmental restrictions.

Texas has been annexed by the United States in 1846, and the next section, "The Ranger," deals with the Mexican War of 1846–48. Otto Macnab is now a Texas Ranger and serves under the regular army officer, Lt. Col. Persifer Cobb. "The Ranger" presents history through the eyes of fictional Otto, and the reader participates in the war's battles and skirmishes. With the end of the war, Benito Garza and his wife retreat homeward, south across the Rio Grande, brokenhearted at the defeat and the destruction and suffering they see on their journey. Michener's panorama of war offers examples of courage but never loses sight of the death and pain that are also the results of battle.

The Cobbs are the fictional characters important in the section called "Loyalties." Col. Cobb returns to South Carolina following the Mexican War and takes over the family plantation, supplanting his brother Somerset. Somerset and his cousin Reuben migrate to Texas with their families to start a new cotton plantation, complete with slaves. The issue of slavery and whether it should be allowed in the new states joining the Union divide the Cobbs and many Texans from the policies of the U.S. Congress. When Sam Houston, serving as governor of Texas in 1861, refuses to deny the United States and swear allegiance to the Confederacy, Reuben and Somerset protect his right to speak but join the Confederate army to fight for the cause of the South. They serve at Vicksburg along with Otto Macnab. The description of that siege, and the efforts of the Cobb wives to keep the plantation going during the Civil War with the help of the slaves, makes historical events come alive through what happens to the fictional characters.

Relations between the white and Indian residents of Texas are the focus of the following section, "The Fort." President U.S. Grant's peace policy with the Indians is to win their allegiance with kindness, convert them to Christianity, and move them onto reservations. The churches are to handle this effort, to the disgust of many army personnel. Earnshaw Rusk, a Pennsylvania Quaker, is sent as a government agent to deal with the Comanches. This chapter of Texas history is filled with violence and bloodshed, with courageous black soldiers in a cavalry unit, with army wives bringing their own touch of civilization to the frontier, with Indians waging a futile struggle to keep their way of life. It concludes with Rusk and Emma Larkin, the Comanches' abused captive, beginning a new life at the fort no longer needed by the army.

"The Frontier" is the chronicle of the establishment of a town on the site of the fort. The Cobbs, the Rusks, the Quimpers, and Otto Macnab are all involved in the story of this part of Texas in the late nineteenth century. Earnshaw Rusk wants a civilized town on the fort site, including stores, schools, churches, and a newspaper, but Emma regrets the changes that will come to the open space. She trains wild horses and raises longhorn cattle to provide a living for the family. Little by little the open range is fenced to protect the cattle imported to improve the longhorn breed. The cattle drives from Texas to Kansas will be a thing of the past when access to all the water holes is cut off and the railroads are built. Also part of the town's development are descriptions of frontier justice where gunfire settles more disputes than courts do, of catastrophic weather, and of Italian stonemasons carving statues for the town's new courthouse. The town has been improved, but for Emma Rusk the cost has been too high. Future generations won't know the free-roaming buffalo, Indians, and longhorns.

As the panorama moves on in time the fictional town of Larkin becomes the example of all Texas towns faced with the changes brought about in the twentieth century. In "The Town" the reader finds natural disasters such as the boll weevil striking the Cobb cotton fields and man-made problems such as certain church groups preaching against the evils of dancing and the rise of the Klu Klux Klan to punish blacks and others who disagree with the Klansmen's theories and behavior. Oil exploration also transforms the town and starts the Rusk family on the way to a considerable fortune. And a new aspect of the Texas story enters with the mania for high school football.

Changes continue in "The Invaders," for new groups come to Texas in the years following World War II. Immigrants from northern states and others from Mexico looking for better economic opportunities add to the mix that is Texas. Even armadillos are part of the invasion, and Ransom Rusk's efforts to control the animals that have decided to live on his land become another example for Michener of the difficulties of coexistence with different groups. As Michener moves the Texas story along in this section by illustrating problems with people and with land through his characters' interactions, he tells about the Morrisons from Michigan who come when Todd is laid off from his job in the auto industry and Maggie loses her teaching post. Todd makes his way in real estate and is soon willing to compromise his ethics to take advantage of opportunities to make more money. He also discovers what it's like to go hunting in Texas—the fun of stalking wild turkey and quail. The Cobbs, a continuing part of the story, move farther west in Texas as water supplies diminish at their previous site. They feel their initial success will continue forever, but their underground water source, the Ogallala aquifer, is falling an inch per year. A tornado is the final invader, causing damage to Rusk's mansion and the town of Larkin.

"Power and Change," the title of the final section, presents modern-day Texas and the complexities of life that face all Texans. Again, it's Michener's fictional characters who make the problems of water rights, relations with the Hispanics, ethics in business, and problems of drugs and alcohol seem real and interesting as they interact and make decisions. Some of the task force members become part of the story's unfolding, and the task force recommendation about what Texas history schoolchildren should learn concludes the saga—with one last Texas extravaganza: Lorenzo Quimper throws a cattle sale complete with food, drink, and entertainment, and Ransom Rusk endows a new museum of art featuring sports. The task force has completed its work.

CHARACTER DEVELOPMENT

In a sweeping panorama of five centuries of history, it is the characters who move the story along, but as people they do not usually change and grow in important ways. Often they represent certain attitudes and belief systems that interpret the events as they happen and as they are remembered by subsequent generations. Yet many of the personalities that form *Texas* stay in the reader's memory because of their actions and reactions and the type of human beings they illustrate.

The members of the task force are interesting in themselves as they "reappear" after each historical section. They are "types" in that each represents a certain outlook and attitude about Texas. Travis Barlow is the professor who tries to maintain academic objectivity toward any controversial topic. The reader sees him in the mediator role but never really knows the man apart from his role. Ransom Rusk is the billionaire who views the world from the perspective of a developer of assets and property, and he feels that only property owners or people of means should vote because they have a stake in society and know what is best for it. Yet his human side is visible when the armadillos invade his estate. He refuses to shoot them when they destroy the lawn and bowling green, and he enjoys playing with these determined creatures. Lorenzo Quimper is a flamboyant supporter of all things Texan, from mesquite logs for barbecues to cowboy boots to Texas football. But he also helps Rusk endow a professorship in Texas studies at the university with Barlow as the first holder and has already donated funds to support professors of poetry and philosophy. Miss Cobb, a representative of polite and gentle behavior, is more open-minded than her wealthy colleagues, but even she is ready to help them throw out the visiting professor who speaks in a condescending manner about Texans and their intellectual contributions to the United States. Professor Garza is another academic type like Barlow, objective and interested in presenting all aspects of Texas history. He is more than able to hold his own against Rusk and Quimper when they want to ignore Hispanic contributions to the formation of Texas.

Professor Garza's sixteenth-century ancestor, Garcilaçao, is one of the more memorable participants in the Texas story. Michener shows Garcilaçao in action as the helper of a brutal mule driver and also in reflection as he accompanies Coronado's futile search for the Seven Cities of Gold. Garcilaçao sees the contradictions in human behavior during this expedition. His first mentor, Fray Marcos, turns out to have told lies in order to say what the Spaniards wanted to hear. Yet he treats all people as human beings and would not have allowed the Indian prisoners to be burned alive. Coronado's assistant Cárdenas orders the burning but is the one who manages to hold the expedition together by finding food and keeping the men's spirits up. At the end of the expedition, when Fray Padillo insists on returning to Indian country as a missionary even though he realizes he may be killed by the Indians he seeks to help, Garcilaçao understands the complete meaning of honor: a commitment to central beliefs along with physical and moral courage. This mestizo boy has interpreted the early Spanish presence north of the Rio Grande, and the reader applauds his eventual prosperity after marrying Fray Marcos's servant and inheriting those gold coins Fray Marcos had put aside over the years.

Fray Damián de Saldaña represents the devotion of the Catholic missionaries. He does his work for the Lord in humility and with great diligence. For example, he labors long hours to dig irrigation ditches that will enable the mission farm to prosper with adequate water. However, this saintly man has his less saintly moments: when the demanding immigrants from the Canary Islands insist on their own irrigation ditch, Fray Damián makes the mission's ditch deeper before the newcomers can divert much of the water. He is one of those sincere souls who brought light to the wilderness, and the human touches make him believable and likeable.

Mattie Quimper and her son Yancey portray two types of American settlers. Mattie is the determined, hard-working person who rises above adversity. She appreciates the space and land to call her own in Texas, and she will run her rough inn and the river ferry until she dies at the hands of Mexican soldiers. She has burned her inn and destroyed the ferry so they won't fall into the enemy's hands while her son has joined Sam Houston's army.

It is hard for readers to find Yancey sympathetic. Refusing to take risks during his growing-up years or even to work hard, he is a worry and concern to his mother. When he joins the army, he matures, gains confidence, and learns how to create his own legend. After the defeat of the Mexican army at San Jacinto, Yancey finds General Santa Anna hiding in the fields, completely demoralized. Yancey is known from then on as the brave captor of the enemy general and trades on this undeserved reputation for the rest of his life. Yancey cheats people and lies about his accomplishments. For Michener he appears to be the darker side of Texas confidence and self-promotion.

Otto Macnab's life spans several of the book's sections. He is an example of the boy who shows courage and determination from a young age and remains steadfast in what he must do. Michener shows Otto in action, as a child struggling with a bear who is trying to get his food, as a mature Texas Ranger carrying out his duties. And he also gives his readers a glimpse of Otto's thoughts on right and wrong. At the age of ten, Otto worries about his father's partner taking cattle that aren't his. By fifteen, Otto is a realist, having learned from the battles in the Mexican War that "for a man to make a mark in this world, he had better have a tough core of righteousness which he should allow nothing to scar . . ." (528). This tough core of righteousness stays with him until he is killed, in the line of duty, by Amos Peavine, arms dealer to the Indians.

Another character who appears in several sections is Benito Garza, son of Trinidad de Saldaña and Domingo Garza. Called a Mexican by the incoming North American settlers, Benito considers himself a true resident of Tejas. He teaches Otto Macnab how to ride and saves his life at Goliad. But the contempt he receives from most Anglos stings his pride. When Benito must choose sides, he goes with his Mexican-Spanish heritage, for he cannot accept the denial of its values and its contributions by the settlers from such places as Kentucky and Tennessee. Known as a bandit by the Texans, Benito sees himself as a patriot as he spends the rest of his life fighting to recover what he considers his own. Michener does not hesitate to show the violence that is a part of Benito but portrays also the person who holds steadfastly to a cause.

The Cobbs from South Carolina and Georgia with their black slaves represent another type of settler moving into Texas in the 1850s. The Cobbs are courageous and determined in establishing their way of life in the new land, and they are convinced that their slaves are happy serving enlightened masters. When Petty Prue Cobb, managing the plantation during the Civil War, sends her cotton under the supervision of two slaves to run the blockade, Jaxifer chooses freedom and crosses the Rio Grande. Trajan returns to the plantation because as a man of honor, he must discharge the responsibility he had been given. He leaves when freedom is proclaimed for all slaves, saying to Petty Prue: "You can say I was faithful, because I was. And you can say I come back when I could of run away, because I did. And you can say I was respectful, because I liked the way you handled this plantation with the men gone, Miss Prue. I tried to be a good slave, but don't never say I liked it" (789). He agrees to work for the Cobbs as an employee but keeps his own place to live. It's a matter of principle that the Cobbs are finally able to accept. Jaxifer later becomes a cavalry troop leader for the army and explains to Captain Wetzel why the army has so little trouble with the black cavalry unit: "We ain't never before had honor, but we got it now, and we will not risk it" (853). Again, the characters with fortitude and their individual honor are those the reader remembers.

Earnshaw Rusk and Emma Larkin portray this same fortitude and honor as they play their part in the settlement of Texas. Earnshaw is the idealist, believing in the Comanche Indians whose allegiance he has been sent to win. Crushed when the Comanche prove as faithless to treaties as the whites, he finds other causes to promote in the town he works to establish. Earnshaw's plans may not always work out, but his sincere and energetic efforts to do what he feels is right make him unforgettable.

Emma, the settlers' daughter captured, violated, and mutilated by the Comanche, has the courage to survive her years in captivity and to make a life for herself in spite of her dark years. She refuses to give up her rights to her parents' land, marries Earnshaw, and raises her cattle. Her last act is to give some longhorns to a national project for restoring the breed. After supervising the delivery of the cattle, Emma dies soon after the car bringing her back to Texas crosses the state line.

Maggie and Todd Morrison, who come to Texas after layoffs in Detroit, are the new settlers. Michener uses the Morrisons to represent two responses to the challenges all new settlers face. In twentieth-century Texas it's no longer Indians and wild animals but opportunities to make money. How a person responds reveals his or her character. Todd is willing to compromise his personal ethics in his pursuit of financial success. The potential for quick money blinds him to a sense of right and wrong, and he is finally killed by the manager of his game ranch who can no longer stand Todd's petty schemes and his use of the farm to make money rather than saving endangered species. Maggie Morrison has greater strength of character, and as she adapts to Texas life, she prospers honestly in real estate transactions. She portrays the person of courage and integrity, although the reader does wonder when Maggie marries Ransom Rusk if she will accept his belief that only people of means should have the right to vote.

THEMATIC CONSIDERATIONS

The social and cultural context of Texas provides many illustrations of one of Michener's most permanent themes: the interactions of different ethnic, racial, religious, and cultural groups and how misunderstandings and lack of understanding of the Other lead to problems between the groups and even atrocities. Throughout the centuries presented in the novel, examples show that no group is immune from attitudes of superiority toward those whose values and ways of life appear to be different. Yet each group makes contributions to the civilization that develops, and the framework story of the novel brings out these contributions in specific ways and urges recognition of their value.

Those Spanish born in Spain present one aspect of this theme: the concern with the purity of the bloodline. And this concern influences the actions of the Spanish born in Mexico. They work to preserve Spanish civilization as they know it, which means forbidding all intermarriage with anyone who might have an Indian or even French ancestor. Don Rámon de Saldaña is obsessed with finding the proper Spanish husband for his granddaughter, yet she marries the son of ranch employees because change comes inevitably and those who can adapt, survive.

The pages of *Texas* are full of the atrocities committed by one group on another, the darkest side of the sense of superiority toward the Other. The Apaches' torture of Franciscan friars is nauseating, as is the Spaniards' burning alive the inhabitants of a captured village. Santa Anna's army kills its prisoners at Goliad, and the Texan army retaliates after San Jacinto. The Comanches mutilate Emma Larkin horribly after torturing and killing her family, and the U.S. Army plus the Texas Rangers basically exterminate the Indians in Texas. And the rangers kill as many Mexicans as they can find as they chase the remnants of Santa Anna's army back across the Rio Grande. The long-term results of all this violence in Texas are to be seen in the continuing difficulties between the Anglo and Hispanic communities. Task force chairman Barlow foresees no easy solution.

Otto Macnab and Benito Garza had already expressed the dilemma faced by Anglos and Hispanics when trying to understand each other's values. Even at age eleven Otto felt the ambivalence involved in two different cultures. Benito's sister Maria was like a mother to him, and her relaxed manner toward life was "in harmony with the birds and the rising sun" (405). But Otto also saw the violence in Benito and his encouragement of any deed if it took advantage of an Anglo. Benito, in spite of respecting people like Mattie Quimper and the Macnabs, sees the Anglos in general as despising his religion, mocking his language, laughing at his actions, and treating Mexican women with contempt: "If they insist on ridiculing everything we stand for, how can they hope to share our land with us?" (424).

The task force members, through their discussions with experts, must come to terms with their own definitions and feelings about the various groups that have created Texas. Through their opinions and the various characters in this fact-filled fiction, Michener presents the paradoxes and contradictions that characterize all cultures and their histories. For example, Ransom Rusk wants to downplay any mention of the influence of Catholicism, but the friar who speaks to the group about the legacy of the early missions reminds them that the early friars' influence would have been nothing without their devotion to the Christian faith. And the contradictions among the Protestant settlers and citizens even into the twentieth century are also brought out in detail. One minister in the 1920s crusaded against horse racing, gambling, and alcohol but won an argument by shooting his opponent in the back. A jury acquitted him of murder. The expert who speaks on "Religion in Texas" concludes by saying that Texas honors religion more than most states: "Basic to everything we do is a reverence for religion, but we insist upon constructing our own theology" (315).

In Hawaii the intermingling of cultural groups creates the "Golden Man," an individual open to new ideas and willing to work toward a more harmonious society. In Texas the frontier spirit predominates, with its emphasis on personal freedom—for those Anglos who had the power. "Texas did not provide a cadre of philosophers who agonized over this basic contradiction of freedom for everyone like me, slavery or extermination for anyone different" (614). The Morrisons' daughter learns that Texas must not be judged by standards of other states, for it was a sovereign nation and still forms an empire off to itself.

This empire faces bravely the many problems of its tangled heritage as it makes its way toward the twenty-first century. And the task force's final report reflects this attitude. Rusk signs a minority report of one, refusing any emphasis on the multicultural aspects of Texas history and supporting a return to the simple, Anglo-Saxon Protestant virtues that, according to him, had made the state great. Professor Garza has his own minority report that urges bilingual education at least through the sixth grade. And no one will join Miss Cobb in her statement that Texas history should be taught by trained history teachers. Quimper points out that there has to be some role for the football coaches in the off season. Barlow justifies his lack of concrete support by noting that he wants the report accepted. "Texas history might be revered, but Texas football was sacred" (1299). The final two paragraphs of the report are revised to summarize what kind of future Texans must work toward: one in which they join moral and intellectual leadership to financial power. The problem of how the Texans of various backgrounds will work out their differences and misunderstandings is not solved in this novel, but in creating a panorama that presents the positives and negatives of Texas history and culture, Michener never loses sight of his idea that a civilization is only as strong as its component parts as they accept each other and work together.

In addition to the relationships of people to each other, Michener also presents the relationships of people to the land and the animal world as an important part of the historical panorama of the story he is telling. In *Texas* the reader sees his concern for the environment in the story of the extermination of the buffalo, the saving of the longhorns, the game farm with its hunters, and problems of water sources and rights.

The last buffalo hunt near the fictional town of Larkin is a poignant reminder that animals give way to people's needs. An aging chief of the Comanches comes from the reservation with fourteen young boys, requesting permission to hunt the old buffalo on the Rusks' land. Only half of the boys have ever seen a buffalo, this long-time source of food and skins for the Indians. The hunt is conducted according to long-established ritual, and the last symbol of the free and mobile life of the Indians is killed.

By the 1920s the longhorns are nearly as extinct as the buffalo, and the U.S. Congress passes a bill with an appropriation to set up a refuge. However, very few pure-bred longhorns in good condition can be found, until Emma Larkin and her herd are located. Emma does not want to sell but is convinced of the project's value and offers calves and cows descended from her prize animals, Mean Moses and Bathtub Bertha. People are beginning to learn that they and animals must learn to occupy the planet together for the health of all.

The game farm is started by Todd Morrison and colleagues, including Roy Bub, the man who digs sewers. It's Roy Bub who loves animals beyond the interest in hunting. He starts buying exotic creatures, those in danger of extinction. The sable antelopes are the crowning acquisition that Roy Bub means to preserve. Shooting them will be forbidden, but a sable antelope is the one trophy Ransom Rusk lacks. However, once he realizes what Roy Bub's goals are for the vanishing breeds, he regrets his trophy, obtained when Morrison knows Roy Bub will be gone, and decides to buy out Morrison and create a game ranch that Roy Bub can manage in the way he sees fit. Rusk is realizing the need for balance in nature.

The question of water is another difficult problem to solve. The cotton-growing Cobbs move their operations to drier lands in West Texas in order to escape the cotton-destroying boll weevil. They plan to tap into the Ogallala aquifer, the vast underground water system formed by springs and runoffs from rain and melting snow and stretching hundreds of miles under the middle section of the United States. Wells, sunk deep into the aquifer, will irrigate the dry land for cotton. But like all resources that are used without being replenished, this one too will start to disappear. After years without the average sixteen inches of rain, the many wells that must be dug even deeper indicate that the aquifer's water level is lowering. Sherwood Cobb is farseeing enough to anticipate future problems in the use of this precious resource. Every user, from the rancher to the oilman to the farmer to the fisherman, appreciates the need for water to be conserved as long as his inherited rights are not restricted. Cobb becomes a member of the water commission, and during the drought of 1983 he works tirelessly to establish a reasonable water-use policy. At the same time he helps those suffering from the drought's effects. When a record-setting cold spell hits the lands along the Rio Grande, he works with Mayor Simón Garza of Bravo, who has the same grasp of reality. The two agree that Texans, like all inhabitants of planet earth, are restricted by what the land will allow, and those who forget that fact are in trouble.

In *Texas* Michener presents the land and its peoples in a panorama that protrays both the good and the bad of the Texas legend and the Texas character, that celebrates what is of value from the past, that shows what is needed to continue into the future. As John Kings has stated, Michener "is able as a writer to remind us of the essential values that go to the making of a healthy society" (Kings 1978, 15). Vision and hard work are illustrated in a variety of ways in this novel, and the importance of fully utilizing human resources as well as respecting natural resources is emphasized.

A FEMINIST READING OF *TEXAS*

Reading this novel from the feminist perspective as described in Chapter 3 requires that special attention be paid to cultural history. Michener is presenting images of women in this narrative against the background of the ongoing story of a certain place during a time period of several hundred years. Historically, in many societies women had specific roles and duties. A feminist reader of *Texas* must keep that fact in mind while evaluating the authenticity of women characters and attitudes toward them in this novel.

Texas history and culture are punctuated by violence, from the voyages of the Spanish explorers to the "frontier justice" dispensed with firearms which lasts into the twentieth century. In this type of world women are viewed almost solely in terms of their relationship to and with men. Michener recognizes this reality and tells the story "as it is." However, he is able to create women characters who go beyond the stereotype of supportive wife and are women of strength and conviction.

The upper-class Spanish culture as transposed to Mexico and then Tejas treats its women as cherished possessions. The promenade of the young women of marriageable age described in "The Mission" chapter shows how ritualized the courtship behavior has become in order to protect these precious objects. Benita Liñán is stereotypically lively and flirtatious as she participates in this parade, but she becomes the essential Spanish wife and mother once she marries Alvaro de Saldaña. Her descendant Trinidad de Saldaña breaks out somewhat from the protective custody of her culture, but her reason for doing so is to obtain a husband. Her grandfather has been killed, her lands have been taken from her, and she writes to a man of lower social status and rides off with him to a new life, to be loved and cherished as the mother of a large family. The stereotype has not been broken, but it is realistic in the context of the culture it illustrates.

With Mattie Quimper, the settler from Tennessee, the strong woman meets the frontier. Mattie is the guiding force in her family. She has found her home in Texas and is determined to keep it. When Jubal suggests returning to Tennessee, she offers him his freedom; she herself plans to stay in Texas, running the small ferry and inn. After Jubal's death, she refuses marriage proposals and lives her independent life until she is killed by Mexican troops.

Lucha López is another fighter like Mattie, only her cause is that of the Mexicans who realize the North Americans settling Texas will leave no place for them. When she meets Benito Garza she has found a kindred spirit. She refuses a home and children to marry Benito and share in the revolution. Her parents will not permit the marriage, but Lucha and Benito find a priest who goes against custom and law to perform the ceremony. She breaks the stereotype imposed on her by her culture and supports her cause side-by-side with her husband.

The Civil War broadens Petty Prue Cobb's image as Reuben's supportive wife; she must run the cotton plantation while the men are off at war. She is equal to the task with the help of her slaves. At the end of the war, with Reuben killed, she marries Somerset, whose wife has died. When he is elected to the U.S. Senate, her diplomatic efforts with President Grant and other congressmen obtain Somerset positions on important committees, for she promotes reconciliation after the horrors of the war. Petty Prue may excuse herself when the men talk politics over their cigars, but she is a self within the constraints of her time and her culture.

Emma Larkin Rusk's experiences on the frontier set her apart from the usual stereotypes. She survives capture and mutilation and refuses the arrangements the army wives want to make for her. She has land and will live on it. Emma marries Earnshaw Rusk, another misfit, and while supportive of his projects, she goes her own way, training horses and saving the longhorn cattle breed from extinction. Her fortitude provides a role model of what a resolute woman can accomplish in spite of adversity.

The more traditional women are the army wives at Fort Garner in the late nineteenth century. They find ways to civilize life in a rude army post without luxuries, and they uphold the conventional moral standards. Louise Reed, wife of the fort commander, tries hard to counsel the straying wife who belittles her husband and his work and begins an affair with another soldier. A wife's role is to love and help her husband, taking pride in his accomplishments. These army wives do their duty as they see it and are authentic within the social confines of their culture.

Maggie Morrison is the most fully realized woman character in the novel's last chapters. Honest in her business affairs, she sees her husband building his real estate empire by cheating his friends subtly: "He had been a good husband and a better father, but she could not escape realizing that under pressure he had revealed himself as a shifty, small-caliber man" (1260). Maggie is able to succeed in a male-dominated business world with her courage, character, intelligence, and honesty. It is not clear in the narrative why she decides to marry Ransom Rusk as the story winds down, but her independent reality has been established through the professional career she has forged for herself.

In *Texas* Michener has succeeded in relating the history of a male-oriented culture that prides itself on its chivalry toward women. One of the task force's scholars, a woman, summarizes how women are viewed in Texas: "You cherished us, honored us, protected us, but you also wanted us to stay to hell in our place. In no state of the Union does a woman enjoy a higher social status than in Texas. She is really revered. But in few states does she enjoy more limited freedoms" (795–96). When Lorenzo Quimper retorts that he is proud of the way he treats women, the scholar responds to his point about chivalry: "Chivalry is a man's determination of how he should treat women. It's his definition, not hers. I would like to see a somewhat juster determination of the relationship" (796). Quimper's attitudes are not changed, Maggie's daughter Beth chooses to become a cheerleader and not a poet, but reading the novel from a feminist perspective reveals authentic women characters and a realistic portrait of women in a particular culture developing over a four-hundred-year span.

10

Alaska
(1988)

The challenges of Alaska, the Great Land, are the material from which James Michener fashions the fifth of his historical, panoramic novels about these United States. *Alaska* was published in 1988, and it traces the development of the land, the animals, and the people of this place of "great beauty but also implacable hostility" (22). The beauty of the mountains, the valleys, the rivers, and the ocean is as overwhelming as the harsh climate that tests all living things. From the first settlers known to later generations as Athapascans to the modern-day oil workers, from the Russian explorers to the gold seekers, from the missionaries to the farmers, all the humans coming to the Great Land are attracted to its richness. Some grow with the land, others despoil it, many fall under its spell, and Michener tells their stories with his usual mixture of historical events seen through the eyes and actions of fictional characters.

Plot development or how Michener tells the overall story will be discussed in this chapter. Character development and thematic concerns will also be analyzed. The chapter will conclude with a consideration of the novel from the viewpoint of a feminist critic.

PLOT DEVELOPMENT

Before beginning Alaska's story, Michener notes which events and people are factual and which are fictional. This technique helps readers orient themselves within the story and reminds them that Michener's narratives interpret history as well as display the events and people that make up its parts. To structure this novel, he uses the collection of episodes that tell of specific events at specific times and in specific places. With *Alaska* Michener dispenses with the framework story he devised to connect the parts of the narrative in such historical, panoramic novels as *The Source, Centennial, Texas,* and *Mexico.* Instead, the anonymous yet omniscient narrator provides the viewpoint from which the characters and their stories are seen.

As he did in *Centennial,* the writer wants to be sure his readers understand the land before they meet its inhabitants. Chapter One, "The Clashing Terranes," provides the geological explanation of the formation of Alaska. The theories presented regarding the movement of tectonic plates under the ocean and land are still being refined by scholars, indicates Michener in his opening pages. The point of view in this chapter is that of the author-narrator, and the tone is informative.

This tone and point of view continue in Chapter Two, "The Ice Castle," as the formation and movement of glaciers in general are explained. Readers intrigued with how things come to be will find this chapter's information of special interest. After explaining the origin of the land connection between Asia and Alaska, Michener brings in the animals. He focuses on the habits of the mastodons and then the woolly mammoths, developing with these descriptions the portrait of the land itself. As he did in *Centennial* and *Chesapeake,* Michener makes a character out of certain animals; in this story it is Matriarch the woolly mammoth whose protectiveness for her offspring is highlighted. Michener's imaginative tale of how the mammoth herd lives and dies will appeal to readers who enjoy animal stories; other readers will find it difficult to accept speculation about the mammoth's reasoning ability. The writer moves the story on to the arrival of human beings when Matriarch's granddaughter is finally killed by two-legged creatures.

Michener uses a starting date of 29,000 years before the present era to bring people into the narrative in Chapter Three, "People of the North." These people are not anonymous, for Michener gives them names and a history to explain how they migrated to the cold, northern lands of Siberia from the warmer south. In the never-ending search for food, a small group of these people manages to cross the land that connects the Asian continent to Alaska at that point in time. The reader learns about their appearance and their culture, which had enabled them to survive in Arctic regions. They are considered the ancestors of the Athapascan Indians.

Eskimos come 14,000 years before the present era in the Michener chronology. Again, the people are given a personalized history for their migration. Oogruk is an outsider in his clan because of his poverty and appearance, and after he is blamed for an unsuccessful whale hunt, he decides to build a kayak to hold himself, his wife, her four-year-old daughter, and his father-in-law for his successful voyage to the new land. The next group arrives on the peninsula near the land bridge between the continents about twelve thousand years before the present era, and their coming is verified by archaeological evidence. This group's life is seen through the eyes of Azazruk, who hears the voices of the spirits and becomes his people's shaman, or wise man. When life becomes too difficult on the peninsula, Azazruk's group moves on, finally settling what is now the Aleutian Island chain. A mummy is found on their new island home, which Michener names Lapak. Azazruk calls the land from which his group had come the Great Land, or Alaxsxaq in the Aleutian people's language. Europeans will condense the name to "Alaska."

Chapter Four, "The Explorers," features the Russian traders, the English sailors, and the American whalers who will bring the European presence to Alaska. The Russian venture involves three historical personages: Tsar Peter the Great along with a Danish sea captain in Peter's service, Vitus Bering, and a German scientist, Georg Steller. The fictional character is a cossack from Ukraine named Trofim Zhdanko. Zhdanko's courage in action in Siberia, where he was sent as a prisoner, brings him to the tsar's notice and he is to be Peter's eyes and ears on the expedition to learn more about the land to the east and to see what other countries have a presence there. Michener moves his narrative along with full descriptions of the weather, land, and peoples that the explorers encounter during voyages that begin in 1740. Both Peter the Great and Captain Bering have died by the time the first Russian group arrives in the Aleutians in 1745 to "conquer" Alaska. Relations with the Aleuts are tense from the beginning in spite of Zhdanko's efforts, as the Russians treat the native inhabitants brutally and kill the sea otter indiscriminately for their pelts.

In 1778 Captain James Cook of England stops in the Aleutians during his well-documented voyage in the Pacific Ocean. For purposes of the story, Michener has the English land on his fictional island of Lapak, and Cook's lieutenant George Vancouver meets Zhdanko and his brutal stepson, but the Russians and English have no one who can speak the other's language.

The American presence enters these waters with fictional Captain

Noah Pym and his whaling ship. His adventures along the north coast of Alaska allow Michener to bring in the Eskimos and their culture. Captain Pym and his crew spend several months with the Eskimos as his ship is caught in the winter polar ice. The Americans bring rum to the Eskimo with disastrous consequences for this group, which cannot tolerate alcohol.

The story moves east from Lapak to Kodiak in the following chapter, "The Duel." By 1789, with nearly all the sea otters in this part of the sea killed, the Russians basically exterminate the Aleuts on Lapak Island by taking all the men to Kodiak. Michener recounts how the great-grandmother left on the island encourages the women to work for their own survival by killing their first whale. The narration of the trip is engrossing and brings to the forefront a new fictional character, Cidaq. As great-grandmother feels there is no future on Lapak, she sends her great-grandaughter Cidaq to Kodiak, but the girl is raped and beaten during the trip. Life for the Aleuts continues to be brutal. The duel between the Aleuts' religion and Russian Christianity involves the reader as efforts are made to convert Cidaq so that she can marry Rudenko, one of her Russian torturers on the ship. A marriage will save him from being sent back to the Pribilof Islands to hunt seals under inhuman conditions. Cidaq is willing to play the game and refuses at the last minute so that Rudenko will be punished for his crimes. The Aleut shaman, Lunasaq, does not approve of playing with religion and asks Cidaq, "Is there anything . . . any one thing you can think of . . . any good thing their god has given us? And is there any good thing which we already had which they have not taken away?" (291). When a new Russian Orthodox priest arrives, he is able to convince Cidaq of the important role of women in the Orthodox faith and of "the wondrous message of redemption and forgiveness and love" (316). She becomes Sofia and says farewell to the shaman and his mummy. The new priest is Vasili Voronov, nephew of Zhdanko's widow, destined by his aunt for church leadership, and Sofia is his first convert. Rudenko is still brutal and beats the shaman who tries to intervene in the wedding and then he beats his wife. The priest helps the shaman, but this last reminder of Aleut religion is eventually murdered by Sofia's husband and his cronies. Aleksandr Baranov, sent from Russia to manage the settlement, has established a discipline of sorts and sentences Rudenko to permanent service on the Pribilofs. The story becomes more dramatic with a tidal wave that kills Rudenko and others, but Sofia is put in charge of the orphaned children and then marries Vasili. Christianity has won the duel with shamanism but at the cost of eliminating nearly the entire Aleut population. "And even those few who survived, like Cidaq, did so only by merging themselves into the victorious civilization" (337).

The next part of Alaska's story tells about the Russian move to southeast Alaska and the ongoing conflict with the Tlingit Indians who live there. In Chapter Six, "Lost Worlds," Michener portrays the Tlingit way of life through the experiences of Raven-heart. He interacts first with the Americans, who bring rum and guns, and then with the Russians, who want to take over Tlingit lands. After a crushing defeat of the Tlingits, recounted with all the violent details, the Russians have some productive years at Sitka, which they call "New Archangel." However, Baranov as a member of the merchant class is scorned by the Russian nobility, and conflicts are part of life in New Archangel. The story continues with the characters, fictional and historical, moving on in their lives and work. After his education in Russia, Arkady Voronov, the son of Vasili and Sofia, returns as the colony's assistant administrator. Vasili goes back to Russia to rise in the church hierarchy. When the Tlingits are defeated again, Sofia works valiantly toward reconciliation of the two groups. The Russians continue their exploration of the Great Land, and Arkady and his wife get to the far north along the Yukon River. However, the colony's eventual destiny is being decided far from its shores. The United States buys Alaska in 1867. The takeover is disorderly, with Russians evicted from their quarters, their cathedral damaged extensively, and Tlingits killed. When Arkady's wife is nearly raped by American soldiers, the couple leaves their long-time home and flees Sitka.

In Chapter Seven, "Giants in Chaos," Michener creates sea captain Emil Schransky to illustrate a part of the lawlessness that prevailed in the historical Alaska of the mid-nineteenth century. Captain Schransky is a law unto himself in these seas. He kills seals indiscriminately, especially pregnant females, and does a booming trade in rum and molasses in villages on both sides of the Bering Sea, teaching the inhabitants to distill their own rum from the molasses. The story of Alaska at this point is one of depletion of the land and its original people but of increasing riches for certain outsiders.

The Tlingits in the Sitka area decide to take advantage of the lawlessness that prevails in that region, too. They infiltrate the town and the surrounding land, not with plans for warfare but with hopes for "fair ownership of the land, assured supplies of food and hardware and cloth, some kind of sensible control of salmon fishings, and a just participation in the lawmaking procedure" (483–84). Worried American settlers travel by canoe to Prince Rupert in Canada to ask for help. The Canadian ship that steams into Sitka Harbor discourages the Tlingits, who realize they won't receive justice in the foreseeable future.

Interesting portraits of two American giants in terms of their influence on the development of Alaska conclude this part of the story. Michael Healy, a captain of a U.S. government revenue cutter, is determined to stop Schransky's illegal and immoral trade in sealskins and rum. Sheldon Jackson, a Presbyterian missionary, is equally determined to establish his church in this vast area. These actual historical characters are seen in action with the land, the ocean, and the people. When Healy gets a well-designed, well-built ship, he does chase Schransky from the Bering Sea. Jackson, with massive lobbying efforts and his own tireless labors, does establish a Christian mission presence in remote areas of Alaska. He is even instrumental in dividing Alaska into spheres of influence for various Christian denominations. Both men made enemies by the way they went about their work, but they served Alaska with ability and determination, notes the narrator.

Michener introduces gold to Alaska's story in Chapter Eight, called appropriately enough "Gold." He begins with an explanation of how gold is formed in the earth and how it can be discovered. The actual discoveries of gold in the Canadian Klondike are shown in action, but the fictional characters in this chapter add the interest movement to the narration. John Klope's trip to the goldfields by boat and dog sled is representative of all the gold seekers in 1897–98. The role of the "frozen North" in all that happens is highlighted as Michener involves his reader in that sense of place that is so important in the historical, panoramic novels. Other characters in the saga are Buck and Tom Venn, father and son, who are traveling with a woman named Missy Peckham. This group approaches the Klondike over the Chilkoot Pass from Skagway, in southeast Alaska. Again, the details and the hardships are a vivid part of the narrative. How the characters react to their experiences illustrates Michener's belief that ordinary people are capable of extraordinary feats of courage and hard work when necessary. Life at the goldfields is as hard as the various ways of getting there, and Michener's mix of description and dialogue makes the reader part of this life. What happens to the Venns, Missy, Klope, and new arrival Matt Murphy tells the story as it applies to the representative participants in the great gold-rush adventure of the end of the nineteenth century.

The second Alaskan gold rush takes place in the Arctic, when three reindeer herders—a Norwegian, a Laplander, and a Siberian—find gold on the sandy beaches at Nome. Chapter Nine, "The Golden Beaches of Nome," tells this part of the story, showing the lawlessness often present in a new settlement as well as the successes and failures of those rushing north to seek wealth and adventure. Tom Venn reappears in the narrative, setting up a store for the Seattle firm Ross & Raglan. Missy Peckham and Matt Murphy also come to Nome, and Missy gets a job as secretary to a newly arrived federal judge. Michener depicts this phase of Alaska's history through the activities of the fictional characters, presenting the details that bring a gold rush to life and portray its decline.

The life cycle of one salmon serves as the framework for Chapter Ten, "Salmon." Nerka comes to life in a lake near Juneau in southeast Alaska. Michener names his fictional lake Pleiades and makes it a center for the action of the chapter. Tom Venn's interactions with the Bigears family also frame this section of the story and give Michener the opportunity to present the Tlingit way of life in the early twentieth century, including the tale of a potlach to raise the totem carved by Sam Bigears. Tom's boss, Malcolm Ross of Ross & Raglan, has big plans for a salmon cannery and chooses a site on a headland facing Sam Bigears's cabin on Lake Pleiades. The story of the Seattle-controlled salmon industry as illustrated by the Ross & Raglan venture is one of a single-minded purpose: take as many fish as possible, ignore any concern for future stock, and work to replace fishermen and cannery workers by mechanical devices. Canadian officials finally protest the tactics of taking as many fish as possible by using traps on the rivers so the salmon can't return to their spawning grounds. The life cycle of Nerka and his fellow salmon is being interrupted for the profit of non-Alaskans. When Missy and Matt come to Juneau seeking new opportunities after the end of the Nome gold rush, Missy sees how the profit motive governing the "outsiders" is impacting the Alaska residents, Indian and white. She has found a cause, even if Nerka and his fellow sockeye salmon are doomed in the Lake Pleiades area.

The story of Alaska continues to be affected by economic control from Seattle. Chapter Eleven, "The Railbelt," begins with the explanation of the Jones Act passed by the U.S. Congress in 1920. This law decreed that goods could be carried from one American port to another only in ships built in the United States by American labor. The fictional Ross & Raglan ships have a virtual monopoly on transportation of goods and materials to Alaska so can set their own prices. With his use of ordinary people such as the Anchorage storekeeper ruined by shipping costs, Michener involves the reader emotionally in the injustices he sees in Alaska's history.

This history moves forward in time when farmers from such areas as Minnesota come to the Matanuska Valley along the railroad from Anchorage to Fairbanks. The Flatch family is typical of the new settlers and they participate in the ongoing events of the story. They are individualized through their special interests: the daughter Flossie has an affinity for the wild creatures of her new home, father Elmer wants to hunt and be a guide, and son LeRoy becomes a pilot, one of the many courageous ones who will enable people to travel to inaccessible parts of the Great Land. Missy and Matt come to the valley, too, on assignment from Alaska's territorial government to represent its interests, and Missy helps the new residents establish their society. The work is hard but the adventures are exhilarating. These characters will all be involved in different ways when World War II begins. Elmer Flatch will help build the Alcan Highway, the road which would finally connect far off Alaska with the forty-eight contiguous states. Michener describes the construction with his customary attention to bringing alive people and events through description and dialogue. Flossie Flatch's part-Indian boyfriend, Nate Coop, serves as a scout in the Aleutians. After the war, questions about statehood for Alaska resurface. Does Alaska have the people or the power to be one of the states of the Union or will it always need help from "outside"? The two sides are represented by Tom Venn, now an even more important businessman, supported by LeRoy Flatch, the bush pilot, and Missy Peckham plus Flossie and Nate Coop. The Venns think the territory cannot manage independently while Missy is sure that the courage of the Alaskans has made them eligible for statehood. Finally, in 1958 the U.S. Congress makes Alaska the forty-ninth state.

The novel's final chapter, "The Rim of Fire," brings the story to the present day, dealing with such issues as the Alaska Native Claims Settlement Act, the oil boom, and Alaska's geography. The interactions of Jeb Keeler with Poley Markham provide the chapter's framework. These two lawyers are eager to help the Alaska natives with the legal ramifications of setting up corporations to administer the newly acquired lands. Vladimir Afanasi, who can include a bit of Russian in his ancestry, represents the Eskimo-Indian commitment to subsistence living—that is, hunting and fishing as his ancestors did. He wants "enough safe land for the houses of my village, enough free ocean to ensure the harvest of the sea" (1155). Schoolteacher Kendra Scott, who comes to Desolation Point near Barrow, discovers the difficulties involved in helping a group adjust to new wealth without losing the values of their culture. And "outsiders" are always interested in the riches of Alaska. Japanese and

Russians discuss plans in their two countries for taking over the state economically for the former and militarily for the latter. However, Alaska's geography is still an important part of its panoramic history. Michener returns to the geological, geographic considerations of the first chapter by presenting the work of a volcanologist who studies earthquakes, volcanoes, and tidal waves and the labors of scientists living on a floating ice island in the Arctic. A fictional tsunami, an earthquake-generated tidal wave, has the last word in Alaska's story. It sweeps away Jeb Keeler, who wants the native corporations to succeed, while sparing Poley Markham, who is looking to profit from their financial failures. The reader is left with the impression that Alaska's future, like its past, will not be determined by those who are there to make their homes.

CHARACTER DEVELOPMENT

Pioneers are the characters in *Alaska*. As such, they represent the courage and endurance needed to settle and develop new lands. In this narrative Michener does not emphasize the family strands that move the story from one time period to the next as he does in such novels as *Chesapeake* and *The Covenant*. There are some connections between generations, but they are not as important as each new group of people who test themselves against the land and its climate. Certain characters do remain in the reader's memory for their personality, their perseverance, or as illustrations of the heroic in human endeavor, but most of the cast is memorable only for showing how history happens because of what people do when faced with new and different challenges.

Among the early Russians Trofim Zhdanko stands out for his courage and endurance in action but also for his human side, which treats the Aleuts as human beings and tries to control the violence and cruelty of his stepson and those Russians whose greed alone drives their actions.

The Aleut girl Cidaq represents the meeting of two cultures, and she is seen in enough different situations to become more individualized. While starving on Lapak she has the courage to support her great-grandmother's efforts to break the taboos against women hunting whales. She is able to survive brutal treatment from the Russians and face the challenges of the new ways brought by Russian Christianity, which she learns about on Kodiak. She accepts the Christian message of love and redemption preached by Father Vasili Voronov and maintains her faithfulness through the years, always working toward reconciliation and understanding between natives and whites. As Sofia, a Christianized Aleut, she even understands when, after years of marriage with Vasili, he must dissolve their union in order to become a bishop and start his climb in the Russian Orthodox church hierarchy. She is a character made vivid by her situation and sympathetic as she identifies again at the end of her life with the Tlingits, another group who must cope with new settlers wanting to take over their land, with little concern for or interest in their way of life.

Vasili Voronov himself is interesting in his representation of the best of the Russian Orthodox presence in a new land. Sincerely wishing to convert the pagan Aleuts, he is thrilled when Cidaq becomes Sofia, and he always respects her as a human being. Vasili shows his own human contradictions as he tries to protect the Aleut shaman from injury, but he also throws the shaman's mummy on the flames to destroy this symbol of paganism. And his conflict is real as he decides that he is called to return to Russia in order to rise in the church hierarchy, leaving Sofia behind. He is memorable through his actions and reactions at a particular time and place.

Missy Peckham and Tom Venn are two of the most fully realized characters in the narrative, partly because they are involved in several episodes of the ongoing story. Their fortitude during the arduous trip to reach the Klondike and their behavior at the goldfields makes them illustrative of the challenges of pioneering in a hostile environment. Because of Michener's ability to make a story come alive by showing his characters involved in their experiences, the reader believes that real people have struggled up the icy steps of the Chilkoot Trail and down the rushing rivers to Dawson. Their paths diverge after the Klondike experience, with Missy devoting herself to issues of the Alaskan peoples and Tom concentrating on economic ambitions.

In Nome, Missy sees in her work for the incompetent federal judge how the corrupt prey on those trying to earn an honest living. When she and Matt Murphy move to Juneau, she vows to work toward an Alaska that will rule itself, make its own laws, have its own freedoms that are not decided by rich men in Seattle. In her sixties Missy goes to the Matanuska Valley, helping the new residents there with their adjustments, working to organize a library and churches. Her feistiness is now directed toward complainers and what she sees as unwarranted prejudices. She tells the Flatch family they have no cause to forbid Flossie's marriage to Nate Coop, who is half Indian and half white, for they should not judge a person on his background alone. In her seventies and eighties

Missy promotes the cause of statehood for Alaska and its residents, whose courage has made them eligible for self-government. Missy Peckham is one of those unforgettable Michener characters whose participation in the unfolding story makes the reader realize that history is people as well as facts.

Tom Venn makes his choice to support the Seattle business interests in the development of Alaska. As a boy earning money for the trip to the Klondike, he is impressed by the city, so the course his life will take is prepared from his first appearance in the narrative. Tom's involvement with Nancy Bigears will not survive his attraction for what the Ross family can offer. Even while accepting the paternalistic attitude of the Seattle business community toward Alaska, he never loses his respect for Missy, "who encouraged him in his work, and imparted to him her wonderfully stable set of values" (1079). His solid character represents those valid contributors to the Alaskan scene whose love for the land balances the lure of its riches—and who are a vivid part of its story.

Nancy Bigears and her father Sam bring the Tlingit Indians into focus as real people in the narrative. Sam's talents working with wood make him a valued builder, and he appreciates young Tom Venn's interest in his land and his daughter while deploring the abuse of the salmon resources by Ross & Raglan's efforts to can more and more fish. Nancy is portrayed as a lively, vivacious girl maturing into a realistic young woman who knows that she and Tom will always disagree on how Alaska should develop. Through these characters the reader can gain new images and understandings of the unfolding story.

The new settlers of the modern era play brief but telling roles in the panorama of the state's peoples learning to live together in this place of spectacular beauty and challenge. The Flatches from Minnesota are involved in the development of the Matanuska Valley. Flossie, who tames Mildred the Moose, adapts readily to her surroundings, and her brother LeRoy is the characteristic bush pilot, who calculates the manageable risks and knows when it is time to stop flying. Jeb Keeler, the idealistic young lawyer from the lower forty-eight states, falls in love with Alaska's landscape and inhabitants. His experiences as he works for the native land corporations highlight the problems of the late-twentieth-century exploitation of Alaska's natural resources. Kendra Scott comes to Alaska to teach Eskimo students in the Arctic, and her attempts to encourage these students lead her to a love of their way of life. But they also lead her to despair about the "cultural fracturing" of this people trying to reconcile the consumer goods of the technological age with the age-old ways of living in the Arctic. The reader sees the stark beauty of the Arctic through Kendra's impressions of the land, the weather, the light, the darkness, and the Eskimo culture as she observes such activities as the whale hunt and the blanket toss. Vladimir Afanasi is the Eskimo who is working the hardest to confront the problems caused by different cultural values, but even he cannot predict the ultimate outcome for his people. Rick Venn renews his family ties with Alaska and his own connection with its challenges by running a team in the Iditarod sled dog race and then joining the scientific team on the floating ice island in the Arctic Sea. These fictional Alaskans are representative of the many characters in the novel who give a sense of authenticity to the story of Alaska.

THEMATIC CONSIDERATIONS

In this story of humans in a land of beauty that tests its inhabitants physically and morally, Michener has emphasized again the theme of human tolerance. As he has done in the other historical, panoramic novels discussed in this study, he shows how groups of people suffer at the hands of other groups, how fear of the Other can translate into cruelty and mistreatment of the Other, how a sense of superiority leads one group to deny the worth of another group by treating its members as inferior. Yet certain individuals counteract the prevailing tendency and form lasting bonds with people of a different heritage and way of life.

The Russian treatment of the Aleuts demonstrates cruelty taken to the extreme. Trofim Zhdanko's stepson shoots eight Aleut hunters "to teach them a lesson." Rape and beating are the common fate of Aleut women at the hands of the Russians, and the women of the fictional island of Lapak are left to die when the Russians take all the island's men to Kodiak so more otters can be killed. On Kodiak the Aleuts face extermination through disease and abuse, yet Russians like Vasili Voronov and Aleksandr Baranov choose Aleut wives, recognizing their worth.

Captain Noah Pym and the sailors of his whaling ship spending the winter in the Arctic ice learn how the Eskimos have adapted to their environment and appreciate the hospitality of this group, without whom the sailors would not have survived. However, Captain Pym's relationship with the Eskimo woman Nikaluk cannot last: "No, Pym saw Nikaluk as a human being equal to himself in all ways except the possibility of her living in Christian Boston. Mr. Corey had been right; she was, in so many respects that mattered, a savage" (253).

Both the Russians and the Americans treat the Tlingits with the same indifference and often contempt for a different culture, giving them gaudy presents for land. The whites and the Indians will fight over the years for control of this land and its riches. The Tlingits will be overwhelmed by the armed might of the whites and will be caught between two cultures as the Americans consolidate their control of Alaska after 1867.

Through his presentation of the Eskimo, Aleut, and Tlingit cultures, Michener indicates his own respect for these different ways of life, especially for their harmony with the natural surroundings. The portrayals of the Eskimos greeting the reappearance of the sun after the long Arctic night, the Tlingit potlatch with its generosity and fellowship, the shaman's effort to help the Aleuts on Kodiak retain some essential beliefs, and the whale hunt in the 1980s are sympathetic and engaging.

The many references to the ravages of alcohol on the Eskimos and the Indian groups present Michener's indignation and sadness at its effect on these people's physical and emotional well-being. The introduction of rum to the Eskimos sheltering Pym and his crew was part of celebrating the sun's return, but later traders would use alcohol to seduce the native population into handing over valuable fur pelts. Whole villages would drink themselves into a stupor, fail to hunt and gather food for the long winter, and starve, for the native peoples were unable to control their craving for liquor. In spite of official efforts to end the supply of alcohol, it remains one aspect of the dark side of the Alaska story, as Kendra Scott finds at Desolation Point.

Michener does not attempt to solve the problem of how two ways of life can coexist to the improvement of both. Nancy Bigears finishes high school in Juneau, one of the rare Tlingits to do so, but leaves the University of Washington after three weeks to return home, saying, "Those classes held nothing for me" (923). She makes a life with Ah Ting, the Chinese foreman who has stayed in Juneau when the other Chinese cannery workers are sent away. The Eskimo children Kendra teaches also find it difficult to reconcile the traditional ways with the new knowledge she brings. The changes brought about by contact with the white man's alcohol, guns, machines, laws, and even his faith are too much to absorb in a few generations for many of the peoples of the north: "this malaise, a sickness of the soul, evolved, with the all too frequent result that those who did not find the refuge in drunkenness found release in suicide"

(1167). Vladimir Afanasi has seen both results in his own family, but he will go on his way trying to fit his social context and its harmony with the environment into the historical context of a technological world that wants to understand both.

One way two cultures meet is through marriage, and *Alaska* has several examples of such unions. Tom Venn will not marry Nancy Bigears as the twentieth century begins because the lure of Seattle is too strong, and he could never be important there with an Indian wife. However, the historical context changes; in 1925, when Tom's son Malcolm meets Tammy Ting, daughter of Nancy and Ah Ting, marriage is the result. Tammy never loses her identification with Alaska and its people, and she supports statehood until it is achieved; she is accepted by her husband and his family on her own terms.

Both Flossie and LeRoy Flatch choose spouses of other ethnic backgrounds. As Missy Peckham tells the horrified parents when Flossie wants to marry Nate Coop, any marriage is a risk: "Marriage in Alaska is often a woman with good sense and an overdose of humanity marryin' a clod like this Nate and civilizin' him" (1002). Flossie and Nate get married, but World War II also has an impact on the civilizing of Nate, for during the fighting in the Aleutians his ability as a scout gives him a new self-respect. He also meets another "half breed," Sandy Krickel, whose mother was Aleut. Sandy's intelligence fostered by her education has made her fit for any society, and Nate learns he doesn't have to accept the white culture's judgment that he is an inferior person. On meeting Sandy, LeRoy Flatch will forget his prejudices and see an attractive woman of ability and character, rather than the Other who is inferior because of ethnic and cultural background. In *Hawaii*, published in 1959, the novel's narrator indicates that marriage between two people of different ethnic or racial heritage was not necessary for the cross-fertilization of ideas and knowledge, but nearly thirty years later such marriages between two human beings who love and respect each other are a natural part of the story.

The connection between humans and the environment is the other major theme in *Alaska*. It cannot be separated from the consideration of greed, for it is greed that leads to the destruction of the environment. The Russians must leave Lapak because they have destroyed the sea otter population, but their passion for the riches to be gained from the furs blinds them to any concern for the depletion of this living resource or for the Aleut women left behind to starve when their men are taken to hunt the otters in the sea surrounding Kodiak. The same killing frenzy motivates Americans like Captain Schransky, who kill the pregnant seals because the fur of the unborn baby is the softest. Both Russian and American officials finally wake up to the senselessness of this slaughter and stop it the best they can.

Ross & Raglan's thirst for profit leads to similar destruction of salmon in the Taku Inlet. Their fish traps are opened on weekends so some of the salmon run does reach the spawning grounds. Tom Venn sees only that the salmon taken by the cannery are going to feed people and does not consider a problem the waste of those left to rot because the cannery can't pack them fast enough. Nancy Bigears throws the two salmon sent by Mr. Ross into the inlet, for she realizes that the businessman does not look beyond the year's profits and fails to realize that waste will lead to the end of a resource that seems so promising. And he is also one of the outsiders making decisions about a land they see only as a source of wealth.

The oil resource may be another like the gold, which will eventually be depleted, but as its extraction from the frozen tundra at Prudhoe Bay is under way, some concern for the animal population is voiced. Flossie and Nate Coop are hired to work with other naturalists in an effort to help the caribou, whose migration routes will be crossed by the pipeline carrying oil to the terminal at Valdez so many hundred miles to the south. The "nature freaks," as the pipeline official calls them, now have a loud enough voice to be heard as humans debate their stewardship of the earth.

The debate about humankind and the use of natural and animal resources will be ongoing, as the "new breed" of walrus illustrates. Eskimos are allowed to kill a certain number of walruses for food to maintain their ancient ways of life. However, many of the animals are killed for their ivory alone, and the headless carcasses are left to rot on the beach.

The animals, the people, the resources in the ground and in the sea—who will develop them, who will control them? The hard work and fortitude that has characterized the past has carried over to the present, but will the future be heroic in the sense that the land and its inhabitants will live in harmony? With the ending of *Alaska*, Michener seems to express doubts. Poley Markham, ready to take over native corporations at the expiration of the Alaska Native Claims Settlement Act, survives the tidal wave. Jeb Keeler, who "had grown honestly to love Alaska and to see it as a unique blending of white newcomers like himself and longtime natives like the Eskimos, the Athapascans and the Tlingits" (1271), does not.

The splendors and the challenges of the Great Land and its terrain and climate, the people who fall under its spell, the wildlife that is an inherent part of it—Michener has presented them all in this panorama of the forty-ninth state and its history. His narrative has illuminated the story of Alaska for the reader.

A FEMINIST READING OF *ALASKA*

To look at a Michener historical, panoramic novel from the feminist perspective described in Chapter 3, a reader must carefully consider the culture and time period in which the women characters play a part. Are the images authentic in terms of their context? Are the women more than objects serving the male characters' interests? A consideration of selected women characters in *Alaska* will concentrate on these questions.

Since the evidence for gender roles in cultures that existed thousands of years before the present era is limited, a feminist critic can note that Michener creates women whose opinions are respected by the men of these early societies. Varnack of the first group to cross the land bridge between Asia and North America refuses to deprive his mother of food during hard times. The Ancient One's wisdom is needed by the tribe more than the small amount of food she eats. In the next group of migrating people Nukleet, wife of Oogruk, is the courageous supporter of her husband and father as the small group flees from the anger of the tribe's shaman.

Among the eighteenth-century Russians, an important role in the fur-trading business is played by a woman. Daughter of a provincial governor, Marina Ismailovna marries a trader from a lower social class because only through marriage will she be able to become involved in the trading business. As Madame Poznikova she expands her husband's business, and when he is killed by bandits attacking their caravan, she marries Zhdanko and continues her commercial ventures. She is an independent woman, finding through marriage to husbands who accept her as a partner a way to deal with the constraints imposed on women by her culture.

The Old One on Lapak Island is another example of Michener's effort to create a woman character who refuses to conform to cultural stereotypes. When the women are faced with starvation because the men have been taken away by the Russians, she challenges the taboos that say women should not hunt the whale. Her great-granddaughter Cidaq agrees with her that "it was nonsense to believe that spirits would want an island of women to starve to death because there were no men at hand to pursue whales in the traditional way" (266).

From a feminist perspective, Cidaq, the great-granddaughter, is one of the most authentic women characters in the novel. Although treated more cruelly than any object on the ship taking her from Lapak to Kodiak, she refuses to let the beatings, indecencies, and humiliations overwhelm her. Cidaq is determined to survive and settle a few scores. Throughout her brutal marriage to Rudenko and her happy one with Father Vasili, her reflective courage gives her an independent reality apart from the men in her life. Left behind when Vasili returns to Russia to become an important church official, Cidaq continues her efforts to reconcile Indians and Russians until her death.

Missy Peckham is another independent woman character. Traveling with Buck and Tom Venn, she backs their efforts with her fortitude as well as her earnings. She acts with the same resolution when she joins forces with first John Klope and than Matt Murphy in the Klondike after Buck's death. When she talks to the Flatches about Flossie's proposed marriage to Nate Coop, Missy indicates she has never married because she fell in love with men who had wives. However, none of these men nor the married state are necessary for her identity; they provide companionship and mutual affection. Missy is also a fighter for the causes in which she believes, such as justice for the natives and statehood for Alaska. The story affirms her life and actions.

Kendra Scott offers another authentic image of a woman character. An idealistic teacher, she is of interest in her own right, caring deeply for the students in her class and trying to understand this Eskimo culture facing the challenges of a technological society. Her relationships with Jeb Keeler and Rick Venn are secondary to her struggles with the emotional challenges of the Arctic and her job.

The other women characters who are part of this panorama briefly are also more authentic than stereotypic from a feminist perspective. Nancy Bigears never loses sight of her Tlingit heritage and values in spite of her attraction to Tom Venn; Tammy Ting Venn does not hesitate to disagree with her husband on the merits of statehood for Alaska; Flossie Flatch Coop will use her love and understanding of animals to study the effect of the Alaska pipeline on the migrating caribou. People rather than events shape Alaska's history as Michener tells it, and as one reviewer put it, "The most remarkable of Michener's people are the women, who dominate the book by their strength and desire to transcend mere survival. They are creations not of a poetic vision but of circumstances in which people must be self-reliant or perish" (Cornish 1988, 18).

From a feminist perspective, Michener has created in *Alaska* authentic women characters who have as much as or more reality than the men in the narrative. Cidaq and Missy Peckham are realized thoroughly enough to become role models, and all the women in the book affirm the value of women's lives.

11

Miracle in Seville
(1995)

Miracle in Seville, James A. Michener's most recent work of fiction, appeared in bookstores in October of 1995. Like his previous novels, *Miracle in Seville* exhibits a vivid setting and compelling narrative. Yet it is a much shorter work, running 107 pages, and has a strong aura of fantasy; in effect, it is a fairy tale for adults. In the hardback edition of the book, John Fulton's drawings of Seville, the people, and the events of the story enhance visually the sense of place that Michener creates throughout the narrative. Fulton is an American *matador de toros* who has been fighting bulls in Spain for over thirty years.

This chapter will touch briefly on plot development, character development, and thematic considerations in Michener's most recent narrative.

PLOT DEVELOPMENT

As in his novel *Mexico*, Michener uses a journalist as narrator and participant in *Miracle in Seville*. Shenstone is sent by his editor to Seville to write the story of Don Cayetano Mota, owner of a famous ranch where fighting bulls have been raised for decades. The quality of Mota ranch bulls has declined through the years, and Don Cayetano, upon inheriting the ranch, has dedicated himself to restoring its past glories. His efforts will be the focus of Shenstone's article.

However, it is an article that will not be written. No one would believe the events that Shenstone witnessed, he feels, and he would lose credibility as a journalist. Some twenty years later, Shenstone reflects on the story he saw unfold, and he relives each day he spent with Don Cayetano.

The use of the journalist as narrator provides a realistic framework for giving the reader information about the classical Spanish bullfight with its four distinct parts. As he establishes the context for the story's events, Shenstone also describes the appearance, personalities, and techniques of four matadors who will be involved in the fights to take place in Seville after Easter, including Lázaro López, the Gypsy. Lázaro is known for his brilliance during the early parts of a bullfight and for his cowardice during a fight's climax.

Bullfights in the town of Puerto de Santa María before the Seville *feria* illustrate Don Cayetano's problems: five of his six bulls are disasters in the ring. Also, López reveals his fear, refusing to face the sixth bull courageously. Don Cayetano mutters that someone should kill the cowardly matador who diminishes the honor of both man and animal.

The story moves to the three-week spring *feria* in Seville. Along with the bullfights, the festival includes demonstrations of the people's religious faith. During the week between Palm Sunday and Easter, there are processions of men bearing crosses, and parades of floats that feature scenes from Christ's final week of life or replicas of the Virgin Mary and other saints. Don Cayetano drags his cross, and Shenstone overhears his prayer to the Virgin before the procession starts: "Mother of God, allow me just once to guide my bulls. Help me to help them perform respectably" (31). He explains to Shenstone that in his dreams, he becomes the bull, with his spirit enabling the animal to act according to the traditions of the classic bullfight. The rancher's spirit leaves the bull just before the animal's triumphal death. Shenstone thinks that Don Cayetano is nearly crazy, but he also realizes that the Spaniard has a tendency toward mysticism and an intense veneration of the Virgin Mary.

As Don Cayetano takes part in the religious events of the festival, Shenstone observes and even participates. The journalist is involved in three incidents during which he is almost certain the Virgin Mary has had direct contact with Don Cayetano. During the festival Shenstone also notices a Gypsy woman who appears to be watching the rancher. He learns that she is López's sister, Magdalena, who asks Shenstone why he bothers to write about a man whose days of glory are over.

Shenstone's observations and participation in the *feria* include the reader in the unfolding of Don Cayetano's story. The bullfights are described with Michener's customary attention to detail; the final confrontation between Don Cayetano and López, the Gypsy matador, is skillfully prefaced by verbal sparring between the two men and the prophecies of López's sister that her brother will be the triumphant matador during the *feria*.

During the last fight of the day, Shenstone realizes that Don Cayetano's dream has been realized: he is his bull, and López intends to kill that bull. After López succeeds in butchering the bull, he is jeered and attacked by the crowd. Don Cayetano is found dead in his ringside seat. Shenstone realizes that he can never report what he believes has actually occurred: Don Cayetano died because López killed the bull before the rancher's spirit could leave the bull and return to his own body. Ashamed that his lost story comes to his mind when he should be mourning his friend, Shenstone comments: "Only then did I see Don Cayetano as he truly was: a man with two abiding passions, to serve the Virgin and to restore honor to his ranch. He had died in the service of both ideals, and few old men can claim as much" (101). He concludes that Don Cayetano has achieved his miracle: the Virgin answered his prayers, and his courageous spirit enabled the bull to fight nobly and restore the ranch's lost honor.

CHARACTER DEVELOPMENT

Character development is secondary to narrative in *Miracle in Seville*. Michener is more interested in telling the story of a man who seeks to restore the lost honor and glory of his ranch with the help of the Virgin Mary than in developing a fully realized character. Enough cultural background is given to make Don Cayetano's religious faith believable— but it's his obsession that remains vivid, not his character.

The reader knows Shenstone chiefly through his observations and reactions to Don Cayetano. His background and personal concerns are mentioned in passing, but he mainly serves as a background against which Don Cayetano's story unfolds. Shenstone interprets the story, and his actions are important only insofar as they play a role in telling or explaining what happens.

The two Gypsies, Lázaro the matador and Magdalena the fortune-teller, are Don Cayetano's adversaries. They are interpreted by Shenstone who both fears and is attracted to Magdalena and considers Lázaro a disgrace to a noble profession. The brother and sister are necessary in order to provide contrast to Don Cayetano's quest. They fulfill their assigned roles well, but are not clearly defined as human beings.

All of the characters have been created for the sake of the story. They are believable within context, but readers will probably remain distant from them—interested in what happens, but not particularly caring about the characters as individuals.

THEMATIC CONSIDERATIONS

Miracle in Seville does not present the usual Michener themes of acceptance of different ethnic and racial groups and concern for the environment. The work exalts courage and the value of striving toward a goal, as have Michener's other fictional works, but it is primarily a portrait of a country, Spain, that Michener has long been enamored of—where bullfighting as a sport is, at its best, an art form; where religious faith is sincere and often dramatic in its expression; and where constant effort is required to sustain personal and family honor. Michener is able to present this Spain through his detailed rendering of place and culture: the reader is in Seville, seeing, smelling, hearing, and experiencing the bullfights, the processions, the parade.

Miracles are possible in the context of the devout faith of the inhabitants of Michener's Seville, although the reader's perception of this religious theme will be influenced by personal beliefs. As he prepares to relate the story, Shenstone himself is still not certain whether a real miracle took place: "I suspect that what I experienced was some shadowy glimpse of a truth we men do not like to acknowledge: that women possess an arcane power to influence men, making them see visions and influencing them to perform acts they would not normally commit. . . . Certainly in Seville I witnessed a battle between two powerful women, and to me they remain as forceful as they were when they involved me in their combat" (3–4). This idea of the power of women is not developed, but the Virgin Mary and Magdalena López are contrasted throughout the story.

Although shaken by events of that final bullfight, Shenstone appears to accept the idea that Don Cayetano has achieved his dream with the Virgin's help. And he seems to believe that the Virgin "had engaged in a plaza brawl with a Gypsy fortune-teller from Triana, but in Spain that's the way things sometimes happen. Their duel was a draw" (107). Michener never indicates that it is a duel between the forces of good and evil, but such an implication can be drawn from Shenstone's comments about the two Gypsies. Don Cayetano does reach his goal and is able to restore the lost honor of his bull ranch. Thus, Michener implies that miracles can be realized through strong and sincere faith.

Miracle in Seville is a novel that stands apart from Michener's already impressive collection of works. It resembles his previous novels in its focus on the culture of a particular place, but it is the only novel to present events that cannot be explained rationally: the narrative has strong elements of fantasy. At the same time, the book exhibits a well-developed story and a vivid sense of place. *Miracle in Seville* is a testament to Michener's strengths as a storyteller.

Bibliography

WORKS BY JAMES A. MICHENER

About Centennial: Some Notes on the Novel. New York: Random House, 1974.

Alaska. New York: Random House, 1988; London: Corgi Books, 1989 (paperback).

America vs. America: The Revolution in Middle-class Values. New York: New American Library, 1969.

The Bridge at Andau. New York: Random House, 1957.

The Bridges at Toko-Ri. New York: Random House, 1953; New York: Fawcett Crest, 1973 (paperback).

Caravans. New York: Random House, 1963; New York: Bantam Books, 1964 (paperback).

Caribbean. New York: Random House, 1989; New York: Fawcett Crest, 1991 (paperback).

Centennial. New York: Random House, 1974; New York: Fawcett Crest, 1975 (paperback).

Chesapeake. New York: Random House, 1978; New York: Fawcett Crest, 1978 (paperback).

The Covenant. New York: Random House, 1980; New York: Fawcett Crest, 1982 (paperback).

Creatures of the Kingdom: Stories of Animals and Nature. New York: Random House, 1993.

The Drifters. New York: Random House, 1971; New York: Fawcett Crest, 1972 (paperback).

The Eagle and the Raven. Austin, Texas: State House Press, 1990; New York: A Tor Book, 1991 (paperback).

Facing East: A Study of the Art of Jack Levine. New York: Random House, 1970.

The Fires of Spring. New York: Random House, 1949; New York: Fawcett Crest, 1972 (paperback).

The Floating World. New York: Random House, 1954.

Hawaii. New York: Random House, 1959; New York: Fawcett Crest, 1973 (paperback).

Iberia: Spanish Travels and Reflections. New York: Random House, 1968.

James A. Michener's Writer's Handbook: Explorations in Writing and Publishing. New York: Random House, 1992.

Japanese Prints: From the Early Masters to the Modern. Tokyo: Charles E. Tuttle, 1959.

Journey. New York: Random House, 1989; New York: Fawcett Crest, 1994 (paperback).

Kent State: What Happened and Why. New York: Random House, 1971.

The Legacy. New York: Random House, 1987; New York: Fawcett Crest, 1988 (paperback).

Literary Reflections: Michener on Michener, Hemingway, Capote & Others. Austin, Tex.: State House Press, 1993.

Mexico. New York: Random House, 1992; New York: Fawcett Crest, 1994 (paperback).

A Michener Miscellany, 1950–1970. Edited by Ben Hibbs. New York: Random House, 1973.

Miracle in Seville. New York: Random House, 1995.

The Modern Japanese Print: An Appreciation. Tokyo and Rutland, Vt.: Charles E. Tuttle, 1962.

"Mr. Megabook's Dream Machine." *Forbes ASAP*, 7 June 1993: 25–27.

My Lost Mexico. Austin, Tex.: State House Press, 1992.

The Novel. New York: Random House, 1991; New York: Fawcett Crest, 1992 (paperback).

Pilgrimage: A Memoir of Poland and Rome. Emmaus, Pa.: Rodale Press, 1990.

Poland. New York: Random House, 1983; New York: Fawcett Crest, 1984 (paperback).

Presidential Lottery: The Reckless Gamble in Our Electoral System. New York: Random House, 1969.

The Quality of Life. Philadelphia: Lippincott, 1970.

Rascals in Paradise. New York: Random House, 1957 (with A. Grove Day).

Recessional. New York: Random House, 1994.

Report of the County Chairman. New York: Random House, 1961.

Return to Paradise. New York: Random House, 1951; New York: Bantam Books, 1952 (paperback).

Sayonara. New York: Random House, 1954; New York: Fawcett Crest, 1974 (paperback).

Selected Writings of James A. Michener: With a Special Foreword by the Author. New York: Modern Library, 1957.

Six Days in Havana. Austin, Tex.: University of Texas Press, 1989 (with John Kings).

The Source. New York: Random House, 1965; New York: Fawcett Crest, 1965 (paperback).

Space. New York: Random House, 1982; New York: Fawcett Crest, 1983 (paperback).

Sports in America. New York: Random House, 1976.

Tales of the South Pacific. New York: Macmillan, 1947; New York: Fawcett Crest, 1973 (paperback).

Texas. New York: Random House, 1985; New York: Fawcett Crest, 1987 (paperback).

The Voice of Asia. New York: Random House, 1951.

The World Is My Home: A Memoir. New York: Random House, 1992.

INFORMATION AND CRITICISM ABOUT JAMES A. MICHENER

Becker, George J. *James A. Michener.* Literature and Life Series. New York: Ungar, 1983.

Contemporary Authors. Vol. 21, New Revision Series. Detroit: Gale Research, 1987: 292–99.

Contemporary Authors. Vol. 45, New Revision Series. Detroit: Gale Research, 1995: 282–90.

Day, A. Grove. *James A. Michener.* Twayne's United States Authors Series. Boston: Twayne, 1964: 60.

Day, A. Grove. *James A. Michener.* 2nd ed. Twayne's United States Authors Series. Boston: Twayne, 1977: 60.

Hayes, John Phillip. *James A. Michener: A Biography.* Indianapolis, Ind.: Bobbs-Merrill, 1984.

Hines, Jr., Samuel M. "Perspectives from the Novels of Michener and Vidal." In *Political Mythology and Popular Fiction,* edited by Ernest J. Yanarella. Westport, Conn.: Greenwood Press, 1988: 81–99.

Kings, John. *In Search of Centennial: A Journey with James A. Michener.* New York: Random House, 1978.

Nicklin, Julie L. "Colleges That Helped Spawn Michener's Career Are the Beneficiaries of His Philanthropy." *Chronicle of Higher Education,* 13 January 1993: A27–A28.

Roberts, F. X., and C. D. Rhine, comps. *James A. Michener: A Checklist of His Works,*

With a Selected, Annotated Bibliography. Westport, Conn.: Greenwood Press, 1995.

REVIEWS

The Fires of Spring

Prescott, Orville. "Outstanding Novels." *Yale Review,* Spring 1949: 574–75.
Reynolds, Horace. "A Stream of American Life." *Christian Science Monitor,* 15 February 1949: 12.
Rolo, Charles J. "David, Write That Book." *Atlantic Monthly,* March 1949: 84–85.
Trilling, Diana. "Fiction in Review." *Nation,* 12 February 1949: 192.

Hawaii

Geismar, Maxwell. "Gods, Missionaries and the Golden Men." *New York Times Book Review,* 22 November 1959: 4.
Hogan, William. "Michener Looks Over a New Breed of Men." *San Francisco Chronicle,* 25 November 1959: 31.
"Pineapple Epic." *Time,* 23 November 1959: 107–108, 110.
Sutton, Horace. "Some Enchanted Islands." *Saturday Review,* 21 November 1959: 40.

Centennial

Cooper, Arthur. "Eohippus Opera." *Newsweek,* 16 September 1974: 82–83, 86.
James, Stuart. "Stately American Novel." *New Republic,* 21 September 1974: 21–22.
Stafford, Jean. "How the West Was Lost." *Washington Post Book World,* 1 September 1974: 1–2.
Wilkinson, Burke. "Blockbuster from James Michener." *Christian Science Monitor,* 25 September 1974: 11.

Chesapeake

Gibbons, Boyd. "James A. Michener Bridges the Bay." *Washington Post Book World,* 9 July 1978: 1, 4.

Mano, D. Keith. "Poop Poop." *National Review,* 15 September 1978: 1153–54.

Wills, Garry. "Typhoon on the Bay." *New York Review of Books,* 17 August 1978: 31–32.

Yardley, Jonathan. "An American Vision." *New York Times Book Review,* 23 July 1978: 11.

The Covenant

Burns, John F. "Michener: The Novelist as Teacher." *New York Times Book Review,* 23 November 1980: 3, 30.

Gannon, Thomas M. *America,* 24 January 1981: 66.

Hoffman, Nancy Yames. "Michenerland: Another Cast of Thousands." *Los Angeles Times Book World,* 7 December 1980: 6.

Winder, David. "Michener's Sweeping South African Saga." *Christian Science Monitor,* 10 November 1980: B1, B11.

Space

Bell, Pearl K. "Soft Soap and Hard Fact." *Times Literary Supplement,* 25 February 1983: 200.

Harrell, Don. "Fact Laden Novel on Space Program." *Christian Science Monitor,* 6 October 1982: 14.

Smith, Michael L. "No. 1 on the Best-Seller List . . ." *Nation,* 5 March 1983: 279–81.

Wilford, John Noble. "A Novel of Very High Adventure." *New York Times Book Review,* 19 September 1982: 3, 26.

Texas

Bueter, Robert J. *America,* 18 January 1986: 36.

Lemann, Nicholas. "James Michener's Ten Gallon Epic." *Washington Post Book World,* 29 September 1985: 1, 13.

Rudd, Hughes. "Four Centuries of Tex Arcana." *New York Times Book Review,* 13 October 1985: 9.

Spitzer, Jane Stewart. "Current Fiction." *Christian Science Monitor,* 30 October 1985: 20.

Alaska

Cornish, Sam. "Michener's Alaska Epic: Fiction, Fact and Imagined History." *Christian Science Monitor*, 27 July 1988: 18.
Jennings, Gary. "A Nice Place for Mastodons." *New York Times Book Review*, 26 June 1988: 7.
Lehmann-Haupt, Christopher. "Michener's Cautionary Tale of the 49th State." *New York Times*, 23 June 1988: C21.
Review of *Alaska. Time*, 4 July 1988: 70.

Miracle in Seville

Griggs, Brandon. "Michener Eager to Explore More Territory in His Well-Traveled World." *The Salt Lake Tribune*, 24 December 1995: E2.
Jones, Patricia A. "*Miracle* Is a Jewel." *The Tulsa World*, 17 December 1995: K4.

OTHER SECONDARY SOURCES

Donovan, Josephine. "Beyond the Net: Feminist Criticism as a Moral Criticism." In *Denver Quarterly* 17, winter 1983: 40–57.
Eagleton, Terry. *Marxism and Literary Criticism*. Berkeley, Calif: University of California Press, 1976.
Keesey, Donald. "Mimetic Criticism: Reality as Context." In *Contexts for Criticism*, edited by Donald Keesey. 2nd ed. Mountain View, Calif: Mayfield, 1994: 187–96.
Marx, Karl. *A Contribution to the Critique of Political Economy* (1859). Translated by N. I. Stone. Chicago, Il.: Charles H. Kerr, 1904.
Register, Cheri. "American Feminist Literary Criticism: A Bibliographical Introduction." In *Feminist Literary Criticism: Explorations in Theory*, edited by Josephine Donovan. 2nd ed. Lexington, Ky.: University of Kentucky Press, 1989: 1–28.

Index

About the Author

MARILYN S. SEVERSON is Associate Professor and Chair of the Department of Foreign Languages and Literatures at Seattle Pacific University. In addition to her specialization in French language, literature and cultural studies, she enjoys working with mystery and historical fiction.